The Outsider

The Outsider

GEORDAN MURPHY

PENGUIN
IRELAND

PENGUIN IRELAND

Published by the Penguin Group
Penguin Ireland, 25 St Stephen's Green, Dublin 2, Ireland (a division of Penguin Books Ltd)
Penguin Books Ltd, 80 Strand, London WC2R ORL, England
Penguin Group (USA) Inc., 375 Hudson Street, New York, New York 10014, USA
Penguin Group (Australia), 250 Camberwell Road, Camberwell, Victoria 3124, Australia
(a division of Pearson Australia Group Pty Ltd)
Penguin Group (Canada), 90 Eglinton Avenue East, Suite 700, Toronto, Ontario, Canada M4P 2Y3
(a division of Pearson Penguin Canada Inc.)
Penguin Books India Pvt Ltd, 11 Community Centre, Panchsheel Park, New Delhi – 110 017, India
Penguin Group (NZ), 67 Apollo Drive, Rosedale, Auckland 0632, New Zealand
(a division of Pearson New Zealand Ltd)
Penguin Books (South Africa) (Pty) Ltd, Block D, Rosebank Office Park,
181 Jan Smuts Avenue, Parktown North, Gauteng 2193, South Africa

Penguin Books Ltd, Registered Offices: 80 Strand, London WC2R ORL, England

www.penguin.com

First published 2012
001

Copyright © Geordan Murphy, 2012

The moral right of the author has been asserted

Set in Bembo 12/14.75 pt
Typeset by Jouve (UK), Milton Keynes
Printed in Great Britain by Clays Ltd, St Ives plc

A CIP catalogue record for this book is available from the British Library

ISBN: 978-1-844-88279-3

www.greenpenguin.co.uk

MIX
Paper from
responsible sources
FSC™ C018179

Penguin Books is committed to a sustainable
future for our business, our readers and our planet.
This book is made from Forest Stewardship
Council™ certified paper.

ALWAYS LEARNING   PEARSON

Contents

Prologue

Monday evening, 15 August 2011
Carton House, Co. Kildare

The shepherd's hook is coming. My time as an Ireland international will not end in glorious triumph or defeat at the World Cup in New Zealand. It will happen in a hotel room in Kildare, my county, a few miles up the road from my family home. Deccie will do it discreetly and people will barely even notice.

The lads in camp agree with me. Rog said it straight: 'Yeah, I think you are gone, Geordie.'

Paulie too: 'Doesn't look good, Geordie.'

They are assessing it coldly, not sugar-coating it. Three fullbacks for two places.

Deccie wants to see me tomorrow morning. This evening he and a few others have gone up to Dublin for the rugby writers' awards.

I was player of the year at those awards in 2003 – just before another World Cup I missed out on. Tonight's ceremony is in the shiny new Aviva Stadium, overlooking the field where I first played in the Leinster Schools Cup semi-final way back in 1996.

That was the start of all this, I suppose. The end is coming in the morning.

I got used to this kind of rejection under Eddie, but Deccie always liked picking me, ever since the under-19 World Cup in 1997.

Still, I guess I've known for a couple of weeks that I would not be going to New Zealand. There are too many wounded bodies in camp. Drico's trapped nerve is a serious concern. He'll need an operation after the tournament – if he makes it. Darce isn't right yet either, but he will be. They both will; durable men are those squat centres of ours. Stevie Ferris has been out since January with a knee. Rob Kearney hurt his groin in France, but he is Deccie's preferred choice at fullback. With so many injuries, seems like the coach had to draw a line somewhere. And that somewhere is the wrong side of my foot. Thirty-three years old. Another bad fracture on the mend. No game time banked since January.

Declan Kidney has moved on.

It must be difficult for him to see me walking around the hotel these past few weeks, knowing he was not going to pick me.

Deccie has his favourites – all coaches do. Felix Jones, the recently established Munster fullback, is one of them; while myself and Rob have been crocked and Luke Fitzgerald proved he was more winger than fullback, Felix has performed impressively.

I have been the coach's pet on many occasions in Leicester. But in green, I've always been the outsider.

I'm in my room in the Carton House Hotel, another night staring at the ceiling, confidence levels slowly, painfully ebbing.

I've been able to taste the rejection for two weeks now. I thought I could cling on for a few more days, but I'm probably not even going to get a run against Connacht next Thursday. Or, even worse, I'll get picked knowing I'm a dead man walking.

I'm angry because I feel let down by Deccie. I've spent the last eight incredibly frustrating months rehabbing an injury more usually associated with motorcycle crashes. I am almost there. My focus has been narrowed on one goal: the plane to New Zealand.

I hoped a miracle recovery would get me back for the Premiership final against Saracens on 28th May. But that was never going to happen. The initial prognosis was career over; then a year; then I haggled the specialist down to eight months.

I'm ready now.

My last appearance for Ireland was in June 2010. Deccie made me captain against the New Zealand Maori. I have been the Leicester captain these past few years so it must have seemed like a rational decision with Drico and Paulie not in the side. I took it as my cue to become a more vocal figure in the set-up.

Then I got injured.

Still, I believed Deccie would play me in the warm-up match

against Scotland at Murrayfield two weeks ago. When he went for Rob, with Felix off the bench, I knew I was on borrowed time.

We had a little chat about it. Unlike his predecessor, Deccie has always been approachable. On this occasion, however, I may have preferred the cold shoulder. He was clearly struggling.

We all knew he was going with his favoured side for the return match against France, which meant Rob at fifteen, this Saturday in Dublin. That leaves Connacht at Donnybrook on Thursday night.

I cannot imagine a more difficult game to get motivated for. Half the guys' death warrants will have been signed, while Connacht will be like a pack of wild dogs. For them it's the perfect pre-season fixture against international players rated above them. For us it's no-win stuff.

But I may not even be there. Tomorrow morning Deccie could release me back to Leicester.

When Deccie told me I wasn't playing against Scotland or away to France, I was angry.

I looked him in the eye. 'Would I be picked if it was just rugby reasons?'

He didn't give a straight answer.

'What I mean is,' I clarified, 'if I was fit, would I be selected?'

'You won't be playing against France in Bordeaux,' was all he told me.

That's when I knew the end was coming.

I am desperate. I've even suggested a run-out for Naas GAA club's junior football team just to prove my foot is fully functional. Whenever the painkillers wear off, the foot is agony. But rugby players are always playing hurt. Comes with the territory. I am fine.

Knowing your last chance of playing for your country has passed yet still being part of the group is a horrible existence.

I've always felt I was good enough to play for Ireland. Always felt respected by my peers because I could do things out of the ordinary. I still do and I still can, but I know it's over.

Some international careers end in glory, like Martin Johnson's at the full-time whistle of the World Cup final. Others conclude in defeat.

My international story looks certain to end with packing my bags and driving the few miles down the road to the family home in Naas. Cup of tea, bacon sandwich, a few quality hours with the nieces and nephews, then back on a flight to England.

Broken, I call my girlfriend, Aneka. I call the brother, Ross. There is nothing they can say. There is nothing I want to hear. But you call those closest to you just to hear their voices.

I just wish I could have a last chance to prove I'm the same Geordan Murphy who catches high balls and scores, or in more recent times creates, tries for a living. Yes, I'm getting old. Yes, the foot is sore. But it seems like the back catalogue counts for nothing.

While I'm in such sparkling form, I may as well tell you about the rest of it.

Yeah, I'm bitter tonight. And pissed off.

Should make for good reading . . .

1. Doing Something Different

'The man who emerged as Newbridge's match winner was
outhalf Geordan Murphy. He contributed 16 points, varied
his game, and his kicking from hand and with the placed ball was
excellent. He also scored a great try after blocking down a kick.
He gathered the ball and his pace and dedication of purpose enabled
him to score in the right corner. He then crowned that fine
effort by converting from the touchline into a fitful wind.
If there is better than him in the position in the competition,
I have not seen him.'

Edmund Van Esbeck, *The Irish Times*, March 1996

'He's not good enough. You may take him back to Naas, that's
his standard. He's too slow . . .'

An Irish schools selector in conversation
with my father, April 1996

Long before I tested my skills against the aristocrats of schools rugby,
long before I started dividing opinion, and long before I was ever
made to feel an outsider in the game I loved, sport consumed my
childhood.

I was always honing my skills. Give me a tennis ball and I would
hop it against a wall all afternoon. In our back garden I played
one-man rugby. Hooker, that would be me, throws to four in the
lineout, still me, ball off the top to the scrumhalf, guess who, outhalf
throws a miss pass to the centre, who chips over the cover for the
flying fullback – me again, a.k.a. Blanco or Campese – to gather,
and dive over in the corner. My mother must have looked out the

kitchen window and presumed the sixth of the litter would prove the oddest.

Every chance I got I would tag along behind my big brother, Ross. Inevitably, I found my way down to Naas GAA and rugby clubs. Ross was seven years older, and he used to tell me I had to figure ways around the big fellas because I was so small.

'Do something different,' he would tell me, and I soon realized that I could.

I taught myself to chip the ball over the big guys' heads or roll it between their legs.

I realized I had something most players don't possess. It's hard to explain. I guess it is simply natural, God-given ability.

My name is George, by the way, not Geordan. The fifth son after Nicolas, Etienne, Brian and Ross, my dad finally decided to pass on his own name.

It didn't last long, though. Mam decided a change was needed when a district nurse scared her half to death one morning not long after I was born.

There was a knock at the door. 'I'm here about George,' the nurse said.

Dad was an army officer, so he was overseas a lot, and here was a nurse at the door about George, her husband. It couldn't be good news.

'What about . . . golf?'

Dad is a four handicapper.

The two women stood staring at each other until the penny dropped.

'Oh George, the baby! Come in, come in. Sure, he is fine . . .'

But the name had to go. I became Geordan, then Geordie, then a whole bunch of other unwelcome nicknames. My uncle Stephen was a Dominican priest based in Trinidad and Tobago, and he told us the Scottish dialect of George was Geordan. Fr Stephen passed away a couple of years back, but my brother Etienne keeps the name (which is French for Stephen) safely minded in our family.

There is decent sporting pedigree in the Murphy household. A lot of it transpired before I was born. My eldest brother, Nicky, twenty years my senior, joined Naas RFC and played in the 1982 Towns Cup final. A broken leg eventually slowed him down but not before a stint with Wanderers in Dublin, playing in the centre alongside the Australian international Andy Slack. By all accounts (and not just those of Murphys) he was a really good player. Nicky knows plenty about the game to this day but keeps most of it to himself.

George likes to assure me that Etienne was the most talented of his rugby-playing sons. He did play Irish Schools, which is more than I can say. A fullback long before I was one. His Irish Schools side were well beaten by a touring Australia team that included Michael Lynagh. Supposedly the one-way traffic got so ugly that several parents in the Donnybrook stand turned their attention to an entertaining two-year-old carefully lining up and kicking an imaginary ball through the goalposts over and over again. Practising my touchline conversions for the long road ahead.

Brian is next. Based in Wexford all his adult life, he was a handy player but never got beyond J1 level down in Gorey RFC. We have plenty of cousins from that neck of the woods – both my grandfather and my mother's grandparents are from Wexford.

Maeve is our only sister. She didn't play rugby, but she has been around plenty of it over the years. She's married to Mark Fitzgerald, who played on the wing for Naas and Leinster Juniors.

Then there is Ross. A six-foot four-inch no-nonsense lock. Our specific rugby gifts are somewhat contrasting – he will have you thinking Bakkies Botha after a few pints – but he had a huge influence on my early career.

My father's game is golf, but he was Leinster high-jump champion once upon a time.

Dad's career in the army meant several trips overseas, to places like Lebanon, Cyprus, Angola and Congo. I was brought on the last of these trips, to El Salvador, during their civil war in the 1980s.

We were there for about eight months as part of a UN peacekeeping delegation until, as George explains it, peace broke out and we were sent home. While there we were put up in a nice house, with a cleaner included. The language barrier between my mother and Marie, our cleaner, was of constant amusement for me.

'Mammy, she has no idea what you are saying.'

I would talk away to Marie, blurting out ridiculous stuff just to make Mam giggle. I could always talk away.

There are GAA roots in our background as well. Being from Kildare and playing sport usually means Gaelic football. I played in the Christian Brothers primary school and Naas GAA club. This early sporting education certainly helped my rugby later on. You can see it with loads of Irish rugby players, like Shane Horgan, Rob Kearney and Tommy Bowe – it is no coincidence that we are all fullbacks or wingers. There are huge benefits to having Gaelic football skills in rugby, especially for a back or even a wing forward. You develop a good engine first and foremost. Kicking, catching and handling skills are also honed from a very early age. I was a midfielder, so soaring for high balls became second nature.

I played in fifth and sixth class for Brother McGovern, who has since passed away. He was one of those teachers whose words resonate long after they've been uttered. I got on great with him. In a school tournament each team had to pick a county in Ireland. I was captain. No one had picked the Lilywhites so I decided I'd captain my own county. We weren't doing very well at the time so it wasn't the popular choice, even among the Kildare boys!

Sure enough, 'Kildare' made the final, and before taking the field Brother McGovern pulled me aside: 'Geordan, if you get your tactics right, you'll win this game.'

I thought I understood what he meant and duly brought my teammates into the action as much as possible, playing with generosity of spirit that would make Brother McGovern proud of me. With a few minutes remaining we were a few scores behind when I gashed my knee against a rock on the pitch. I went down in agony, thinking no pain would ever again be this bad. Brother McGovern came on and poured some 'magic water' on the wound. When I stopped grimacing I realized he was annoyed with me.

'I told you to get the tactics right!'

'I did, Brother. I passed to . . .'

'Don't pass the ball to anyone – just keep it yourself. Trust yourself and take your points.'

I played Gaelic and soccer until I was about seventeen, when rugby became serious. The Leinster Schools Senior Cup saw to that.

Still, a few mentors from Naas GAA would be on every now and again to rope me in for a game. I would be knackered after rugby training but I was always glad to be playing once the ball was thrown in.

Not long after gaining praise for my place-kicking in Newbridge I got a call from the Kildare minor football panel asking if I'd like to come out training. I went over with Brian Flanagan, the flanker and captain of our school rugby team. We trained a few times and I even played a match against Tipperary at left halfback. I may have annoyed a few people when doing one of my rugby party-pieces. I was solo-ing out of defence and a Tipperary player was coming to challenge me so I put the ball behind my back as if to pass and then stepped the other way while keeping the ball. You can take three steps in Gaelic before having to bounce or kick the ball into your hands. I only needed two steps to stand the Tipp fella up and I was away but there was uproar on the sideline.

I've rarely ever mentioned the fact that I played with the Kildare minors.

Sometimes in Ireland there can be an element of begrudgery – 'Sure he never played championship!' – so I just kept it low key. Don't want people getting the wrong idea. Still, I would have done all right, maybe even played senior inter-county if I'd stuck with it.

Dermot Earley Jr was also on the panel. A really genuine guy, Dermot was one of the best midfielders of the last fifteen years and a bit of a legend in Kildare. His father was an army man like George, so we had that in common. Dermot Senior, who played for Roscommon from 1965 to 1985, is widely regarded as one of the greatest players to have never won an All-Ireland medal. Everyone presumed he had played his last game when, at thirty-seven, he left the field with a broken jaw in the '85 Connacht semi-final, but two weeks later he kicked six points as Roscommon lost the final to Mayo.

A Lieutenant General and chief of staff of the Irish Defence Forces until his retirement in 2010 when he passed away that summer.

I still see Dermot Junior from time to time and we chat away about our respective careers. Or about something entirely different. It would have been a pleasure to have ended up playing football with him for these past ten years.

But I went another way. I was training practically every night as Kildare ramped up their sessions, and when I got home I'd be too knackered to open my books. Mum and Dad were giving me grief about studying. I had become fairly central to Newbridge's unusually successful year. I was the outhalf, the goal-kicker. People began wondering out loud about what would happen if I got injured playing football. I loved Gaelic football and it improved my skill set, but rugby was my calling.

When I was younger I'd write stories about playing for Ireland at Lansdowne Road and for Kildare in Croke Park. I never made it to Croke Park with the Lilywhites, but I did with Ireland.

As a child you have dreams. When you get older, you forget your dreams, only remembering them when you realize you are living them.

For ten years playing rugby, Jimmy Ferris was right beside me. I am from Jigginstown, just west of Naas, while Jimmy grew up in Kill, on the other side of town. We landed into Newbridge, as twelve-year-olds, on the same day. I was tiny. The nicknames on the rugby field tended to stick: 'chicken legs', 'twiggy', 'matchstick man'. That is, until I started giving them something else to talk about. Playing football against fourteen-year-olds when I was seven certainly helped, but the D team was our first port of call. Bottom of the bar-rel. I had played in the back garden (on my own, although Campese and Blanco were always out there with me) while Jimmy had been down to Monkstown RFC with his dad's club so we weren't clueless. Just ended up on the fourths, not that we really cared. They bumped us up to the B's after a few weeks, and it got serious as you are look-ing at the guy in your position on the A's and thinking, 'I'd like to play there.'

I quickly discovered that Jimmy would always have my back. One day a couple of third-years attempted to take our sweets off us as we came out of the local newsagent's. I objected and was quickly surrounded. My reaction was to freeze. Jimmy's was to give one of them a dig. We took off. I escaped but they caught Jimmy, handing him a beating. He was a tough nut and seemed happy enough that I escaped.

We clicked after that. We had to do Saturday school and he would pick me up on the way in to Newbridge. My mother would always have a bacon sandwich ready for him. That's probably why he never forgot to stop. There were morning classes and then we'd go off and play sport in the afternoon.

Jimmy was stronger and faster than me, and in 1993, a few weeks before the Cup started, he was called up to the seniors despite being just fifteen.

On wet days in Newbridge a big puddle would form between pitches, and we used to do what we called Klinsmanns – an imitation of the famous goal celebration by the German striker Jürgen Klinsmann. The idea is you dive, head first, and glide on your chest across the water. After training one day, Jimmy led the charge. He neglected to spread his arms, and felt a crack in his neck when he landed. He showered, dressed and went to study, but couldn't move his head. Naturally we bombarded him with spit balls, oblivious to how much pain he was experiencing. He couldn't sleep that night, so it was off to Naas hospital in the morning with his mam. The X-ray gave him the all-clear. A nurse gave him a soft collar just in case.

The X-ray was reviewed the next day and an ambulance sent to his house. Back into Naas General Hospital, still told nothing; he was sitting up in bed reading a newspaper when the doctor came in.

'Lie down immediately!'

They strapped him to the bed before transporting him up to the Meath Hospital in Dublin. He remained like that, strapped in, for the next eight weeks. Staring at the ceiling. We all visited him. It was surreal, and hard for us to comprehend at that age.

Jimmy's C5 vertebra had been crushed and the C4 and C6 were cracked. He was just lucky. If he had dislocated the vertebrae he might have been paralysed. Or even died. All from a Klinsmann dive.

Thankfully, he recovered, but he was in a Robocop brace for the next few months.

That should have been the end of his rugby-playing days, but it wasn't.

The under-16s went to Narbonne that summer and Jimmy was brought along in a mascot capacity. That was the trip when the epic Joey Gleeson/Geordan Murphy rivalry was finally settled. Joey was the resident number ten in Newbridge until I wrestled the jersey off him at junior level, but he had it back by the time we arrived in the south of France. He may have missed a tackle or two on the rock-hard pitches, so I was shifted from centre and had a stormer. We beat Narbonne under-17s. Joey was a quality Gaelic footballer and went on to represent Kildare. When Joey and Jimmy came over to Leicester for big games over the years, there would always be a moment, after a fill of gargle, when Joey would look around and mutter: 'It should have been me . . .'

The table would explode with laughter. They are still my good friends today.

I was outhalf on the Newbridge senior team in 1995, and Jimmy had made a remarkable recovery from the broken neck to be picked on the wing. We were a talented but youthful bunch that season, a year or two younger than most opponents. I was still only sixteen. Black-rock beat us 17–0 in the quarter-final of the Leinster Schools Cup en route to winning the competition outright. It was pretty much the same Blackrock team we would meet a year later. I didn't keep that newspaper cutting, as 'Gordon Murphy' was mentioned only for striking a drop goal off the crossbar.

My big brother Ross was having better luck, winning a Towns Cup that year with Naas. They had a Kiwi coach named Kevin West, who was also sent in to us in Newbridge. Westie had played openside in the same back row as Zinzan Brooke, arguably the game's greatest-ever number eight, at the Marist club in Auckland. After a few run-outs for the Auckland Blues, he moved into coaching in his early thirties as further progress at flanker was blocked by Sevens legend Eric Rush and legendary All Black Michael Jones.

Westie's father-in-law, Ian McKinley, was the assistant principal of Auckland Grammar and he organized an exchange programme to which myself, Jimmy, Dermot O'Sullivan ('Dos' henceforth) and Paul Noble (aka 'Ronnie') were accepted. Westie went home for the summer so he was able to keep an eye on our progress. We shelved the Leaving Certificate for a year and headed off to New Zealand in May 1995 for four months.

Auckland Grammar is the school that developed Graham Henry as a coach and produced Doug Howlett, the All Blacks' all-time top try scorer. Think Grant Fox, the Whetton brothers and the great All Black captain, Wilson Whineray. Sir Edmund Hillary — one of the first two men to climb Everest — went there too.

On the exchange I was paired with Kerry Stanley, and I stayed with his family in Auckland. Ronnie stayed with a Chilean family, guy called Sebastian Berti. Jimmy's set-up was the most interesting. He was housed in East Tamaki, Otara — straight out of the *Once Were Warriors* film — with Johnny Tapu's family. To say the area was rough doesn't do it justice — a man was shot in the alley behind the house one night — but Jimmy was well looked after. All the local 'bros' would come round and we'd play touch on the road.

At Auckland Grammar I played 3A level, the equivalent of under-16s at home. Except this was not Ireland; there was no Irish equivalent; this was the most intense rugby environment on the planet.

Until you make the First XV, everything is done by weight class in the New Zealand underage systems. 3A players, under 75 kilos, were usually within a year of progressing to the Firsts, so it was a serious standard. (The other three Newbridge lads, being too heavy for 3A, had to ship countless bone-jarring tackles from the massive Polynesian boys.)

In direct contrast to home, kicking possession away was blasphemy — a last resort. But anything inventive was encouraged, so my boot became a valued weapon for keeping opponents camped in their own 22. It was a brilliant environment for an Irish teenager who loved his rugby. I became a human sponge.

A few days after we arrived in New Zealand, the four of us were dropped straight into a Sevens tournament at King's College, another famous rugby breeding ground. All the major Auckland secondary schools were present, which meant practically all the players were Islanders. We got smashed. Jimmy was concussed in the first minute of the first game. He woke up to a big Samoan looming over him. Dos, a powerful centre in his own right, was next to be taken out. Ronnie, the biggest of us all, was hauled off, covered in blood. I stayed out of the way – quick hands and even quicker feet meant I didn't get nailed on this occasion, but huge collisions were unavoidable playing rugby in New Zealand. You embraced it or you were discarded.

Dougie Howlett was the superstar at Auckland Grammar. He was on the New Zealand Schools team and looked destined to become an All Black. Ronnie recovered from the opening weekend to make the First XV for a few games, running in a rake of tries on the opposite wing to Howlett. He did so well they asked him to stay on for another year.

We played against St Paul's on a bog in the rain – unsuitable conditions for someone like me who thrived on the firmer surfaces – but everything clicked that day. I controlled the game's tempo, bounced up after every late hit and looked for the ball again. Ran hard at the line and put others into space, but mainly I kept our bigger opponents pinned down with some competent line-kicking. That's what the day required.

We went on to win the 3A championship with a little help from my goal-kicking, and it was mainly because of my kicking that I was asked up to the seconds for an invitational championship at the end of the season. Oddly, there was no emphasis on place-kicking down there. All four of us Newbridge boys kicked for our respective teams.

My 3A coach, Richard Skelly, who went on to coach New Zealand Schools and the the New Zealand women's team, asked me to consider a full academic term at Auckland Grammar. They would fatten me up and I could play First XV within a few months. No thanks – I wanted to take all the tools they had given me back to Newbridge.

We couldn't play enough rugby in New Zealand, lining out at under-21s for the Varsity and Carlton clubs on the weekend. They don't play football on the street, they don't head off for a swim or tennis on a sunny afternoon, it's grab a ball and play some touch rugby.

We went to the Test match against Australia – this was the brilliant 1995 All Blacks side that had done everything but win the World Cup final in South Africa a few weeks after our arrival. Jonah Lomu fever had swept across the nation and he ran in their only try in a 28–16 victory at Eden Park.

We had been talking of taking a wander around New Zealand for ages, so eventually we just skived off for two weeks. Ronnie's brother Rob, a decent player for Greystones and Bective Rangers, was playing in Greymouth, which is a good bit down the west coast of the south island. We were right up the top of the north island. Sure, the four of us would rent a car and drive the length of the country.

We walked into the dodgiest rental agency we could find. Jimmy had a provisional licence. The guy at the counter said he couldn't take it. What about cash, then? He took one look at the dollars and handed over the keys.

Ronnie made the most convincing case to be the driver, only to fail at the ramp out of the car park. We distracted the man who had just handed us the keys as Jimmy figured out how to do a hill start.

Off we went. First stop Rotorua. Four kids in an edge-of-town boozer. A metal can was doing the rounds so we handed over a few quid. Moments later, a stripper began her show on the pool table. We didn't know whether to laugh or cry. The giggles took over as we ran out the door.

We were sleeping in the car that night – to save beer money.

Next port of call was Wellington. We got the ferry over to Picton on the south island, where we made our first major error. It took three hours before anyone questioned our chief navigator: 'Ronnie, shouldn't the sea be on our right, not our left?'

We had taken the wrong turn off the ferry. A night on the piss in Christchurch was the only solution. Next day it was all sorted by the map: we'd drive cross country through Arthur's Pass National Park. It was a mountain range. Lots of signs warning of closed roads, but we trekked on through. Sure what could go wrong?

Ever seen *The Lord of the Rings*? This could be where they filmed the mountain scene when the Hobbits are submerged by the snow pouring off the mountain.

We were the Hobbits. Halfway across Arthur's Pass we accepted our stranded and perilous situation. A lorry came by so we flagged him down and made our escape off the pass.

It was only coming back to get the car the next day that we realized just how dangerous it had been. We eventually got to Greymouth by the recommended route. We looked at the map.

Another feature of the drive was the constant smell of burning – Ronnie, who did most of the driving, had one foot on the accelerator and the other on the brake all the time. We also had a theory that we should drive as fast as possible to save on fuel. We didn't have a clue. It was great fun.

Auckland left a lasting impression. It made me realize I could have a future in the game. If I wanted it badly enough. After four months down there I wanted it more than anything else.

The four lads we stayed with in Auckland followed us back to Newbridge for the next academic year. I don't imagine they learned as much about rugby in Ireland as we did in New Zealand. Johnny Tapu was a serious underage player, but unfortunately Ireland was too cold for his Polynesian bones. He was straight to bed after school every day.

'Too cold, bro. Too cold.'

He'd tog out for training the odd time, smash some poor unfortunate who held the ball a fraction too long and then lose interest. He'd be shivering. Beanie on, hood up and back to bed as soon as possible.

'Too cold, bro. Too cold.'

Kerry and Sebastian made the bench of our senior cup team in 1996.

Dermot O'Sullivan's exchange student was Matt Newman – a giant, powerhouse winger who became an integral part of our attacking game. The O'Sullivans are a great Kerry rugby family – John, the younger brother, ended up playing professionally in France with Agen, while Dermot ended up playing for Grenoble and Perigueux in France, after stints with Connacht and Munster, before injury slowed his progress. The other brothers, Brian and Alan, also featured prominently for Tralee RFC, with Brian captaining Munster Juniors. Matty liked Ireland so much that he came back a year or so later and was working for the O'Sullivans in their shop and tavern in Tralee, living in the house. One day, just before he was due to go home, Matty took his own life. It shook us all – a terrible, unexplainable tragedy.

The provincial Schools Cup competition means a lot to Irish rugby people. It is a huge deal in Leinster. The crowds at Cup games are staggering – thousands turn up.

At that time, from a Newbridge perspective there was an elitism associated with the big south Dublin schools, as well as Belvedere and Clongowes Wood. They had their rugby traditions and were seen as better than us. That's how we felt, anyway: like outsiders.

The social barriers have broken down somewhat because rugby has grown so popular all over the country. Players in provincial towns like Naas or Tullow who show real potential, like Sean O'Brien, don't get passed over any more. It is harder to miss raw talent. Or harder to be missed if you are that talent.

At Newbridge in the mid-1990s, though, we felt we weren't rated. Before Christmas 1995 we were given another reason to feel aggrieved. The Leinster Schools squad was announced and none of us made the cut. The selectors had picked the team without seeing how we had improved during the pre-Christmas league, which we won, playing open, attacking rugby. We moved everything wide simply because we had a small pack and buckets of talent in the backs. The selectors wouldn't have been watching, because none of the big five compete in that competition. As far as we could tell, the representative teams were a closed shop.

We couldn't wait for the Cup to start in January. Nobody knew it, but we were genuine contenders. Those four months in New Zealand had changed everything. The four of us brought home a new attitude to our training sessions that the other lads embraced.

Jimmy was now at scrumhalf, I was outhalf. We demanded quick

ball and then looked for space. If there was none, we'd create it. First
up in the Cup we beat Templeogue before I had one of those untouch-
able afternoons against Castleknock. The New Zealand experience
made these early rounds seem almost like child's play. We entered the
last four with no doubt in our minds about our ability to compete.

In the semi-final against Clongowes Wood, at Lansdowne Road,
I scored what is still one of the more memorable tries of my career:
blocked a kick by my opposite number, scooped it up, stepped a guy
and sprinted over before their stocky young fullback – Gordon
D'Arcy – could grab hold of me. Darce was already brilliant back
then: a near-unstoppable low-centre-of-gravity running machine.
He lit up the '97 and '98 schools competitions as Clongowes made
both finals, winning the second. But after the '96 semi-final, it was
Jimmy and myself who were making the news. Edmund Van Esbeck
in the *Irish Times* called Jimmy 'a scrumhalf of rounded skills and
perceptive judgment. His passing was excellent and his ability to
break at pace caused Clongowes some problems.'

Little old Newbridge College had made it to our first schools final
since 1970.

Blackrock College was synonymous with the Cup, and Blackrock College stood in our way. This was supposedly the best team
they had ever produced. Brian O'Driscoll was a seventeen-year-old
bench-warmer. Their twin towers, Bob Casey and Leo Cullen, are
well known to all rugby people nowadays. David Quinlan (who
later played for Northampton) and Ciarán Scally would also go on
to be capped by Ireland until injury shortened their careers. Their
captain Barry Gibney, a fine openside flanker, was capped by Leinster at twenty, and Peter Smyth was the Leinster hooker for several
years. They also had flyers like Tommy Keating, David 'Magic'
Johnston and Michael Price, who also went on to play professional
rugby.

They were some team, but we were a special bunch ourselves, aug-
mented by a few skins from Auckland Grammar. And so, despite
their reputation, we were confident about beating Blackrock on
St Patrick's Day. The Clongowes match had given us vital experience
of playing at Lansdowne Road. We felt ready. Westie was really

smart in the way he prepared us. Great man for the old mind games, he had us pumped up and focused only on ourselves.

We knew to avoid kicking to touch: the ball had to stay in play due to the sheer size of Leo Cullen and Bob Casey, who would dominate the lineout. It really was Dream Team stuff. O'Driscoll wasn't even sprung from the bench when Dave Quinlan, a centre, was carted off, concussed, in the early exchanges. Everywhere you looked they had a player capable of winning them the game. Their opening try came from Quinlan's replacement, Shane Kelly. We stayed with them for as long as we could, but they were so powerful, so controlled and had been playing and winning together for five years. We had nothing to be ashamed of when they opened us up in the second half.

Despite the heavy 37–3 defeat, I played well that day. My performances got me selected on the Possibles XV, at outhalf, to face the Probables in the Irish Schools final trial a few weeks later at St Andrew's College in south Dublin. The aim was to secure a plane ticket to Australia that summer – a seven-match tour culminating in a Test match against Australia Schools.

Blackrock captain Barry Gibney, along with several of his teammates, had already stormed through Australia unbeaten the previous summer with the Leinster Schools, so most of the places were booked well in advance. Yet there was no certainty about outhalf. Bryn Cunningham, who eventually became a stalwart at fullback for Ulster, was in the mix, but I knew this was a huge opportunity.

I went out and played the game of my life. Kicked goals, ran in a few tries and generally ripped it up. I was eventually swapped over to play behind the Probables pack.

Dad was really pleased with how I performed, but he said very little on the way home. He seemed disappointed. Peter Stringer's old man, who was also on there, still comes up to me scratching his head about what happened next.

A few days later I checked Teletext to seek confirmation of my inclusion in the tour of Australia. That's how it was announced back then. I was shocked to see no sign of 'G Murphy (Newbridge College)' on the list.

The Clongowes semi-final should have been enough in itself.

No other kicking or running outhalf had stood out during the Cup. I had done both – kicking and running amok. But after what happened at the trial in St Andrew's I was certain I would be selected. Dad could have told me otherwise but he didn't have the heart. The old-school politics of Irish rugby had been revealed to him as I was trotting back over the halfway line like a peacock, having converted my own try. Dad sidled over to a selector he recognized for a 'Not bad, is he?' chat of the sort that a father gets to do once, maybe twice in his lifetime if he's lucky.

'Nah, he's not good enough,' came back the reply. 'You may take him back to Naas, that's his standard. He's too slow.'

Too slow! That hurt. Dad told me about the conversation only after my Teletext agony. I'd be stuck in Naas while the elite under-18 schoolboys – including three other number tens (one of whom was the future Ulster fullback Bryn Cunningham) – went on tour of Australia.

We reckoned that the selectors' minds had been made up before the trial match. Blackrock was rightly getting something like ten picks, so there must have been a scramble for the remaining slots. Ulster and Munster needed their share. The other big Leinster schools too. That didn't leave much room for a skinny outhalf from Newbridge, no matter how well I was playing.

Over the years, Dad regularly saw the selector in his blazer at post-match international functions as he climbed up the IRFU committee ladder. Colonel Murphy would stand in his path as the man visibly cringed: 'Still too slow, eh?'

There was a link between Newbridge and Bective Rangers RFC up in Dublin. I was asked to play under-20s with them. There were other offers as well, but Kevin West made the most compelling case: 'There's no point in playing against all the boys you have been up against for the past few years. What are you going to learn? Do me a favour and come play one season for Naas in the Junior One League. Test yourself against men. Play alongside your big brother. You can still go off and play under-20s next season in Dublin.'

It was an unconventional path, but it made sense. Westie was the best coach I'd ever encountered, so I knew my game would continue to improve. And being dropped straight into the men's game was a bigger challenge. Jimmy made the same decision – we came as a double act back then. Two halfbacks for the price of one.

We also went to college in Waterford IT together. I did a course in Legal Studies (why, I don't know), and Jimmy did a business degree. We took up dual status to line out for Waterpark, who were in All-Ireland League division three. We would travel to Naas on Thursday nights for training, play for Waterpark on the Saturday, and back up to Naas for a Sunday game.

Waterpark were perceived as the superior club owing to their league status, but training was farcical. We played touch rugby. After that we would do some tap-penalty moves. It was a joke.

I played about ten games for them that season, culminating with a game up against one of the Ulster clubs. The coach pulled Jimmy and me aside and actually told us not to pass to anyone else. It was the only way we were going to win. 'Jimmy, you pass to Geordie; Geordie, you kick to the corners, drop goals or make a break. Just win it on your own.'

Brother McGovern tactics all over again.

In contrast, Naas was a well-oiled machine. There was a problem, though. Westie had a plan for me that he neglected to mention until I arrived at training the first night. Naas had an English guy named John Corbett as their established number ten. I had watched him and Ross playing together since I was knee high. He was a big, classy outhalf.

It presented a slight problem, but Westie didn't see it that way. He had regularly run me at fullback for attacking moves in training for Newbridge. Come the Cup it was agreed that I was more valuable behind a small pack in the decision-making role, where I could dictate the terms of engagement. Fullback, from my perspective, was more about trusting others to get you the ball. I wasn't used to that.

'No, Westie, I play ten.'

'Just try it, Geordie.'

I hesitantly back-pedalled into the patch of grass behind everyone else, thinking, 'This is bullshit. Maybe I've made a mistake. I should be up in Dublin, running the show at under-20s.'

Outhalf is the number ten, the midfield general. Fullback – well, he's the goalkeeper who, at best, occasionally gets to charge into the line. That's how it seemed to me at the time. How wrong my perception of the position turned out to be.

We ran a move off John, where he put me into the wide channel with a skip pass, while the centres ran straight decoy lines to fix defenders. It was a moment of clarity. With acres of grass laid out in front of me, I barely had to veer outside the second centre before facing my opposite number in open country. Moving so fast now, I had multiple options to skin him: step off the right and head for the corner; step off the left and go under the posts; chip and chase; or draw the tackle before setting the winger free. Once he planted his feet, it was over. I can't remember which option I took, but I glided in for a try.

Westie blew his whistle.

'Again, but this time Geordie . . .'

My whole perception of the game changed in that instant, my eyes suddenly opened to a different sport. John and Jimmy knew how to find me. I just had to pick lines, which came so naturally. Even if I was tackled, there would usually be a pass off either shoulder. Other times I'd just trail the runner and, if he had enough about him, the offload would come and so would the try.

Fullback gives you so much space, and plenty of responsibility too: I could win games with my eyes back there, picking the soft shoulders of props and locks stranded in no-man's-land.

I had no difficulty with the other responsibilities of the position either: my grounding in Gaelic football had me well prepared for the aerial bombardment, and the kicking was easier than at outhalf, as I had more time.

Yeah, we had a grand time that season.

I could roll out my full bag of tricks. A good few tries came from the move that had the GAA folk in uproar: entering the line at pace, I'd go to pass but flip the ball behind my back instead and keep running. The defender always buys it the first time. I did it for Leicester years later in a Premiership game, and it worked again. I test-drove another famous gimmick for Naas: the dummy-chip and chase. No chip, just a chase. Basically, a Gaelic football solo. It is best saved for the last defender – that's right, embarrass your opposite number, they love you for it. Kick the ball upwards but when he jumps to block, catch it and step around him. Another certain try when it worked.

And everything worked that season. Mainly because I didn't plan anything. Just played what was in front of me.

I was overlooked for the Leinster Juniors squad, a representative team made up of players from junior-grade clubs like Naas, so my confidence took another knock. Barry Gordon from Carlow was picked ahead of me, so I had still never played any representative rugby and there were Ross and Jimmy wearing their Leinster hoodies, having been selected. I thought all the gear was so cool. As a kid, earning that kind of status is a huge boost. It reinforces your belief in your ability, makes you bulletproof. I was jealous.

Finally, I got a break. The IRB changed the date of birth for underage teams in 1997 so I became eligible for the Irish under-19s. The World Cup was in Argentina that February and I got picked for the squad. Finally.

There was one small problem. Naas had a top-of-the-table clash against arch-rivals Carlow just two days before the long-haul flight to Buenos Aires.

Dad and Ross were both on to Westie: 'Geordan's not playing.' But after speaking to Westie I decided to play. Of course he wanted me on the pitch, but I bought into his argument:

'This is what rugby is all about, you can't wrap yourself in cotton wool.'

After a shaky opening few minutes, I copped on and just played my usual game. We won, and I arrived at the airport the following Tuesday unscathed.

I was an outhalf again, for Ireland at a World Cup, and I wasn't complaining. I got picked largely off the back of my form for Newbridge in the 1996 Schools Cup – the Castleknock and Clongowes games. Nobody seemed to even know I was a fullback now, as no selector was down watching Naas play junior rugby on a Sunday afternoon when they could be taking in an under-20s game involving Lansdowne, UCD or Blackrock.

The Ireland under-19s coach was a quietly spoken schoolteacher from Presentation College, Cork. This was my first encounter with Declan Kidney.

Despite having a decent side – which included Leo Cullen and Bob Casey, along with a few other Blackrock guys who were already old hands at this touring stuff – we were hammered by Argentina in the semi-final. All I remember is the unbearable heat on the pitch and visiting a teammate, Tom Keating, in hospital after he ruptured his spleen. I played at ten but didn't see much of the ball against the hosts and their massive pack. By the time we played Wales, in the third-place play-off, we were shattered, and lost again.

Deccie was very good with us, a genuine motivator. He was constantly trying to change our mentality as Irish rugby players, to make us believe anything was possible. A year later he guided the next wave of under-19s to the World Cup in France, where they beat the hosts in the final with Drico, Paddy Wallace and Donncha O'Callaghan in the team.

Despite being included in the under-19 squad, I never heard anything from the Irish Academy. It hadn't been split into provincial systems at that stage, and they took fewer players then than they do now; but I never believed I wasn't up to the standard. I was now on the IRFU's radar, but they weren't investing any further man-hours in my progress after Argentina.

So I returned home and saw out the season with Naas. We finished joint top of the league, but Carlow won on points difference. There followed some great experiences of playing Towns Cup in the muck, wind and rain.

I remember one game in particular: Edenderry in the Towns Cup quarter-final. At that time I had complete confidence in my own ability: I wanted the ball to come my way so I could attack. Go to the line, find the weakest link. If there wasn't one, I would chip or launch a garryowen and catch it over their heads.

Ross wouldn't leave me alone beforehand.

'Whatever you do, don't get involved in the shite! These lads will, well, you know yourself, Edenderry, like, they'll just want to kill you.'

I wasn't too worried. Most of the Edenderry lads could never catch me. If I got tackled and stood on, I'd just get up and get the ball again. Then they would be sorry. Fear didn't come into my mind. Edenderry had some huge units in their side, but to me that has always meant plenty of immobile, slow trudgers. I just had to find them in the open field.

Ross was still trying to get my attention.

'Do you fuckin' hear me! Stay out of the messing – leave that to me.'

I ignored him, game blinkers on, and anyway he had to move up for the kick-off.

Adrenalin was coursing through my veins. Man's rugby. Towns Cup.

I knew I wouldn't be long getting the ball. Sure, I was only a kid so they were always going to test me. It came down my throat right from the kick-off. Perfect. I caught it and planted it deep in their 22.

Ross was still glaring at me. I know, I know, stay out of trouble.

Another ball rained down. I caught it under pressure, stepped into space and cleared it miles downfield again as one of their bigger men leaned in with a late shoulder. I grabbed hold of him. Big mistake. I was no longer operating on my own terms. I'd entered Towns Cup territory. I knew a hail of digs would follow if he got an arm loose, so I hung on tight. Ross arrived and cleaved him, only to be surrounded by their big lock and number eight. He had one hand on my jersey and was yelling for me to get out of the mêlée. I obliged.

Ross still says it was the worst beating he ever took on a rugby field. My jersey was a little stretched, which was disappointing as it was already too big for me.

Ross is the sort of big brother every boy should have. I remember Jimmy being clobbered in another match and Ross spending the next twenty minutes landing or standing on the poor guy. Tortured him. You didn't mess with Ross's scrumhalf, especially if it was Jimmy.

He always had an eye out for us.

We beat Edenderry that day and made the Towns Cup semi-final in '97. Carlow were lying in wait. They had the midlands legend Andrew Melville playing at number eight, along with other stalwarts like Lenny Peavoy and Barry Gordon. They beat us 5–0. I missed two penalties (the local paper quipped that I must have left my kicking boots in Argentina), but Harry Sothern, their place-kicker, also had a bad day in difficult conditions. That Carlow side deserved to win. They went on to do something not seen since: climbing all the way through the ranks over the next few years, gaining promotion into senior rugby and ending up in division one of the All-Ireland League.

Little did I know, as I played in those unglamorous yet brilliant Towns Cup matches, that within a few months I would be gone not only from Naas but from Ireland. I assumed I'd stay with the club the following season, maybe get dual status to tog out for a big Dublin team as well. I let the college course slide after Christmas anyway.

In truth, I hadn't really formed much of a long-term plan.

Thankfully, Westie had. He wrote letters to every Premiership club in England, explaining that Naas had two young players worth looking at. The IRFU structures had, for the most part, ignored me, but Westie was guiding me towards professionalism.

I found out later that he wrote in those letters that I possessed a skill set which exceeded anyone he had ever coached or played with, apart from Zinzan Brooke, his old teammate in Auckland.

Bob Dwyer, Australia's World Cup-winning coach in 1991, was now running things at Leicester. Dwyer was the only one who replied to Westie's letter, calling him up to say he would be interested in meeting Jimmy and me at their training camp at the University of Limerick that summer.

Westie drove us down. We watched the Tigers train and had a chat with Bob afterwards. He expressed concern about my size, but Westie assured him I had the talent to make up for it. With no video evidence to provide proof, he tried to explain what we could do.

'Only Zinzan Brooke . . .'

'All right, all right, I'll take a punt,' said Dwyer. 'Send them over for a three-week trial in August.'

2. Cub Life

Never, in my wildest dreams, and there were plenty, did I believe Jimmy and I would be signed up by the Leicester Tigers. I just thought our trial, like the summer in Auckland, would be a great experience that could only improve my game.

We arrived over there a few weeks after Leicester's Martin Johnson had led the 1997 Lions to victory in South Africa. Eric Miller was already there two years, so it wasn't an impossible notion that an Irish kid could make it at this massive English club. Miller, Neil Back, Will Greenwood and Austin Healey had all impressed for the Lions. Any rugby-mad teenager like me had watched the brilliant *Living with the Lions* documentary about that tour. It had made these men seem like mythical figures, and suddenly I was going to the place where they trained. It would be cool, I thought, to see them on the pitch next to us.

Sure enough, on arrival there they were. About forty-five Tigers were togging out. We were told to follow them.

'Shit, Jimmy, I think they want us to train with the firsts.'

It was true: we were dropped straight into a pre-season session. I don't think it would happen now.

The second team needed a fullback, so within minutes of arriving I was running against the Leicester Tigers. The first move called was a double skip pass from our centre to the winger. I turned to this big guy inside me, 'You got that pass, bud?' As you would in a club game. In Naas. If he had any doubts, we could run a tighter line.

'Yep, I got it, pal,' he replied in a distinct Scottish twang, turning enough for me to see the word 'Joiner' on his back. I wanted the ground to swallow me. Craig Joiner had seventeen caps for Scotland at the time.

That was Monday – there was a trial match on the weekend so everything was building towards that.

After training, the assistant coach Duncan Hall gave us a lift to the family that was putting us up. There were pictures of Martin Johnson and his brother Will everywhere in the house.

'Shit, Jimmy . . .'

'I know, Geordie.' He looked as scared as I sounded.

David and Hilary Johnson showed us up to Martin's childhood bedroom. Until then, we had just assumed that Martin Johnson arrived on planet Earth as the Goliath we saw on television.

Hilary Johnson was a remarkable woman. She ran competitively for Durham before becoming a PE teacher. She eventually started running marathons before graduating to 100-km, ultra-distance races for Great Britain. That must be where Johnno got his engine.

Hilary had a heart problem and needed a pacemaker. She used to tell me that she would run until her pacemaker zapped her; then she'd walk until her heart rate dropped back to normal so she could start running again.

She took time to talk to us every day to see how we were getting on. Her house was also the first place I ever came across with protein shakes and high-fibre carbohydrate drinks.

'Drink them up, boys.' We did.

The trial match was a selection of potential recruits against the established Academy XV. Serious stuff. It couldn't have gone any better for me: I scored tries in the first two attacks. Converted them as well.

There was a winger for the Academy boys named Nnamdi Ezulike from Nigeria. His running style made it seem like he was barely moving, but he was rapid. At one point, Nnamdi was put in the clear and was coming straight at me. I had him covered, until he changed direction and I felt a chill of panic go through my body: *I'm going to get absolutely smoked here*. I turned and gunned for the corner flag. Fear got me there in time to put Nnamdi into touch with a shoulder just before he could free his hands.

Bob Dwyer was standing behind the dead-ball line.

'Come off.'

What? Nobody ever wants to be pulled. He had to check who I was. Somebody told him.

'Murphy, you are playing for the seconds next weekend.'

Away to Gloucester, in Kingsholm. Our team was ridiculous. Dean Richards at lock, Niall Malone, who was capped for Ireland, at outhalf, Will Johnson at number eight and a crazed-looking blond flanker around my age named Lewis Moody at openside wing forward. And chicken legs at fullback.

It was my first outing in front of The Shed – Gloucester's hallowed ledge for their ultra-passionate home support. Deano's presence guaranteed it was packed. In the opening minutes he belted a guy in a ruck right under The Shed's gaze. Then he raised a defiant arm at them. The place went up.

Jesus. I had played in a Schools Cup final in front of 20,000 people at Lansdowne Road, but this was different, way more intimidating. The crowd were on top of you, especially when you were waiting for the ball to drop from two hundred feet.

We drew 17-all. I did my bread-and-butter stuff well enough to get a few pats on the back afterwards.

I was due to play for the Academy on the third weekend, but the match was cancelled. On the day before Jimmy and I were due to go home, Hilary was waiting with our dinner, protein shakes and the usual questions about training.

We gave our usual answer. 'Great!'

'Have they offered you anything?'

'Eh, no.'

'Right, boys, into the car.'

She drove us to the training ground and marched straight into Bob Dwyer's office. No messing about: 'Bob, are you going to keep these lads or not?'

Bob said yes on the spot. Three-year deals.

'What about their education?'

We could continue our studies at De Montfort University.

Contracts were produced, signed, and the deal done: twelve grand a year, digs and Uni covered. Hilary didn't take a commission.

My folks were happy so long as I continued my studies. I took up a course in Chartered Surveying. Again, no idea why. Lucky-dip stuff. No career appealed to me.

All I knew was that I had just become a professional rugby player for the Leicester Tigers. The environment, its work ethic, the quality of player – all of it was contagious. Our heads had barely stopped spinning – New Zealand, Lansdowne Road, Waterpark, Argentina, Naas and now Leicester, all in the space of two crazy years.

Me and Jimmy. Our partnership wasn't going to last for ever. Nothing ever does in professional sport. But you only learn that when things change.

Myself and Jimmy stayed with the Johnsons for a few months before moving into town: 33 Rydal Street, just around the corner from Uni. One of Richard Cockerill's houses. There was a gang of Tiger cubs in the area, so we all knocked around together – the Wednesday Club, as Neil Back christened us. Thursday's morning session was never easy.

Paul Gustard shared number thirty-three with us – a flanker who eventually clocked up 110 appearances for the Tigers before moving on to London Irish and then Saracens, where he is now defence coach. Paul thoughtfully came up with another nickname for me: 'Pencil'.

Mrs Johnson also introduced us to Hugh Owen, the only prop to score four tries for 'The Extras' – the seconds team. Hugh took us under his sizeable wing. James Gosling lived with him just around the corner. Lewis Moody was also close by. Others in our gang were Leon Lloyd, James Overend, Neil Fletcher and Nick Redpath. Nick, who also moved into our place, was a hard centre who ended up at West Hartlepool. He proved handy to have around of a night if things got a little heated.

We all spent a lot of time together, creating a mini-family – that is, in the *Lord of the Flies* sense. We also socialized with our college mates. On Saturday nights we'd come back from either seconds or a development team game, have some food and play *Jonah Lomu Rugby* on the Playstation for a few hours. Loser paid the three quid in to the Student Union, but sometimes we never got out the door. Cockers was a regular visitor but never in a landlord capacity.

I did a couple of half-hearted semesters at De Montfort University, but my studies got shelved once I reached the crossroads between lectures or training.

Really, Dean Richards made the decision for me. Bob Dwyer was sacked in early 1998 and things changed at the club. Or, more accurately, things went back to the way they used to be before I arrived. Training began at a non-negotiable 10 a.m. Dwyer used to repeat the 10 a.m. session in the afternoon so you could organize your day around college and rugby, but Deano insisted that the whole squad train together.

Other things changed which didn't exactly benefit Jimmy or myself. We had developed into utility players, cursed by our versatility. Jimmy got pushed on to the wing because Austin Healey, Roly Edwards and Jamie Hamilton were the other scrumhalves. It helped that he was lightning quick – he even gassed Philippe Bernat-Salles in a match against the Barbarians.

At the end of our second season we both signed two-year extensions. But Jimmy was struggling with a knee injury and didn't play much in our third season.

Kevin West called Jimmy one day. Blackrock club had been relegated to division two of the All Ireland League and they hired Westie to bring them back up. He inherited a phenomenal squad of aspiring professionals – most of the schools team that overran us in '96, with Brian O'Driscoll also joining from UCD. Ciarán Scally had been forced to retire with a knee injury, so Westie needed a scrumhalf and a grizzled second-row. Ross was brought up from Naas on dual status and Jimmy was offered a chance to go back to Ireland. He took it, and I knew he was doing the right thing. He had finished his business degree, and his injury was going to make it hard for him to advance at Leicester. All the provincial squads had been signed off, but Connacht eventually recruited him for their European Shield campaign. He did three seasons in Galway before his shoulder caved in.

Jimmy's fairly consistent string of injuries eventually caught up with him. There was the broken neck as a teenager, the knee in Leicester, the shoulder in Connacht and, worst of all, his arthritic hips. He had a hip replacement last year, aged just thirty-two. Initially, he thought it was a groin problem. He put off the operation for six years, even playing a few more games, but when tying shoelaces became a major task, the op became essential to his long-term health.

He needs the other hip done as well. Not that he's bothered, and he still looks in decent physical shape from all the boxing training he does. Now he is working away in private banking, making a living and getting on with life. A few years ago he went back to his father's club, Monkstown RFC, as director of rugby. He stepped away last season due to work and the birth of his first child, but I'm sure he will return to rugby some day. Jimmy left the place in good hands – Kevin West is the current head coach of Monkstown.

We played together as twelve-year-olds on the Newbridge under-13 D team. Ten years later he was going home. It was some journey. By the end of it I was deeply embroiled in the Leicester way of doing things. It is different from other ways.

At Leicester, friendships are born out of a work ethic which has always been the cornerstone of the club. The club also has its own customs, some of them brutal. There were regular beatings handed out as a welcome on your first day at training. I must have been useful enough in other areas to be shielded from most of this carry-on – the forwards were a logical enough bunch to realize that pounding me was of little benefit to them. Anyway, you tended to get overlooked when Austin Healey was around, constantly mouthing off to them.

I get on really well with Austin – most of the time. He was never bothered who he pissed off, but I found him likeable. A few months after I signed for Leicester, he pulled me to one side.

'You know something, Geordie, you are too nice. You need to be more of a wanker. Like me. I don't really give a shit about people, I enjoy pissing them off. There is plenty of time to make friends after you have finished playing rugby.'

'Thanks, Austin. I will take that under advisement.' But my attitude was to keep the head down and work. I was respectful of the older Tigers. An arrogant attitude was a certain way of getting your head kicked in at training.

Austin got knocked out a good few times. In his autobiography, aptly named *Me and My Mouth*, he remembers winning a lot of fights, but I don't remember him winning any. One time, out for a few drinks, we got into a row that got slightly out of hand. I was leaning over the table chatting and, as I was only wearing a T-shirt, you could see down the back of my pants. Austin felt obliged to inform me of this by casually pouring his entire drink down there. I turned to see his Scouser grin.

'Wot you going to do about it, Geordie?'

'I guarantee you: I'm going to knock you out.'

'Bring it on, Geordie. Bring it on.'

I decided against jumping up and whacking him in the face: revenge would be better served cold. This prompted him to fire off a string of abuse. A while later his phone rang. He turned away to speak to his missus, foolishly turning his back on me. I crept up behind him and locked him into a choke hold, cutting off his supply of oxygen, before leaving him laid out on the floor of the pub, out cold, the phone still in his hand and his girlfriend on the other end.

'Austin . . . Austin!'

I went back to Leon Lloyd and Darren Morris at the table. When Austin woke up, his blood was boiling.

'Well, I told you I was going to knock you out.'

He was adamant that I was out of order. It kicked off. A few apologies were needed the next morning.

This was child's play compared to what went on among the harder edges at the club. After matches, there was a tradition whereby the likes of Dean Richards and John Wells owned the back seat of the bus. Anyone else who wanted to sit there would face extreme violence on the way. Paddy Howard made it to the back once by crawling beneath the seats while a scrap was raging above him. It meant he was always allowed to sit there. It was vicious. I remember Craig Joiner getting a good beating off Cockers. We still do it occasionally nowadays, but it is not so popular with the coaches since Jordan Crane got split open after the 2009 Premiership final.

Deano and the older crew – Cockers, Darren Garforth, Graham Rowntree and Johnno – used to travel down to England training camps in one car, and a similar tradition developed. Someone got the short straw and had to drive. The rest would get on the beer. They would arrive at Penny Hill or wherever covered in blood.

Those trips created an aura that still exists. It is certainly tapped into by the club whenever defeat is staring us in the face.

When I first came over, there was a lot of contact stuff at training. There is less of it now because the game has changed, but it used to ensure a punch-up at training every week. The coaches rarely interfered. Neither did I, sensible enough to know I am no fighter.

Lewis was, and is, the complete opposite. It could blow up with him in a game of touch. On Wednesday there used to be a game with no referee. Saturday matches rarely reached the same intensity – that was the point. If someone got chinned they would be groggy and then angry, but they'd have to keep it bottled until the next session. The beauty of this scenario was the next contact session tended to be the weekend game, so all the frustration was emptied out on opponents, while the guy who clattered you was right there beside you.

Johnno was forced into knocking Lewis out one day. It was priceless.

We were doing a bag session. Lewis was particularly wired. This was 2004, and he had just returned after a few weeks laid up with injury. He was doing his best impression of a dog chasing a frisbee on to a busy road, oblivious to all consequences. Alex Tuilagi took a ball at full tilt and powered through two bags, continuing up the touch-line. Lewis was holding the first bag but he got blown away. Red mist descended, he dropped the bag and tore after the eighteen-stone frisbee. Alex, unaware that he was being stalked, slowed at the try-line, allowing Lewis to cream him with a right forearm aimed at dislodging the ball. Lewis caught him a tad high. Alex understandably took this as an act of war, but the real concern was that Henry Tuilagi would join in. We were all on red alert. We knew Lewis wouldn't back down. Facing one Tuilagi is bad enough, but two would have got very messy.

Thankfully, Johnno arrived on the scene before Henry.

'Lewis, what the fuck are you doing?'

'Fuck off, Johnno!' Lewis lashed out, but Johnno had him at arm's length and instinctively dinked him on the chin. Lewis's legs buckled, so Johnno had to gently lay him out on the turf.

Lewis woke to the Tuilagi brothers' massive smiling heads.

'Come on, bro, up you get.'

He was steaming angry until a shower cooled him down. Then he laughed it off, but mainly because the weekend was just around the corner.

Leicester used letters instead of numbers on the jerseys until the 1998/9 season, so I was the last fullback to wear O instead of fifteen. No idea where I left that jersey.

There were international matches in November 1997 so I got my first chance in the Cheltenham and Gloucester Cup against Rotherham. Ran in a couple of tries. I finished the Loughborough Students match with 31 points as we won 71–7; Marika Vunibaka also ran in a hat-trick of tries on his debut.

Not that the giant Fijian seemed all that interested. The great Waisale Serevi, who joined Leicester in 1996, had recommended we bring him over. The lads called Vunibaka 'Samuel L' – *Pulp Fiction* had been out a while and he had the same facial hair as Jules Winnfield. I'm not sure if he spoke English – he was the silent type – but it didn't matter: he was superhuman quick, as I learned one night at training. We were playing touch. The Fijians were freezing. The club had these shiny tracksuit bottoms. Serevi intercepted a pass so I turned to track him, just to see if I could catch up. It was the sound that freaked me out, the shell bottom legs rubbing off each other like propellers on an old airplane as Samuel L flew past, hunting down his mate. He couldn't get a work permit and ended up solidifying his reputation with the Canterbury Crusaders a few years later.

The problem with Serevi was that he didn't have a position. Out-half, obviously, but Joel Stransky had won the 1995 World Cup for South Africa from that position. Still, Wiz scored some beautiful tries. I remember one in particular against Pau down in France when he sold a ridiculous dummy, chipped a guy, caught it and threw another dummy before goose-stepping clear. The French crowd stood and applauded the sight of a maestro at work.

To train with him was unbelievable. I learned how to catch silently, absorbing the force of a ball falling from the sky softly into my hands, from watching how Serevi did it. But his genius was Sevens, not the fifteen-man game.

I kept scoring tries, six of them in an invitational game against a President's XV down at a small local club in Burton-on-Trent. With Andrew Leeds, a former Australian international who eventually switched to Rugby League, and the South African Michael Horak vying for the fullback residency, I sneaked up the rails largely unnoticed.

That anonymity ended on 10 January 1998 against Coventry at Coundon Road in the Tetley Bitter Cup. I didn't realize it at the time but Leicester versus Coventry was a huge deal. This was a local rivalry, separated by the M69, going back to the dawn of time.

Jimmy was due to make his debut but the pitch was flooded, and Austin was back fit a week later. I was nineteen, and playing fullback in a team that included Joel Stransky, Neil Back and Martin Johnson.

Ross had promised to fly over for my first big game. Sure enough, he turned up in Leicester with no way of getting to Coventry, so we gave him Jimmy's old Nissan Cherry. Ross dropped me to the hotel outside Leicester.

'Follow the team bus, Ross.'

Martin Corry saw him and said, 'Follow us, mate.' Eric Miller's blue BMW disappeared into the distance a good few times as the Cherry peaked at a very shaky 60 mph down the motorway. Corry ensured Ross wasn't abandoned, and when we got to Coventry he even pulled back the cones so that he could leave the car in behind the team bus.

(Martin Corry is a gentleman – Honest Coz. It was always going to be difficult following Martin Johnson as club captain, but to have to do it for England as well became a nightmare as the defeats mounted up, post the 2003 World Cup. Plenty of other guys had their eye on that job, like Lawrence Dallaglio. Cozza carried it with typical dignity.)

Ross was sitting beside David Johnson, Martin's dad. He got a phone call during the match from Kildare FM. Ross, glued to my movements, handed over the phone to the Lions' captain's father – without mentioning he was live on the radio. Mr Johnson did an impeccable job explaining to the good folk of Kildare about my bedding-in period.

Twenty-five minutes into the game I did something that made everyone sit up and take notice. It was an arm-wrestle but we had a 13–8 lead. Their fullback sliced a clearance about five metres inside the Leicester half. It bobbled into my hands. I was about twenty metres in from touch. There was no one near me, so as I moved over the halfway line I did what I would do for Newbridge College or Naas RFC: I let go a drop goal.

Will Greenwood, who was just back from making a serious impact on the Lions tour of South Africa, was on the sideline. Afterwards he came up and told me I had a bright future in the game. Then he told me that as I pulled the trigger from 46 metres out, Bob Dwyer's face went bright red as he yelled: 'Ah, what the FAAACCckk . . .' but as it sailed between the posts a smile cut across his features and he finished the sentence: '. . . he's got it!'

It was the second best drop goal I ever struck (the best was against Saracens a few years later, from further out and into a gale). It changed people's perception of me at the club. I was no longer just some skinny kid from Ireland, people found out my name. People like Will Greenwood. The surge of confidence that goes through your body after being patted on the back by an established player is immense. It makes you believe you belong.

My league debut came against London Irish on St Valentine's Day. Leeds had departed and Horak was injured, so I was promoted from the seconds. Austin and Leon were my wingers. Lewis had cemented a place at flanker, Martin Corry was at number eight, while the front-row ABC club was made up of Rowntree, Cockerill and Garforth. Johnno led us out.

Bob picked me for the next five games. Then he was sacked after falling out first with the players and then with the board. He dropped Deano for Eric Miller, then fell out with Will and then, fatally it seems, dropped Austin after a training-ground row.

Bob gave me my start, and was going to keep picking me, I think.

He was there only seventeen months, but that's the small window when my rugby career was launched.

(Bob ended up at Bristol and tried to sign me a few years later. I went down for a look with my agent, Justin Page, and was genuinely impressed. They had already recruited Felipe Contepomi, Agustin Pichot and Jason Little, so I would have got plenty of ball. They were a good side and Bob had given me my break and was now offering more money to follow him. I thought about it, but Leicester was a better-equipped club, always slightly ahead of the curve. I decided I wanted to stay, make a name for myself at Leicester and win trophies. I trusted the Tigers.)

In the late '90s Bath were the leading club in England. Until winning the cup the previous season under Dwyer, Leicester hadn't won it for sixteen years. The league title had been captured twice in ten years. We had also lost the European Cup final against Brive in '97.

In came Dean Richards. I was immediately concerned. Sure, Deano had seen what I could do, but he was a hard-nosed, no-nonsense, old-school character.

Another source of concern was Tim Stimpson, who arrived after my first season. Not only was he an England and Lions fullback, he was a place-kicking, six-foot-three-inch, sixteen-and-a-half-stone England and Lions fullback.

But I backed myself against him every time. You have no choice in that situation. I have always believed in my own ability.

There was confusion over my position. Joel Stransky, who took over as backs coach under Deano, promptly decided I was an outhalf again. He saw the residue of my old position in my habits and believed it was a natural fit. I found myself having the same argument I had had with Westie, but in reverse.

Joel was very hard on me, but in a good way. I didn't feel bullied, because I could take it, but I struggled to reach the standards he demanded. This was the man who dropped the winning goal in the 1995 World Cup final, so I obeyed his commands and it made me a better player, even if it took several years for me to realize it. I liked him any time we were away from the training ground. He changed the way I passed the ball – hitting the man outside without any spin, a foot in front of him, at chest height so it could be taken and moved on quicker. He also changed the way I kicked. Like all great Springbok tens, he had a massive boot, and he wanted to add ten yards to my punts. Getting accustomed to the new techniques took months, but he kept on my case and it did prove beneficial to my kicking game.

It took a while before I could get the club to leave the outhalf idea well alone. It's not that I didn't like playing there, it's just that you must be playing there all the time to really thrive in the position. Same goes for fullback.

Deano was all about the tough love as well. He is a former copper with hands like shovels, and he has an intimidating sideways look that gives the impression he's coming in for the kill; but he's deaf in one ear and really he is just leaning in to give you his full attention.

Peter Short ripped his ear off once on the bus home from a game. Deano, John Wells, Johnno and Garforth were the backseat residents. Peter had to get there or die trying. Deano had recently had an operation on his ear and the stitches were still fresh. He and Peter were wrestling. It was good-natured stuff by Deano standards – he had Peter in a headlock – but then Wellsy, another former copper, called a sudden halt to proceedings.

'Whoa, whoa – there is a lot of blood.'

'What?' Deano enquired, inspecting his still struggling victim. Shorty had ripped his ear off. It was dangling there like a piece of jewellery. We had no doctor on the bus. Well, we did, but he was pissed.

'Aw, shit,' said Deano, 'give me the Sellotape.'

I liked Deano. He didn't coach so much as manage the club. John Wells and Joel Stransky and, later, Paddy Howard were given the reins at training, while Deano literally ran every other aspect of the place. He became the club, his personality and attitude seeping into every corner.

I damaged my ankle once and was using a support outside the sock. It really helped, but I heard our physio getting a bollocking from Deano about it. He didn't want me wearing the brace as it made me look soft, and that meant we all looked soft. I got strapped inside my sock instead.

This mentality seeps into your brain after a while. I don't like any strapping now. I feel uncomfortable with it.

Inevitably, Deano took issue with my size. I had my wages sliced in half until I reached a target weight. This has always been difficult for me: my metabolism works too quickly (even in my thirties). I used to get up in the middle of the night to drink protein shakes. I got up to 79 kilos. Deano wanted me at 82. After six weeks of half-wages I was living on pennies, and so stressed that I began losing weight!

In May 1999 we won the league up in Newcastle, on the defending champions' home patch of Kingston Park. I came on at outhalf for the injured Paddy Howard. That's how the season had gone for me – off the bench at ten and occasionally shifted into the back three. Still, I felt part of the squad. Phil Larder had come a year previously and put a solid shape to our defence. It became everything to us. We brought the title back to Leicester.

The lads were staying up north that bank holiday weekend for Matt Poole's stag do in Whitley Bay, and I was invited. Matt, who runs a lot of Tigers events now, played in the second row with Johnno for years. There were thirteen of us, so the round was twenty-six drinks. Everyone bought a round. It was unbelievable, but I was made to feel part of the group.

Winning that league was the best trophy I ever won, because it was the first. I had played in a Schools Cup final and a Towns Cup semi-final, but I had no medals. After that, we expected to win the league every year. Or, more accurately, we demanded it of ourselves.

After we beat Newcastle there were still two weekends left in the season. I played fullback against Swansea and West Hartlepool in a 72–37 coronation at Welford Road. We celebrated heavily afterwards. The next day, Monday morning, Lewis landed at my door.

'We're going on the beer down the Student Union.'

'No, I don't want to go out.'

'No, we are going.'

'I can't afford it.'

'We are going.'

He was not going to stop. A few afternoon pints, then. I knew it became a nightclub at 9 p.m. so I wore runners and a cotton tracksuit: they couldn't possibly let me upstairs.

A student introduced Lewis to suicide tequilas. Sniff the salt, put the lemon in your eye and drink the shot.

'No, mate, that's not a suicide tequila, this is . . .' Lewis sniffed the lemon, poured the salt in his eye and drank the shot as his eye started to foam and burn.

When 9 p.m. rolled around I was longing for my bed. I looked around, no Lewis, so I took this as my chance to escape. As I walked towards the exit a flash of blond hair planted me across two tables full of drinks.

The bouncer waved us upstairs, where Lewis decided to do a stage dive. He announced to the nightclub that all sixteen and a half stone was coming into the crowd. The dance floor parted like the Red Sea. Being a good club man, I tried to catch him, but we both slid across the dance floor into a speaker.

'Good lad, Geordie.' He trusted me after that.

The next season, 1999/2000, I played at ten, at centre, at winger and occasionally at fullback. Or just outside-back replacement.

That was a problem that I addressed against Bath in the Boxing Day war of 1999. The Rec was a swamp. The game was tied up at 6-all when I was sent on for Nnamdi on the right wing, but I switched with Tim and lined up at fullback. Mike Catt immediately sent a high ball down my throat. I caught it and we made good ground. Then I made an important tackle on Kevin Maggs. Next I made a line break, fed Cozza on the wing and trailed him for the return pass to sprint over for the match-winning try.

Deano said afterwards it was my ability under the high ball that prompted the substitution. So he trusted me. Most importantly, he saw that my future was in the backfield. At least the outhalf debate was over.

I was picked fairly regularly after that until I damaged my shoulder scoring a fingertip try to defeat Bath in the cup. I came back in March, as a place-kicking fullback. Tim was in the starting fifteen but we often swapped roles, especially in attack, as it was established I could do more damage in the wider channels with ball in hand.

I made twenty-four league appearances that season and scored nine tries. I had become a central part of a club that had the English domestic game in a stranglehold. We captured our second league title with eight points to spare over Bath, who we beat 43–25 on the last day of the season. I crossed for a try, but Neil Back's hat-trick was a better indication of where the damage was done.

After those great victories, I'd sit as close to the middle of the bus as possible without getting drawn into the rows, thinking: 'What the hell am I doing here?' But I felt loved. Respected too. Playing for pennies, yes, but I was part of something special.

3. Back in the Mix

Felix Jones lands awkwardly. Tom Croft and Aneka are beside me on the couch. Since the double leg fracture in 2003, I can't look at these replays any more. Makes me nauseated.

I leave the room, but I can hear Aneka and Crofty groaning as they see what happened to Felix. Only then it dawns on me: an Irish fullback is injured. And I have no mobile phone. It is in some gutter halfway between Camden Street and Harcourt Street. Or down the back seat of some Dublin taxi. In the early hours of Friday morning it all got a little hazy. I blame the Tipperary fellas.

OK, let's rewind a few weeks.

On Monday morning, 1 August 2011, the week of the first World Cup warm-up against Scotland in Edinburgh, Deccie called me in and said, 'Look, there is no place for you in the twenty-two against Scotland and probably not against France next week.'

I remained calm, putting my practical hat on: World Cup or not, it had been eight months since I played any rugby. I needed a bloody game. Ireland wouldn't give me one, so I flew to France on the Thursday to join up with the Leicester pre-season camp in a grim, quiet village in the south of France called Saint Affrique. Trained Saturday with lots of fresh faces, like being at a new club. Niall Morris, the Blackrock fullback, had joined from Leinster.

Trained again Sunday, before playing the next night. I am a different animal in a striped Tigers jersey, mainly because I can call the shots when I feel it's necessary. The ball will go through my hands whenever we attack. That has always been the way. They trust me.

Montpellier pasted us 50–24. I did all right. Made a couple of mistakes, but good mistakes that reminded me about the game. Ah yes, I know this game. It's like meeting an old friend again: the bullshit gets shelved after the initial formalities.

I was tackled a few times and the foot bent normally. It's always a little sore. It's sore right now. I'm at about 90 per cent. My toes are numb, pins and needles all the time, but when I run it feels good. I always feel good when I'm running. Loved being out there again. Those months of rehab had been a living hell.

About fifteen minutes into the second half our scrumhalf Sammy Harrison saw a sock near the ball at the bottom of a ruck and stamped on it. Scrumhalves do that. They have to. Unfortunately, the ankle was mine.

'Fucking hell, Sammy!' I yell, limping away from the ruck.

'Oh, sorry, Geordie. Sorry!'

The sideline reacted immediately to my one-legged hopping routine.

'You are due to come off anyway,' Matt O'Connor assured me.

'No, I'm fine.'

The usual response but I'm not sure.

'You are coming off.'

I'm in pain. I come off. The ice machine is ready.

'Relax, it's not the foot, it's my ankle. But I'll take the ice, please.'

Crisis averted. The rumour mill on Twitter wasn't long cranking up.

@RugbyUniverse

> Geordan Murphy, having linked up with Tigers to get game time, appeared to limp off when he left the pitch in pre-season friendly.

I'm not too familiar with tweeting, but my phone was cooking, so I provided some clarification:

> 'Played 55 mins. Foot felt great. Lost to a decent Montpellier side but lots of positives! Thank you all for the messages!'

Rog and Drico were on, singing my praises:

Brian: 'Welcome back twiglet!' Another unwelcome nickname due to my brittle bones.

> Rog: 'Can't keep a good thing down . . . it's a nice day.'

I glanced at the blog of a guy who had asked for a retweet a few days beforehand. I'd obliged.

I scrolled down to his World Cup squad:

Fullbacks:

Felix Jones, Rob Kearney

Nice one, mate!

I was back, finally. There was a sliver of hope which lasted all of forty-eight hours. For the trip to Bordeaux, Deccie confirmed Rob was starting, with Felix to be used off the bench again.

This is an out-and-out disaster for me as Leicester don't have another game. It is confirming to the general public something I had known for weeks.

I'm out. Felix is in. My international career is over.

The lads in camp could do the maths. Three into two doesn't go and Deccie has made up his mind.

The Irish World Cup squad headed off to France, I flew back to Leicestershire. I didn't see the game in Bordeaux. It was scheduled to be on ITV4, but as I sank into the couch *Minder* came on instead. I was left with Michael Corcoran and RTÉ radio online – tough to know where the ball was on the pitch, but brilliant. It sounded as though Rob was returning to form, though he pulled up before the end. Felix came in and did well with a chip and chase. That's the ounce of confirmation Deccie was probably seeking.

What really choked me up was that the long road back had been for nothing. I wouldn't even get a chance to prove myself.

I wanted to smash the radio remote control off the wall. But then I'd be stuck watching *Minder*. I sat there on the same part of my couch I was attached to for most of February and March when I was practically a cripple. At least that gave me some perspective.

The injury happened against Northampton at Welford Road on 8 January. There were about ten minutes left. We were winning, but it was close. This is the big East Midlands derby, so the Saints were piling into us, we were clinging on. A kick sent the ball zipping along the turf. Their winger, Paul Diggin, got there ahead of me and offloaded from the ground, allowing them to rumble to about five metres from our line. I ran back around and found myself in the ten channel and, keen to make up for not gathering the kick, went to tackle one of their backrow forwards. I hit him and he stopped, but Craig Newby flew into the other side of him just as another one of their forwards belted into Craig.

That's when I heard the sound.

My right foot was planted on the ground, so when I took the force of Craig and the Saints' forward my knee opened out but my foot stayed square in the turf. When I broke my leg in 2003 I knew instantaneously that I had broken my leg, but this was a weirder sensation. First I thought I'd done my knee: I felt a pop and heard a crack. But there was no pain from the knee, so my next thought was that it must have been my ankle dislocating and fracturing.

Bobby Sourbutts, the Leicester physio and the patron saint of fractured and torn causes, arrived on my shoulder.

'I've dislocated my ankle, Bobby.'

He checked, 'It's in place, Geordan.'

I assumed I had subluxed it – popped it out then immediately back in, like I've done with my shoulder in the past.

'Can you get up and walk off the field?'

You always want to get up and walk off at Welford Road.

All of a sudden, I am Jack 'Cap' Rooney, the veteran quarterback in Oliver Stone's film, *Any Given Sunday*. I can hear the camera flashbulbs, my offensive line are all looking down at me. I am the Leicester Tigers' captain. I have to get up, lean on Bobby and walk off this field. This is a big thing at the club. If anyone has a phantom injury they get a lot of grief. To use a stretcher and be back in training any time during the next month is a guaranteed way of picking up the nickname 'Lazarus'.

You walk off just in case it is only nerve damage sending fake messages to your brain. I was conscious of all this. I tried to stand but unbearable pain seared up the right side of my body. And, trust me, I've known pain on a rugby field.

'No, I can't walk off. Get me a stretcher.'

One of the lads said: 'Are you sure, Geordie?'

'Yeah, I'm sure. Stretcher.'

Waves of pain now. Rushing in and breaking, rushing in and breaking. Two words in my mind: World Cup.

To take the edge off, I was given some gas to inhale in the changing room. But I was in trouble and I knew it.

The medics thought it was syndesmosis. There are two bones held together at the bottom of the foot; syndesmosis is when they split. A lot of rugby players have been diagnosed with this recently. Dean Richards would have called it a twisted ankle, but it keeps a player sidelined for six to eight weeks.

I had heard of this and knew that walking shouldn't be a problem. Nor should I be in excruciating pain.

I showered and hopped across the pitch to the post-match reception because some friends had come to the game. The pain got worse, so I hobbled over the road for an X-ray. Nothing showed up.

The general opinion was that it was nothing serious. But I have got used to this body of mine over the past few years, and I knew something was very wrong. I was in agony and all I could take was paracetamol.

One of the physios, Dave Orton, was staying with me so he drove us home. (Traditionally, if anyone from the club needs somewhere to stay, 'Geordie's place' is the first port of call – I've had quite an interesting array of characters pass through my door.)

I went up to bed, but that didn't last long. I tried sitting in a chair. No comfort there or on the windowsill. Three sleepless nights followed, before Bobby took me down to Basingstoke to see James Calder, one of the UK's foremost foot/ankle specialists, on the Tuesday. Aneka sat with me in the waiting room for what seemed an eternity as Bobby and James reviewed the X-ray. When they called us back in I could tell by Bobby's face that some bad news was coming. He had gone pale.

I had dislocated the cuboid bone on the left side of my foot and had fractured my fourth and fifth metatarsals.

'How long before I can play again?'

'Well . . .'

'I know I will probably miss the Six Nations, but the World Cup is in September.'

The only response I got was: 'We can knock you out and put it back in place now, but we won't be able to operate until the swelling comes down in another two weeks. We can't tell until then.'

'OK, no problem.'

Bobby told me about six months later that Mr Calder's initial prognosis before I came into the room was that my career was over. The injury is seen in fatal motorbike accidents when the person's foot is caught in the peg, or in equestrian accidents when the foot is caught in the stirrup.

I spent two weeks lying on my sofa with the foot up in the air, waiting for the swelling to ease. Every time I put it down, that tide of agony flowed in. My life was reduced to pill popping and just sitting tight.

They eventually opened it up and put a long metal plate over my cuboid with four screws a centimetre and a half in length. The plate looks like a long Lego brick. I still have it at home. They also slid two metal wires down to my toes to stop the foot from flexing so that the cuboid had a chance to remain in place.

The minor miracle here is: the cuboid did stay in place during those two weeks on the sofa. Mr Calder had said it was like a jigsaw piece – if it fell out once it might keep doing so.

'How long?' I asked him again at the end of January.

'A year.'

'Definitely?'

We talked some more. I got him down to eight months. Definitely two, three months off my feet. I limped out of there, thinking seven months. August became my immediate aim. I did everything humanly possible to turn twelve months into seven. That included three sessions a week in a hyperbaric chamber. You are in there for an hour and a half. Small room, four metres across. A steel tank, you have an oxygen mask to breathe through. They drop you down to 30 metres in this decompression chamber. You breathe pure oxygen. If you take the mask off you can still breathe normal air. Your ears pop as you go down. It supposedly speeds up the healing process by saturating blood plasma and haemoglobin with oxygen. Desperate for a reduction in healing time, I was willing to try anything.

*

After the operation I was told to take a break. Go on holiday. I decided to stick around, and by the second month I started training again. World Cup. Nothing else mattered. I was determined to do everything required of me to get back in contention.

I did that. Now the door was being shut in my face. All for nothing.

Deep down I'd been clinging on to the hope of some minutes against France at home until I got an email saying I was in the squad to face Connacht. No more caps, Geordie. I can feck off on the Friday. Back to Leicester. It was 2003 all over again. But worse, because this is the end of my international career.

Togging out for Monday training is depressing. Lots of new players drafted in – Johne Murphy, Darren Cave, Denis Hurley and Ian Whitten. Leo is captain. The atmosphere is pretty low, what with John Hayes, Marcus Horan and Mick O'Driscoll being told that morning they were only on standby for the World Cup. Your Test career is over but would you mind showing up in Donnybrook for a meaningless run-out against Connacht? Thanks. We're on the Just-In-Case list.

The boys took it the right way. We gathered for the last supper. There is always an iPod dock sitting at the food and beverages station. Some bright spark stuck on *The Muppets* theme tune. It immediately became our anthem. We are the Muppets. Lads singing away. Dirt-trackers will always call themselves something insulting. The Skittles – just there to be bowled over. The mood lightened. Even Hayes, Horan and Micko were laughing away.

A few of us went out for dinner that night. We had just sat down when my phone lights up. Deccie. Here comes the axe.

'Who's that?' Stevie Ferris asked.

'Hi, Deccie . . .' The faces around the table were priceless.

'You are at dinner, I'll catch you in the morning.' He was off to the rugby writers' awards in the Aviva Stadium. I hung around the team room, just in case.

Training the next morning was a rugby session, with weights in the afternoon. He called me in between.

'Can you come speak to me?'

Leinster Suite, Carton House. A little irony there – I never did play for Leinster. He has his sad face on. I looked at him and said, 'Well, this is not going to be good news?'

'I'm really disappointed to say I don't have a place for you in the World Cup squad, Geordie.'

I sat down. There it is. Rock bottom.

In the past, as a younger man, I would swallow my tongue. Take it and move on. I was not going to flare up and go crazy, although part of me wanted to. I respect Deccie and I knew he was in a difficult situation. He had made his decision. He had had to do this with Micko, Hayes and Marcus yesterday – men he has known and coached for many, many years. He must have been under enormous strain.

But I still had a few things to say. I disagreed with him. 'I am really disappointed. I feel you haven't given me an opportunity to prove my fitness and to prove I am still good enough to be part of all this. You have given other guys an opportunity. That hurts. I feel I deserved more than that.'

He conceded that this was the case, but I wasn't finished: 'It looks like you picked your squad three weeks ago and I have been strung along, worked as hard as I ever have, for nothing.'

He disagreed.

'Well, that's how it looks.'

He disagreed.

'It doesn't matter what you say – whether it was subconsciously or not, you picked those two guys and never gave me a shot. That's why I am disappointed.'

He accepted this in silence. I've known Deccie since the under-19 World Cup in 1998. He deserved more than the conversation ending on a sour note. I looked at him and said, 'I know it hasn't been easy to do this.'

'You are a very good guy, Geordie. If we were picking the team on good blokes you'd be straight on the team.'

I giggled. 'Well, Deccie, it's a shame rugby is not a nice guy sport.'

'Look, I don't know what's going to happen,' he went on. 'But if I have to call you up, I'll be happy to do that. I would like to give you an opportunity.'

However, there was no clarification that I was next in line. 'I still want you to play in the Connacht game,' he added.

As soon as I walked out of the Leinster Suite my focus switched back to Leicester. At least now I knew it was over. Move on. Leicester will probably have to do that to me one day as well. That's the game.

So, I was Geordan Murphy, ex-international. Leicester Tigers club captain. That was something I could still control.

It was obvious in Montpellier that the club would benefit from having me around during the World Cup time, having lost six Englishmen, plus Alex Tuilagi to his beloved Samoa, Martin Castrogiovanni to Italy and Horacio Agulla and Marcos Ayerza to Argentina. Ten men down, they were hoping I wouldn't get picked so there would be one old head to guide the ship.

I thought: what's the point in this Connacht game anyway? Training had been messy. I called Tigers' director of rugby, Richard Cockerill.

'I can give you twenty minutes against Lyon on Saturday, Cockers.'

'Yeah, no worries, mate. Do whatever you want to do. You don't have anything to prove to us, Geordie. With the way everything has gone these past eight months do you really want to force yourself to play two games in two days?'

He was incredibly sensitive to my situation. 'Why don't you stay home and have a few beers? Come back in Sunday.'

I rang my head coach, Matt O'Connor, just to be sure. What makes him and Cockers such a good team is they don't always agree.

'You can pencil me in for the game against Nottingham on Friday week.'

'Are you going to play against Connacht?'

'Yes.'

'Well, you should probably come back and play against Lyon.'

I agreed but explained that I had trained with the lads and couldn't walk out now as it would be my last ever game for Ireland.

Cockers phoned again on Wednesday. 'Don't get injured tomorrow night, mate. We really need you.'

'Cheers, Cockers!'

'No, look Geordie, make sure you play and play well – you never know what's going to happen and you don't want to piss anyone off. Take it from someone who has pissed a helluva lot of people off in rugby.'

I was already on that wavelength, but it was still good to hear him reinforce it.

The next port of call was the family home. Mum and Dad were more upset than me. We are a big family and everyone wanted to show their support. It's the last thing you want, but they really meant it. The nephews and nieces were running around. Zoey, who is seven, came over with a picture of me in my gear and a note underneath: 'I'm sorry it's so bad.'

Ah, God. She heard her parents and grandparents talking and had enough about her to know a great injustice had been cast upon Uncle Geordan, who plays rugby on the television. She didn't know what all the fuss was about, but a picture was needed and she was sorry it was so bad. Thanks, Zoey, it's a keeper.

Because I had spoken to Deccie, I felt I'd said my piece. But my family are my family, so Declan Kidney got a fair wallop of abuse that evening from the brothers.

I dropped a fairly obvious hint on twitter: 'The obese lady has opened her vocal cords!!'

That was the end of my tweeting career as well.

Thursday, 18 August 2011
Ireland v. Connacht, Donnybrook

Donnybrook is where I first played in front of a big crowd. Junior Cup as a fourteen-year-old. There were more people present that afternoon than this night. Still, I am going to enjoy my final game in a green jersey.

I am not sure whether the team really gives a shit. Leo says all the right things: if we don't go out and win, it will be an embarrassment. We are wearing the green jersey. I've played with and against him at underage and for two seasons at Leicester, the man is a pro.

I speak next. 'This is a game where you earn respect from your fellow players. That's all that matters. If you shirk your responsibilities, your peers will form a certain opinion of you. But if you front up it goes the other way.'

My last words in an Irish dressing-room.

The first half is scrappy. Leo and Micko cross for tries but the scrum goes backwards. People are forcing it. Mistakes. Messy stuff.

It is a hot night. We are going side to side, but as the forwards start carrying more the gaps become apparent. We come out after half-time and get some quick ball. I run a decent trailer for a try. The foot is definitely feeling better. Granted, I am still in the process of weaning myself off the anti-inflammatory tablets I've been gobbling like Smarties these past eight months. We win 38–3.

I was worried about my engine, but I could have played another eighty minutes. I feel fresh, but that doesn't matter any more: I am finished.

Only one thing for it – go on a complete and utter bender. My flight is Friday lunchtime. It starts with a pint in the hotel – the Radisson on the Stillorgan dual carriageway. Johne Murphy tore his hamstring so can't come into town. Donnacha Ryan joins myself and Denis Leamy. Donnacha was twenty-third man for the French game – you do all the build-up work and then sit in the stand. He kindly drops us in to meet Isaac Boss. My mates Jimmy and Paul Kelly are also there. A few more pints lead us to Flannery's on Camden Street, then Ryan's across the road – it's a Tipp pub, so Leams wants to stick his head in. They look after us. Haven't tasted whiskey for a few years, but that drought is ended. The pace goes up another notch when we get to Whelan's. Copper Face Jack's is the inevitable last port of call. I didn't drink over the summer so it hits me hard. Everything is very hazy.

I wake the next morning back in the safe confines of my palatial hotel room. iPhone gone, but who cares. Johne comes in to survey the wreckage. He calls Aneka, to ensure I have a lift from Birmingham airport. He cancels my phone as well. I get dressed, throw everything into my bag and get a taxi to the airport. Miles from sobriety.

Despite being a little shaky, we go for dinner with Tom Croft and his girlfriend. Tough evening; I am hanging while Tom is about to embark on an adventure of a lifetime.

★

Saturday, 20 August
Leicester v. Lyon, Welford Road

I am in the Cat stand on corporate duty. Club captain. World Cup reject. A room full of people feeling sorry for me. Once more it's 2003 all over again.

'It's OK, Geordie.'

PA: 'But hang on, folks, he will be back for the Tigers soon!'

'Yaaaay!' go my corporate fans. I'm definitely still hungover from Thursday night/Friday morning. I contemplate hiding in a toilet cubicle.

Hardcore Tigers fans come over to say it is great to have me around for the tough weeks ahead. No one ever grows tired of genuine support.

Still, no iPhone. It seems like the ideal weekend to be uncontactable. The calls and texts would be raining in, and I don't have to field any of them. I'll sort it out Monday.

The game was at 2 p.m., so I have plenty of time to get home for the French match in Dublin at 5 p.m. On the couch with Crofty and Aneka, I am watching, but not really tuned in – Jesus, it is going to be tough to get through the entire World Cup. At least I'm due to work for ITV. Again, just like the 2003 World Cup.

Felix goes up for a high ball and falls awkwardly on his back. When the camera pans to his face I get the shivers. I know that vacant look.

Long day, I go to bed early. Wake Sunday morning feeling like a human being again. I should probably check my email. My laptop is dead. Nice. You feel naked when the gadgets of modern life are stripped away.

Use Aneka's iPhone – avalanche of messages, nothing from the IRFU. I go to the shop, buy the papers. There is still nothing definitive about Felix's injury. Maybe he's fine. I need to do something. Feck it, I'll kill two birds with one stone. Sinead Bennett co-ordinates Irish team affairs. Flights, schedules, etc. I ring Sinead.

'Hi, Sinead, Geordan here, lost my phone – Thursday night on the beer – can you email me over the spreadsheet with all the lads' numbers? Oh, and, em, you can contact me on this number if you, eh, need to . . .'

She seems surprised to learn I've lost my phone. I have a chance here.

An hour or so later, Aneka's phone rings. Irish number. Deccie.

He has a few things to say. He explains why he told me about not being picked before I played the game on Thursday night. He didn't want me leaving Friday without sitting me down and saying it to my face. He didn't think there would be another opportunity. I understand that. He sounds really downbeat. I have a fairly good idea who he was just speaking to.

'It is good news for you, Geordan . . .'

So bad news for Felix.

'You'll be coming to the World Cup with us.' Happy, yes. Disappointed for Felix, yes. Eventually the selfish emotion wins out.

Felix has all the tools to become a fantastic fullback. I saw him play for the Ireland under-20s in 2007. Luke Fitzgerald got called up to the national squad, so Felix got his chance against Wales and took it. Ireland won the Grand Slam with Cian Healy and Keith Earls also in the team.

Felix also showed well for Leinster against Leicester in a pre-season friendly some time later. The club were looking for a fullback and I suggested him. As I had done with Johne Murphy: if Munster hadn't signed him up, he could have been the guy to come over and probably eventually replace me.

I got to know him these past few weeks. I wouldn't say we are best buddies but I'll ring him in a few days, just to say I'd been where he is right now and to remind him I'll be out of here very shortly. He just turned twenty-four.

The first few days of an injury like that are tough, but it gets better. Well, it gets worse for a while with the torturous monotony of rehab, but eventually it does get better.

After speaking to Deccie I go to Leicester's annual start-of-season barbecue, where all the wives and girlfriends can meet up. It's a family day.

I feel a bit sheepish walking in. Cockers is happy for me, but it is a blow for the club. Eleven regulars on World Cup duty.

Matt, typical outspoken Aussie that he is, but one I get on very well with, lovely man, very good coach, takes one look at me: 'Aw, fuck off, mate. What you doing here eating our food?'

Talk about coming full circle. In four days I have drowned my sorrows, refocused my responsibilities as club captain, and now I'm turning my attention to England for what will definitely be my last international in Dublin. Then I'll head off to the World Cup in New Zealand.

Monday, 22 August 2011
Carton House, Co. Kildare
Deccie asked that I keep it quiet. Obviously told my folks and the brothers. They shouldered the bad news, they deserved the good stuff too.

Early flight from Birmingham. At passport control in Dublin, the lady asks if I'm going to the World Cup.

'Yeah, I am.'

She's going to New Zealand in a few weeks herself.

'See you down there, Geordan.'

She's glad I was going after 'what happened in 2003'. Irish people still associate me with that Murrayfield injury.

I don't think anyone in camp expected Tomás O'Leary and Luke Fitzgerald to be omitted. I assume Lukey's and my name were on the same 'Possibles' list. Not having seen the game in Bordeaux I don't know what happened there, but from what others have been saying his form dipped. That means nothing. Luke Fitzgerald was a Lions Test winger two years ago. I think it became apparent during the Six Nations, when Rob and myself were injured, that he is not a natural fullback.

Fergus McFadden has made the cut. I played with Ferg in the Connacht game. He has been pushing for a while now and has earned the respect of everyone with his attitude to training. Until Deccie's call, I was nervous that he might get in ahead of me, but we're both on the plane.

The older lads seem happy about the reappearance of my mug. They know what being here means to me. I have played a lot of

Tests with Rog, Drico, Darce, Paulie, Leams, Bestie, Fla, Leo and Donners.

Training is suddenly a big deal this week. Just thirty of us. I have weights first up but I am late, walking into the gym at 12.05 p.m. Everyone is working away. I feel embarrassed; after all these years I'm only here due to someone else's misfortune.

Seanie O'Brien, Leo, Ferg and Isaac stop what they are doing and come over. Most of us had played against Connacht. The only side to have won a pre-World Cup warm-up! We have a laugh about me drowning my sorrows and losing my mobile.

There is a team meeting in the afternoon, to formally announce the squad, where Deccie sits everyone down and goes through the list name by name. That's when it really hits home.

Myself and Donncha O'Callaghan give each other a knowing wink. Elder statesmen and messers, we have committees and off-field activities to organize. There will be blood.

There are plenty of Leicester players in the England squad, so I speak more than usual in our preparations. We know they are coming with revenge in their nostrils after the beating Ireland handed them last March. I am asked about Manu Tuilagi in Friday's review. Not much to say: he's not lightning fast but he has a massive handoff and is super powerful. Darce did well against him in the Heineken Cup quarter-final a few months ago.

I approach the coaches about our structures. Now that I am on the plane to New Zealand I want to contribute all my experience and knowledge to the team. I also feel I have nothing to lose any more by speaking my mind.

So many guys in the squad are very good ball players, but sometimes I think we don't organize enough. I have suggested moves and generic shapes that will make it easier to slip into more effective attacking positions as the phases mount up. Some of the things we do are difficult to organize and guys keep popping up in the wrong place. It means we end up playing it through the hands a lot and just smashing it up. There is an over-reliance on our big ball-carriers to bust open opposition defences. As an attacking entity, we are too predictable. Against decent defences, we are simply not creating try-scoring opportunities.

I have been coached by a number of Australians – Bob Dwyer, Paddy Howard and Matt O'Connor – and they always seek to open it up, constantly adding to the play book. We don't need hundreds of backs moves, but our phase organization needs to evolve.

After losing to Scotland and twice to France in the warm-up matches, Deccie intimated that a change in tactics was coming. The coaches give me the same answer: we will implement some new stuff next week.

Now is the time to do it, I feel. We are keeping it too simple.

Alan Gaffney has some good ideas, but he has a laissez-faire attitude – you guys are out there so you should organize it – and doesn't impose himself on the game plan. Riff is old school. I don't want to give it to him because he is too nice a man, but there isn't any modern attacking strategy being implemented at Irish training sessions. Maybe he is not being allowed to coach.

In any case, it is the major issue just weeks out from the World Cup. Les Kiss's brief is defence, so obviously he doesn't want to encroach on Riff's department.

Next week, I am assured, next week.

This week I am the Irish fullback again, winning my seventieth cap against England at Lansdowne Road. I may never play at the stadium again. Next week in Queenstown is time enough for the big picture.

4. The Irish Question

When I wasn't selected for the Ireland under-21s in 1998, Graham Rowntree and some other senior players at the club, including Austin, suggested I declare for England.

'England! No way, mate,' was my initial reaction.

'Well, Ireland haven't been on, have they, mate?'

What could I say to that?

In that first season at Leicester, nineteen years old, I was exposed to more top-class rugby than anyone my age back in Ireland, yet I remember thinking there was a better chance of being called up to the U-21s if I was togging out for Naas.

There was an obvious problem. I was swimming against the tide. When the game went professional in 1995 a raft of Irish players signed for English clubs. But the likes of Victor Costello, Paul Wallace and Malcolm O'Kelly returned home when the Irish provinces got their act together. Even Keith Wood orchestrated a move to Munster for the 1999/2000 season.

Going home wasn't an option for me. I was still only finding my feet as a professional, improving on a daily basis in the purest of rugby environments.

For a while, the thought crept into my head that I wasn't good enough. When I left home, most representative Irish players two years older than me were streets ahead; but when I started to outshine my underage peers in England I knew that gap had been bridged.

In the 1997/8 season Leon Lloyd, a good pal, was playing for England under-21s. A big, quick wing or outside centre, he wondered why I wasn't getting a look in for Ireland U-21s. I may have given him the impression that the standard in Ireland was far superior! This was plausible – Ireland beat England at U-21 level for the third straight time that season.

But Leon made a valid point. His friend Ryan O'Neill from

Bedford was selected on the right wing for the Irish U-21s in 1998 (Girvan Dempsey from Terenure was at fullback). Leon wanted to know how Ryan got called over from England to play for Ireland, despite being a year younger, yet I was ignored.

'Don't know,' was all I could say.

I *didn't* know, but I could not avoid the conclusion that I would have to be exceptional to get selected for my country.

I was called up for the Irish under-21s squad ahead of the 1999 Six Nations, but that didn't commit me to Ireland at senior level, and Leicester teammates again raised the idea of declaring for England around that time. These weren't in-depth, serious conversations. I wasn't going to be immediately selected by Clive Woodward; my teammates were just looking out for a young club man, and of course they were biased towards England. They said I was a contender, based on my form in comparison to the other back-three players in the Premiership.

The forty-man Ireland U-21 training squad went to France in November 1998. We lost against Toulouse and Bordeaux selections, but I could see genuine talent in almost every position, even if most of them had yet to play provincial rugby. I was one of three full-backs, with Tommy Keating from Blackrock and a very young Gordon D'Arcy. Darce didn't make the team then, but Warren Gatland picked him in the World Cup squad and capped him against Romania in the pool stages, which was fair enough because Darce was an electric attacker. (Gats had even tried to take him on the tour of South Africa the previous summer but the Leaving Cert got in the way.) As a schoolboy Darce was a freakishly good fullback, always broke the first man, Christian Cullen-type runner with sizzling pace. It's a real testament to him that he reinvented himself as a completely different type of player at inside centre.

I was still considered a place-kicker and there weren't too many of them around, so I became a fixture in the U-21 side at fullback. We should have won the Grand Slam. One bad night cost us.

Strangely, it didn't come against a French side that included Sébastien

Chabal, Damien Traille, David Skrela and Cedric Heymans. We stuffed them 24–9 in Musgrave Park. Bryn Cunningham started at outhalf, but an eighteen-year-old named Jeremy Staunton came off the bench that evening to grab a late try. Jeremy is at Leicester nowadays. Back then he was so naturally powerful that I didn't realize he was two years younger than most of us. Jeremy was capable of amazing feats when the mood took him and he shot through the ranks, ending up on the senior Ireland bench later that summer in Australia. I assumed he would gather a shedload of caps. It never really happened for him; or, to be more accurate, Ronan O'Gara happened to him and to Irish rugby.

(I remember meeting Rog one night around this time in Kiely's, a well-known watering hole up the road from Donnybrook stadium. I was good mates with the then Munster hooker, John Fogarty, who introduced us. Rog, an interesting character with a glint in his eye, was curious about every aspect of life at Leicester: the environment, the big names and how we went about our business. His voracious appetite to succeed was obvious, and I liked that we could meet up to chat about it all. Everyone has figured out over the years that Rog is different from the rest of us. I have always liked his outspokenness, mainly because his point of view tends to be so refreshing. Not your usual rugby man, but a special rugby man all the same.)

Bob Casey led the way against the French under-21s, and the other forwards ploughed in behind him. Leo Cullen was a number eight back then, joined in a seriously effective backrow by Garryowen's Paul Neville and Richie Woods from Blackrock.

I nailed four penalties and floated the touchline conversion of Staunton's try between the posts. I know Heymans and Traille went on to become world-class backs, but I can't remember much from them that day except a nice moment when our young inside centre splintered Traille in an early collision. His name was Brian O'Driscoll.

Two weeks later we played Wales in Caerphilly on a windy, mucky Friday night. A young Stephen Jones kicked us off the park. I had a decent game, cleaning up messy ball sent my way by Jones and running it back at them when possible. We didn't deserve to win that night, eventually losing 28–18, and the Slam was gone before anyone really started thinking about it.

The next day we went to see the senior match against Wales. It was a one-off at Wembley: the Millennium Stadium was still being built, so Wales borrowed English football's spiritual home. It was the last-ever Five Nations, before Italy officially joined, and unique in that two championship matches were taking place in London on the same day as England played Scotland at Twickenham. It was a great trip. We were sitting behind the posts at the end where Keith Wood stepped Scotty Gibbs for Ireland's first try. Ciarán 'Skids' Scally, a twenty-year-old scrumhalf, had also bypassed the under-21s and was already on the Irish bench. It was a reminder of what could be achieved.

Truth be told, most of us were in the horrors from the night before. It had started in the dressing-room with some beers and it spilled into a local nightclub. Well, more of a barn dance. A bunch of girls weren't long approaching us in our blazers, asking who we were.

'Ireland under-21s,' we happily replied.

'We know who you are. *You boys* are why we are here. We want to fuck rugby players!'

I was terrified – drop me in a bucket of tits back then and I'd come up sucking my thumb. I didn't have a clue what to say so I retreated to the bar.

Next up we annihilated England 23–5 at Templeville Road, the home of St Mary's RFC. Staunton was brilliant again as the starting number ten. Lewis Moody was keen to hunt me, but he was too busy tracking our backrow from ruck to ruck. They also had Iain Balshaw and Mike Tindall in their backline, but our pack refused to give them any possession until victory was secure. I slotted a few penalties and converted Peter Stringer's late try, our third after Keating and Drico also got over to make it four wins in a row over England at under-21.

We coasted the rest of the championship, beating Scotland 22–13 in Sterling and running riot against Italy up in Ravenhill.

That campaign enhanced my reputation in Ireland. I returned to Leicester, satisfied that I'd played to the level I had been operating at in the Premiership.

I could see that there was a wave of exceptional players coming through. O'Driscoll was a year younger, but there was a touch of class and sheer will to succeed every time he went to the line with or without the ball. He just needed to be identified as an outside centre, regardless of who else was around. Ireland – well, Gatland – figured it out before Leinster, bringing him on the senior tour of Australia that summer, along with Scally and Staunton.

I never actually wanted to play for England – and they never made a formal approach – but looking back it would have been a profitable career move. England internationals had (and still have) more earning power than Irish internationals, through sponsorship deals and match fees, as well as their international contracts. But that was never a driving force behind my rugby decisions.

The Irish media caught a whiff of the fact that I would soon qualify to play for England on residency grounds, and they reported it. That probably quickened my call-up to Irish senior training the following January and had something to do with my being capped on the summer 2000 tour of the Americas.

If I hadn't been capped when I was, and it had dragged on for another year or so, well, let's just say it would have been very hard to turn down an offer from Clive Woodward to play international rugby. Test level is what every player aspires towards.

I could see that England were entering a golden period. The red rose over my heart would have itched a little if I'd gone up to collect a World Cup medal in 2003, but it would have been some group to be a part of. In many respects I already was a part of it at Leicester, but there were other exceptional England internationals – Jonny Wilkinson, Richard Hill, Jason Robinson, Matt Dawson and Lawrence Dallaglio – who would have been a thrill to play alongside. There were so many unbelievably talented players and natural leaders in that squad; I wonder if English rugby will ever see their likes again.

Ireland's preliminary 2000 Six Nations squad gathered at the Aer Lingus training ground near Dublin airport. I was a little overawed by it all. I was used to training with big names at Leicester, but being in a senior international camp was different again.

There were guys there I knew well, like Bob, Rog, Strings and

Drico – who had already impressed on the summer tour against the great Australian centres Tim Horan and Daniel Herbert, before emerging as Ireland's main attacking weapon at the 1999 World Cup.

My progress, while steady, was slower. I was handed over to Deccie Kidney and the Ireland 'A' team while Drico was about to do something that will probably never be repeated by an Irish man: running in a hat-trick in Paris as we beat France.

After a tanking by England at Twickenham, Gatland came under severe pressure and he reacted by making massive changes. Rog and Strings were installed as the new Irish halfback pairing, Simon Easterby was brought in at flanker, Mick Galwey got a recall from exile and the great international careers of Shane Horgan and John Hayes were launched.

I was on the bench for the game against the Barbarians at Lansdowne Road before we left on the summer tour. (No caps were awarded.) All I had to do was hold my own against my opposite number when I came on, playing wing. As a gentle introduction to international rugby, the opposing winger was Jonah Lomu. There is a picture of a terrified and very small-looking version of me stooping low as Jonah came charging at me. Luckily, Eric Miller arrived to put him down, but I still have the mark of Jonah's studs on my leg. (Next time I shared a field with Jonah we were on the same team.)

Later in that game I twisted my ankle up in the left corner, at the Havelock Square end, putting Shane Horgan away. The turf collapsed underfoot and my ligaments were damaged. It wasn't too serious, but a sixteen-hour flight to Buenos Aries two days later would not be the best treatment so I was told to rehab at home. I would miss the Argentina game, but if I passed a fitness test the following Friday they would fly me to Massachusetts, where we were playing the US Eagles.

I remember the stress of that week. My parents didn't know what to make of it all, taking turns shuttling back and forth to the local pub for bags of ice for my ankle. Mary O'Connor, a physio down in Naas, got me right.

On the Friday I went up to Dublin for the fitness test with the IRFU head of fitness, Liam Hennessy. The ankle wasn't right, but

I strapped it up, swallowed a rake of painkillers and grimaced through the running drills. Liam went easy on me and I was allowed to travel. Would it have been different if they hadn't been worried about me declaring for England? Maybe.

Ireland lost 34–25 to Argentina, so I landed into a fairly serious environment. The US Eagles needed to be put away in a convincing manner.

Any sense of awe or intimidation at the first training session dissipated once the game of touch began. This was my territory. Sprinting up the touchline, I slipped a no-look, behind-the-back offload to Justin Bishop. It stuck and two defenders were left grasping at thin air as Bis raced clear.

Eddie O'Sullivan, the backs coach, blew up.

'Why are you doing that?'

I had enough cop-on to know this was a rhetorical question.

'There is no need. You got to eradicate that fancy shit from your game.'

In many respects 'that fancy shit' *was* my game. The backdoor pass, trickery with the boot and anything that bamboozled defenders was encouraged at Auckland Grammar, nor were there any complaints at Leicester. Both are hugely passionate and serious rugby environments that encouraged me to play instinctively, because more often than not what I did benefited the team. Jason Robinson, England's brilliant cross-code winger, once said it was very hard for a defender to predict which way he was going to go when he didn't know himself.

In my career I have been blessed with coaches who never inhibited me. Kevin West had a huge influence, shifting me from outhalf to fullback; Bob Dwyer always advocated moving the ball quickly into space, where I was encouraged to find myself; Joel Stransky may have tried returning me to outhalf, but his tough-love method was aimed at improving the fundamentals of my game. Paddy Howard told me to go with my gut, play what I saw.

Eddie was a new experience. Yes, the fancy pass was a risky pass, but what troubled me was that he seemed to ignore the fact that it worked. It must have looked like showboating, but if you get to know me it becomes apparent I am not a showboater. I didn't just try things off the cuff; ever since Ross put the idea into my head as a seven-year-old, I had been constantly honing new ways of beating players.

My first Eddie rocket. It wouldn't be my last.

It was immediately apparent that we had very different opinions about how the game should be played by someone in my position. From that point on I think he saw me as a potential liability. At Leicester I was viewed as the complete opposite – they constantly encouraged me to get my hands on the ball and create something out of nothing. Take opponents on, get myself into positions to put others into space where it didn't seem any existed. Whereas with Ireland I had to stay on the end of the line and wait for the ball to come out. If it ever did. I had no choice but to accept that. This, more often than not, was the Irish way and it meant I struggled to consistently show the best elements of my game in a green jersey.

Our 83–3 victory over the US Eagles at Singer Family Park, in the town of Manchester, New Hampshire, on 10 June 2000 was quickly forgotten by the rugby world, but not by me. The first cap always stays with you. About 3,000 supporters turned up in 90-degree heat. I'd love to watch the game again some day because I remember trying to hide my limp. The opposition were so poor that my two tries didn't count for much. My second was Ireland's thirteenth. The rout was drawing to a conclusion when I saw an opportunity. The Americans had no cover behind their defensive line, with nobody sweeping across, so I knew there was a simple try to be had. I entered the line from fullback, chipped the centres, re-gathered and strolled clear.

Afterwards, my former Leicester coach, Duncan Hall, came over to congratulate me. Duncan had been Bob Dwyer's assistant, but had since got the Eagles head coaching gig. Just shows how small the world of rugby is.

The unofficial rite of passage after winning your first cap can be heavy going. At least the tradition of having a drink with every player – a drink of his choosing – wasn't so bad that night, because there were so many debutants; I found it easier to hide. The Munster boys came down heavy on Marcus Horan and Frankie Sheahan. There was Guy Easterby and Tyrone Howe as well. The opposition are allowed to do the same so, in theory, a guy could get collared for forty-three drinks. The post-match reception was in a pool hall, and it turned into a sing-song. It was a great introduction to the camaraderie of international rugby.

My brother Nicolas had been living in Boston since the early 1980s, so he came to see me get capped. My old man said he was the most talented rugby player in the Murphy family! Ross and his wife Brenda flew over, making a holiday of it, and they drove up from Boston with Nick. That made the first cap even more special.

I wasn't supposed to be involved against Canada a week later. The management knew I was carrying a knock, but strange things can happen on tour.

Thinking I was in the clear, I went out drinking on the Wednesday with the other dirt-trackers up in Markham, Ontario. There was a bit of trouble the next day. One of the lads had urinated in public, and a complaint got back to the coaching staff.

There were plenty of walking wounded after a long season, not helped by the summer adventure through the Americas from Buenos Aires to Canada, and so I got promoted to the bench on the Friday.

Fletcher's Field was a small stadium, so the punters were right on top of myself and Rog as we stretched in the in-goal area. A local decided to lean in and remind us where we had been a few nights earlier. Rog gave him the filthiest of Rog dirty looks. Justin Bishop pulled up injured so I was thrown in with my dodgy ankle. All I remember is Rog following me into the fray as we sneaked a draw, 27-all.

My first international at Lansdowne Road came the following November. We destroyed Japan 78–9, but in my mind, at the time, I had a shocker. A sloppy knock-on in the opening minutes had me all depressed later that night. It was my opening line on the main stage as Ireland fullback and I fluffed my lines. That performance was described in the Irish media as confirmation that I wasn't ready for the step up to international rugby, making my good form for Leicester largely irrelevant.

The Japanese outing also fed into Eddie's stated belief that I was more winger than fullback. It was true that I was wearing number fourteen at Leicester, but I attacked from fullback as much as Tim Stimpson. I thought of myself as a fullback who was quick enough and good enough to get into the starting XV as a wing, but not, at that point, to displace Stimpson. The perception that I was not a fullback was damaging me so badly in my efforts to break through with Ireland that after a couple of seasons I explained the situation to the Leicester backs coach, Paddy Howard, making it clear I wanted to play fullback for Ireland. He had no problem handing me the number fifteen jersey and we continued as normal. Almost immediately I started being described as a fullback even though nothing had really changed. I would run from fullback off set attacking plays with Tim switching to wing. It happened several times in a game, mainly because we were getting such a rich supply of ball, and it certainly confused defenders trying to number up. After a while it just happened naturally – we would switch. I would be itching to attack from fullback and Tim facilitated that, as I did him in return.

The Sunday morning after the Japan game I was told to pack my bag and leave our base at the Glenview Hotel in Wicklow to link up with the Ireland 'A' lads in Limerick, who were facing South Africa's dirt-trackers that Wednesday.

The 'A' coach, Deccie, immediately gelled us all together by tapping into the whole history of great Thomond Park nights against touring sides. Plenty of the 1999 under-21s were in the squad – Bob and Leo still motoring along, Peter Smyth, Marcus Horan, and Jeremy at ten. We tanned the Springboks 28–11 in my first memorable Thomond Park night (I would have one more in my career).

Girvan Dempsey was picked at fullback for the Test match against the Springboks on the Saturday at Lansdowne Road.

Looking back, maybe I wasn't ready. There is no way of knowing. Maybe I needed to mature a little, and accept that things wouldn't always go my way.

5. Winning

Austin Healey and I were chatting at the ten-year reunion for the 2001 team. Austin was up to his usual shit-stirring.

'Geordie, who'd win between today's Tigers and us?'

Obviously, as the current club captain, I made some valid points: 'The game has changed an awful lot, Austin, as you well know in your new-found capacity as a television pundit. Power levels have increased dramatically . . .'

'Aw, bullshit. We'd smash you. We'd smash you like we smashed everyone else.'

I let it go, because Austin can't really be denied; the 2001 and 2002 teams did smash everyone. Never mind Austin combining with Rod Kafer or Paddy Howard at twelve, the finishing abilities of Leon Lloyd or Freddie Tuilagi, and Tim Stimpson's assured place-kicking; it was, above all, about our awesome pack: Rowntree, West or Cockerill, Garforth, Johnson, Kay, Lewis, Back and Corry, with Josh Kronfeld, Perry Freshwater and Will Johnson in reserve. They were murderous in their intent. They had to be, because Stade Français, Llanelli, Perpignan and finally the men of Munster put up some vicious resistance. But our guys were unstoppable when the blood started to boil.

We were led by one man.

Johnno is the best leader I ever followed on to the field. That is said with the utmost respect for Keith Wood and Brian O'Driscoll, but I'm sure they would understand, having been captained by Martin on the 1997 and 2001 British and Irish Lions tours.

People tend to say Johnno's actions spoke louder than his words. He would be the first man to put his body on the line in every game, unless Backy got there first, but I always found what he said at vital moments in games to be equally important.

I am not talking about rousing speeches before we charged out of the changing room, which he would do when necessary, but what he actually said to teammates as the play was unfolding. He would relay instructions that didn't seem to make sense at the time, but because it was Johnno saying it you obeyed.

His rugby brain was a huge component in making him a great captain. I'm certain Johnno was still talking in the last minute of the 2003 World Cup final in Sydney. The last England attack was launched by Lewis Moody gathering off the top of the lineout. A crash ball was taken up by Mike Catt, then Matt Dawson sniped into the Australian twenty-two. Watch what happens next: the two men who played such an integral part in Leicester dominating the northern hemisphere rugby landscape from 1999 to 2002 take control of the situation.

Wilkinson was sitting in the pocket, poised to strike his drop goal. Dawson was at the bottom of the ruck, so Johnno knew another carry was required. He took a flat pass from the acting scrumhalf, who was Backy. The dying seconds of the biggest game of their lives and they made a crucial extra play to give Dawson enough time to regain his feet and ensure that Wilkinson had a number nine passing him the ball. That's Johnno making sure another fraction of a percentage point was stacked in England's favour. Both men always knew what needed doing because they had done it so many times before. Johnno carried those few inches into a ferocious wall of gold jerseys because it was the correct play at that moment.

The rest is rugby history.

I could always hear him talking. I might slip through a gap, but before I'd accelerate to warp speed his voice would land in my skull.

'Hold on, Geordie.'

He'd know there was a certain try two or three phases downfield if I followed instructions. You trust him once, see the result and immediately understand why men say they would follow him into the fires of hell. If he told me to hold on, it might be because he knew my break would probably be gobbled up shy of the line, and I'd be isolated by my own speed. In that situation, 'Hold on, Geordie' meant stall, take the tackle and let the arriving forwards expose whatever chink he had recognized in the opposing armour. Other times, 'Hold on, Geordie' would have to do with position on the field or time on the clock. Take the tackle and let the Leicester eight grind it down.

At other times he would read what I planned to do from my body shape. He could see the offload I was about to attempt would not come off.

'Hold on, Geordie.'

I would take contact, knowing his massive frame would melt the man who got over my body at the breakdown. The other defenders lingering in the vicinity got swept away as well. And he would smash at least one of them as punishment for contemplating dropping a knee or forearm on my thirteen-stone frame while I was exposed. Backy would be nearby, Lewis and Cozza not far off either, splintering someone with absolutely no consideration for whatever part of their body was rattling that weekend.

The true brilliance of this was fully comprehended only in the video room on Monday morning. Only then would I see the winger in my blind spot or the results three phases on. But Johnno saw all this in real time, at pitch level.

He was that good.

You find places to go that you didn't know existed when playing alongside such a man. When he is gone you realize the void must be filled or his legacy will be sullied. So you go deep into the reservoir. You saw Johnno do it, so you must strive to live up to that example.

It was the same for him, following the examples of men like Dean Richards and John Wells. Or 'Dusty' Hare and Peter Wheeler before them.

That is my interpretation of what we call 'The Leicester Way'. You honour the great servants who filled the jersey before you by refusing to bend. It is a tradition of excellence and sometimes violence, but mostly it is a tradition of winning.

As a bloke, Johnno is not what you might think. Never mind the public persona. He doesn't suffer fools, but the guy you saw on television standing on the Irish side of the red carpet isn't the man I know. Sure, it *is* the rugby player I know – an Englishman with an overwhelming desire to dismantle the opposition – but he is actually great company.

When I arrived at Leicester he was the Lions and England captain. The same Lions had just won a Test series in South Africa for the first time since 1974. I walked into a room packed full of like-minded internationals, all searching for their next Everest. They found it in the Heineken Cup, and they got such a thrill from scaling the North Face they had to do it again.

Europe didn't matter in 1999 because we weren't in it. Our attitude was: they couldn't call it the European Cup without English clubs, and without us. That is not meant as a slight on Ulster's achievement in '99 – they beat the best France could throw at them – but it was our perspective at the time.

In 2000 we had to watch Northampton beat Munster in the final. Bath had already won it in 1998. Many of the 2000–1 Leicester team had lost the 1997 final to Brive – Austin, Johnno, Backy and the ABC club of Rowntree, Cockerill and Garforth. None of these men was going to allow that to happen again. They were also disgusted that our chief rivals, Bath and Northampton, had achieved something they had not. I was a fully fledged Tiger by this stage, and had completely bought into this mindset.

I was also coming into great form, wandering the pitch in search of opportunities and scoring tries. The foursome I scored against Saracens in the Heineken Cup quarter-final in January 2001 was the English media's cue to put my name up in lights. None of the tries was particularly special; I just got on the end of some line breaks. Still, the press tipped me as a potential bolter for Graham Henry's British and Irish Lions squad, due to tour Australia that summer. The comparison was made with the uncapped Will Greenwood in 1997. I sought to play down such talk, saying that becoming an Ireland regular would do me just fine. I never made it as two Bath fullbacks, Iain Balshaw and Matt Perry, were selected – although Tyrone Howe, who also made his debut in the US Eagles match the previous summer, was called up as a replacement winger.

In the spring of 2001 we were on our way to a third successive Premiership title, and we were being mentioned alongside great Leicester teams of the past, including the 1919–20 men, who scored 192 tries in forty-one games, and the 1979–81 hat-trick-winning John Player Cup sides.

Our success was built on smashing every opposing pack that came to Welford Road. No team had won in the league on our patch since December 1997, and we weren't bad on the road either, losing only ten times in those three league campaigns. Under the guidance of defence coach Phil Larder we conceded just 346 points in twenty-two games, eighty-two fewer than the next-best club, Wasps.

Wasps had arrived from mid-table as our main challengers, but we were not concerned by them just yet. They still had some way to go.

I started seventeen of the twenty-two league games in 2000–1, scoring nine tries. I played more times in that league season, twenty-nine, than in any other season.

After being crowned Premiership champions we had to enter a fairly ridiculous play-off system, involving the top eight teams playing for a separate title. The play-offs overlapped with the later stages of the Heineken Cup, so we experienced the most excruciating run-in. We beat Gloucester in the Heineken Cup semi-final at Vicarage Road, and seven days later we had London Irish in a play-off quarter-final. The following weekend Northampton were at Welford Road for the play-off semi-finals, before we were off to Twickenham for the first-ever play-off final against Bath.

Johnno barged through a bunch of defenders for the opening try, becoming the first person in English rugby awarded a try by video referee. I had a hand in the second of our three tries, scored by Austin, as we ran out 22–10 victors.

The wins over Bath and Northampton didn't mean as much as topping the league for a third time, but English wars always leave you with an empty tank. Only after dealing with our local rivals could we switch our full attention to Europe.

Six days after Twickenham came the European final against Stade Français. We all knew that European success was how the rugby world would judge us.

A six-day turnaround means really only three days' preparation. The first twenty-four to forty-eight hours after a game is about recuperation. Most of the team were in ribbons – I know Johnno was carrying a neck injury – but nobody wanted their injury to be defined as serious. Everyone wanted to go into battle against the French in Paris. We trained very lightly on Wednesday and Thursday, Friday was a travel day, Saturday was match day.

That day was an amazing experience for everyone at the club. Parc des Princes was no longer an international stadium, but it had so much character. It's where I had watched all the great French backs tear up Irish backlines in the 1980s and 1990s – Serge Blanco, Didier Camberabero, Patrice Lagisquet and Franck Mesnel. This was their theatre.

I was trying to think about that as I ran on to the pitch, but really, on one of the rare occasions in my life, I was too petrified to focus on anything.

Only when I saw the crowd did I start breathing again. We had been told there wouldn't be many Leicester fans – a few thousand maybe. Johnno had us braced for trench warfare, but this was not merely a daunting visit to The Rec or Franklin's Gardens. We had graduated to the Coliseum. It was 19 May 2001 and for once *we* were the Christians being fed to the Lions.

The Parisian streets tend to get clogged up before major sporting events like this so we had police outriders. They shot off with their sirens blaring, smashing on car windows to clear a path for us to the old stadium. The locals won't budge unless they are removed. Just the French way, I suppose. When we got there the bus went straight underneath the stand, so we never saw what was happening above ground.

It felt like that scene from *Gladiator*. Deano, this time, is Oliver Reed moments before we head out – exhorting us to die with glory. Johnno, naturally, has become Russell Crowe. I'm the guy standing beside him, pissing my pants as they lift the gates.

'Whatever happens, we have a better chance of survival if we stick together.'

Oh, Jesus. I shouldn't be here.

I remember looking around at Graham Rowntree, Dorian West, Darren Garforth, Martin Corry, Ben Kay, Backy, Johnno and his brother Will. You could feel their tension too, but they seemed almost annoyed by it all.

How dare these French bastards make us taste fear.

My fear that day was of the more common variety.

When we walked out, the noise was unreal – like having your ear to a radio tuned to static as the volume is cranked up. Forty-four thousand people losing their minds. When that happens in a stadium it is literally mind-blowing.

The hairs on the back of my neck stood up. Unbelievably, half the stadium was green! My brothers were there with a gang of Naas men, but I didn't expect to see so many Leicester people. This was 2001, and the only club with real travelling support back then was Munster.

The pack huddled around Rowntree, aka Wig, as he needed to urinate on the pitch. This is a common occurrence before a rugby match, and it was especially common when Graham was playing.

All of a sudden the French frontrow sought to square off with their opposite numbers in the middle of the field. Actual gladiator stuff. They were animals: Sylvain Marconnet, Fabrice Landreau and Pieter de Villiers. Wig abandoned his slash to join Dorian and Garf on halfway. This is what those boys had always dreamed about. The ABC club on the European stage! Just like Cockers standing toe to toe with All Black hooker Norm Hewitt during the haka in 1997. Cockers was on the bench that day. Probably for the best; otherwise the stand-off could have got out of hand.

I watched all this unfold half in shock. I was still only a boy. The fear was so all-consuming that I could barely breathe. *This is not Towns Cup and I'm not ready.*

Then the ball is kicked off and you are just in it. I had been a Leicester Tiger for four years at this point. You play from memory. You become a man, I suppose.

The game itself is a blur. About ten minutes in, I got hurt – a bruised pelvis, an excruciatingly painful injury. I made it into the second half before succumbing to the pain. Diego Dominguez, the great Argentine fly-half who played for Italy, was a kicking machine, and he put on a show that day, hitting nine penalties and a drop goal. The man was freakishly accurate. It meant we had to respond with tries to have any chance of survival. Forty-three seconds into the second half, Paddy Howard put a cross-field kick into my arms. I chipped on and Leon gassed after it to touch down. Backy also got a try, but it was another player's sensational break that I remember best from that day.

I have mentioned Austin Healey the loudmouth, so I would be remiss not to talk about the talented, versatile rugby player.

We were ten points down when Johnno got sin-binned for punching Christophe Juillet. We held the line without our leader. Everyone dug in and we conceded only three points.

Austin provided the inspiration for victory, switching from scrum-half to fly-half and creating Leon's second try with a sensational break. Tim Stimpson's touchline conversion made it 34–30 and denied Dominguez a chance to win it on his own. They needed a late try, but our pack refused to bend.

The aftermath in our changing room was chaotic. Perry Freshwater dive-bombed into our bath. Others were just sprawled out, enjoying a beer. The forwards were shattered and could hardly move, and I was in a fair bit of pain myself. But it was a great feeling all the same. I have a photo of Johnno pulling the two little babies of the team, me and Lewis, into a bear hug.

As the Tiger cubs, Lewis and I were given the trophy to walk into the post-match function, on a riverboat on the Seine. It had been made clear to us: 'This is not a replica, gentlemen.'

Lewis grabbed it, not realizing there was a solid gold top on it, dropped it and watched in horror as the gold ring went clanging across the floor. It had to be Lewis: my housemate, my best mate at the Tigers and all-round nightmare.

My personal life took a turn for the good around this time and I suppose I have Lewis to thank for it. Or, more accurately, the future Annie Moody.

In 2000 Jimmy and I moved into a house with Lewis in Ruskington Drive in Wigston Fields near the Leicester training ground. Lewis's girlfriend Annie was friends with a girl called Lucie, and I first met Lucie one evening that year in Ruskington Drive when she came up from London to visit. She was just breaking into the music business. We got on well, but she had a boyfriend and nothing happened between us for over a year. I didn't have the balls to do anything about it anyway. I was still terrified of women. Clueless. She interpreted my fear as gentlemanly behaviour.

I met her again about a year and half later in London. She was single, we started going out and it went from there.

After a few years I built an apartment in Leicester and she moved in. We had a great relationship, but it was tough going because of what we both did for a living. We'd go through long periods without seeing each other.

For most of the six to eight weeks she'd be off I would be on tour. As the Leicester season was starting I'd come home, but she would be on the road. Her dad was from New Zealand but she had little interest in rugby. Not that it mattered. It was my first ever proper relationship, and it lasted seven years.

We could so easily have been tabloid fodder but we both consciously avoided that. 'Rugby player dates pop star' was inevitably going to create headlines. Over the years when she was invited to movie premieres and stuff like that in London, her agents would push her to go and be seen – with me. But for me to be photographed at these events was the antithesis of a little thing known as the Leicester Way.

I heeded the advice of people I trusted in the club, but I knew anyway that my face popping up in entertainment magazines and tabloids wouldn't go down well. Imagine what the ABC union would think of it all? I would have got pounded at training. And rightly so. Anyway, I didn't have a huge amount of interest in tracking down to London to stand on a red carpet like a spanner. There were a handful of pictures of us together which the media regurgitated, but that was it. *Hello!* and *OK* magazines offered us decent cash for a photoshoot of us at home, but we politely declined.

I asked her to marry me after a concert in Amsterdam in August 2007. She said yes, and I promptly disappeared into Ireland's World Cup camp for two months. She, meanwhile, was writing in Nashville.

Our careers continued to dominate our lives as the wedding was planned around us. Her parents were lumbered with a lot of the organization, and that was unfair. The hotel was provisionally booked, but rugby was my focus, music hers. We were supposed to get married in July 2008. We faced facts around February. Let's not get pressured into doing things. I respected her saying it to me.

It was tough explaining the postponement to my family but my sister Maeve was her brutally honest self. She will tell me whenever I've played poorly in a game without sugar-coating.

'Well, that's that done,' she said.

Maeve was right: the long-distance relationship didn't work. We tried for a while, but within a few months it ended. We have remained friends, and for that I am glad.

6. Playbook

Saturday, 27 August 2011
Ireland 9, England 20, Aviva Stadium, Dublin
Another meaningless Test match, but it means the world to me. My farewell to Lansdowne Road, I reckon.

Didn't inject myself into this game. I'm used to getting my hands on the ball way more. At Welford Road I can call moves on myself. Not here.

At Friday's captain's run it crossed my mind that this was probably the last time I would go through this routine in this place. Even though it's been renovated in recent years, it's still Lansdowne Road.

Five months ago England were unable to cope with the physicality of our forwards, so we knew what was coming. They came in search of payback. Paulie O'Connell spoke about welcoming this challenge with open arms, but we disappointed our guests, and Paulie, with our lack of intensity.

Myself, Andrew Trimble and Tommy Bowe hatched a few counter-attacking plans, but when the opportunity arose the ball went to ground. We'd put a try together last November against Argentina, but not today. I always seek to bring my wingers into play. We didn't have time to work on stuff during collective training, so we made time ourselves to plan two or three little moves depending on where we were on the field.

It was all of sixty minutes before a chance came along. Mike Tindall kicked an ugly left-footer, a Drico special, skidding off the turf. If it bounced into my hands I would have been over their 10-metre line in an instant. I saw Tommy moving in the corner of my eye. That meant Trimby was doing likewise. It was raining. The ball hopped awkwardly over my head, forcing me to turn and gather on our 10-metre line. In a tight game there are two choices: kick into their 22 or launch one into the clouds. Eleven points down with the pitch cutting up, this is the time to attack. It was the right decision, just didn't come off. An English hand got in the way and we got a scrum out of it.

I'm still second-choice fullback but I feel I've done enough to at least make Deccie mull over the number fifteen jersey. I have my young clubmate, Manu Tuilagi, to thank for that.

Thirty minutes gone, England were 13–6 ahead when I had to chase the youngest Tuilagi. Scooping up possession in his 22 off our overthrown lineout, Manu broke the line and took off. Raphäel Ibañez's mug must have popped into a few people's heads in the stand. It was up to me, and nobody else, not only to catch Manu but to haul him down. This is an example of rugby ceasing to be a team sport. Very simple, one man chasing another. The runaway freight train, pursued by a still slight thirty-three-year-old tentatively returning from a potentially career-ending foot injury.

I had only one thought: Fly, Geordie, fly! I spread my wings for the first time in eight months. He had a ten-metre head start, but, as I told my Ireland teammates less than twenty-four hours ago, he isn't lightning fast. Within a few strides I realized I was going to catch him. That was when my troubles would really begin. As I closed in on Manu, a split-second decision needed to be made. Do I hammer into his thighs? No, too many would-be tacklers bounce off those tree trunks. Ankles, maybe? I've seen him slap down our best defenders in training. He had already ended David Wallace's World Cup with a crunching tackle. Manu's blood was boiling after Wally had carried him through midfield a few phases earlier. England jersey but islander attitude: you smash me, bro, I'll smash you right back.

It was already his day – he'd brushed past Keith Earls for an early try. England were battering us. Now, I'd be remembered at Lansdowne Road for being put on my arse by a guy who, as a little boy, used to collect the empty beer bottles around my feet in his family's back garden.

Manu switched the ball into his left hand and slowed. If he got me cleanly with that giant Samoan paw I'd be eating dirt or, worse, flung into the stand.

I caught up with him around the 22, but it took until the 5-metre line to derail the train. I waited for the fend before moving around his back, using his weight against him by rolling him over my body. With the ball trapped under my leg, I expected a massive shoeing, probably from Crofty, who is rapid and would not be long getting to the ruck, and possibly a sin-binning, but it popped out for clean English possession. They had numbers out wide – story of the game, really. They went through the hands with Darce's slip in midfield creating a two-man overlap, but Courtney Lawes butchered a try by flinging a pass into touch.

Tuilagi's try came off a wheeled scrum. Eoin Reddan was forced to tackle James Haskell, Stevie Ferris went over the ball but our defence wasn't set in time. My man was the super-quick and slippery Ben Foden. I don't think I drifted too early, but I was probably five yards too far to the right, even if my primary responsibility was to mind Foden while Tommy was eye-balling Mark Cueto. Still, we should have tightened up a bit for Earlsey. It's not as if he's had a bunch of opportunities to play thirteen for Ireland. Everyone could have helped a bit more. Earlsey will be disappointed, sure, but it is so rare that Brian is ever left to make that sort of tackle by himself. There were a few mistakes leading up to that try but Earlsey, playing centre instead of Drico, will be blamed for a missed tackle in midfield. I know how he feels.

Afterwards it was while the English boys were giving Manu grief that I ran him down. 'Ah, he has too much respect to leave his club captain in the dust.'

Manu giggled: 'That's right, Geordie.'

He is an incredibly respectful kid. He learned that at home.

Ever been to a Samoan house for dinner? Now that is an experience you can't forget in a hurry. Forget *The Godfather* – the Tuilagis take respect and family values to another level.

It is known as the Island Barbecue. Mountains of meat. And lots of taro – the imported island potato that makes them so strong. The Tuilagis are good people, good friends. They have always treated me like a family member.

They are the most talented clan rugby has ever known. No question. Seven brothers, of whom six became professional rugby players.

(Olotuli doesn't play as he is the *fa'afafine*: in Samoan culture, one son in a big family is brought up to fulfil the role of a 'third gender'.)

I've played with each of the others at Leicester: Freddie, Henry, Alex, Andy, Sanele Vavae and Manu. The eldest sibling, Fereti (Freddie to us), switched back to union from St Helens in 2000. Henry was at the Tigers from 2003 to 2007, and Alex has been a huge figure at the club since 2004. Andy played for Leicester in the 2005/6 season and Sanele Vavae was with us from 2007 to 2009.

Their father, Tuilagi Vavae, is a chieftain of their village, Fatausi-Fogapoa, and was a deputy speaker in the Samoan government. His wife is Aliitasi.

Henry is the biggest and the scariest, and he is still playing with Perpignan. He barged through each member of the Springbok back-row – Schalk Burger, Juan Smith and Dannie Rousseau – on three separate charges at the 2007 World Cup. He also knocked out the big Canadian lock, Jamie Cudmore, with a fair, front-on hit in the Top 14 final of 2010.

The first time I went to the Tuilagi BBQ in Thorpe Astley, a suburb of Leicester, I found the hospitality immediately humbling.

I told them a story about going into a garage in Otara, the tough Maori area in Auckland. Me and Jimmy Ferris, two tiny white teenagers, wandering down the wrong street. The guy behind the counter was a massive Samoan unit.

'Where you from, bro?'

'Eh, I'm from Ireland.'

'AHHhh, no way, bro, I'm from the islands too.'

'No, Ireland.'

'Yeh, bro, me too!'

The Tuilagis all loved this. I was an Islander! Just like them. Geordie and the Tuilagis.

Meat was stacked three feet high on the table, but they were apologetic about the quantities.

'We tried to get a pig on a spit for you, Geordie,' Alex explained. 'They wouldn't let us have it.'

The brothers went to a local farm the day before and asked for a pig. They were told it takes a week as it must go to the butcher's.

'Nah, bro, can we not just have that one there?'

'Yeh, bro, he looks like a tasty one.'

'No, you can't have that one!' replied the farmer.

'Why not, bro? We are going to DIY it for our guest, you know Geordie Murphy.'

The farmer was a Tigers nut, but he still wasn't giving the pig.

They are the best barbecues of all time. You sit in the garden, drinking beers, listening to chilled music as the boys cook up a feast. Only one rule: you are not allowed to lift so much as your pinky. If, after a few cans, I try to get up to bin the empties, I will be immediately surrounded by Samoan brothers.

'What you doin', Geordie?'

'I'm . . .'

'Nah, bro, don't disrespect us. Kids!'

Little Tuilagis appear. I know to be nice to them – one of them was Manu. They scoop up the rubbish as a cold one is placed in my hand. When the food is ready, meat gets dished out by seniority, but as the guest I trump even the chieftain. We eat everything.

The contrast in their demeanour once they get out on the field is stark. But take a look at Alex or Manu after a big hit or a charge up-field: they are smiling ear to ear.

I've forgotten the number of times I have taken a big hit and offloaded just in time to put Alex away. Next time my tackler gets the ball there is a strong probability his ribs will be on the receiving end of a Tuilagi shoulder charge.

Manu is like the rest of them (except for his allegiance to the Red Rose – in fairness, he was raised in England these past few years). He smashes some poor guy, all the while grinning like a toddler coming down a slide for the first time, tongue lolling out. He loves the physical stuff, and I love playing with him and his brothers.

I think Manu's going to make a massive splash at the World Cup.

I speak to Keith Wood in the tunnel after the England defeat. Woody seems happy about my late call-up. He tells me about his decision to retire after the 2003 World Cup, when he was just thirty-one. His body made the decision for him, having taken too much punishment, including an elbow operation four weeks before the tournament that nobody knew about.

This is probably my last hurrah. Two more seasons with the Tigers and then I could be done from rugby altogether, so it is about squeezing the last drops out of my ageing body.

Tuesday morning, 30 August 2011
Radisson hotel lobby, Dublin airport

I am devastated for David Wallace. He has been responsible for Ireland getting over the gainline for so many years. More so than Victor Costello, Axel Foley and Eric Miller combined, and that's saying something. I always enjoy Wally's company as well.

Felix has enough time to play in another World Cup, but Wally doesn't, and it is a horrific injury. His knee is mangled.

I rang Felix Saturday morning. Left a message. Told him I had been in his shoes, and was gutted for him. I know I am the guy benefiting from all this, I told him, but if you do want to chat about anything, give me a call. Any time.

When you get injured like that it is usually a few days before you can get back to people. And sometimes you never do. It is a tough time but, hopefully, he will get other opportunities.

Wally's departure opens the door for my good mate Shane Jennings. Jenno is a leader. I've been speaking to him the past few days on an iPhone app that turns your phone into a walkie-talkie. Jenno cackles over the line at 8 a.m. Sunday morning.

'Come in Geordan, over.'

'What are you up to, Shane?'

'Please say over, over.'

I am glad he is going to New Zealand. He was wondering why I hadn't responded to his messages.

'Sorry, mate, I lost my iPhone last week on the piss after Connacht.'

Silence.

'Over!'

I congratulate him on his even later call-up. Jenno has a slight case of obsessive-compulsive disorder, so packing at such short notice for such a long period of time was a major event. I messed him about a little. I'd do this a lot during his two years at Leicester. We'd be having a few beers and Jenno would arrange all the bottles regimentally on the table. He would go for a piss, only to return to chaos, bottles strewn all over the table. Without a word, he'd sit down and methodically rearrange them back into line, barely even aware he was doing it.

When Jenno got comfortable in the Leicester environment, after a few weeks, he started to showcase a huge array of skills. Offloads out the side door in contact and the like. He's like an eighth back, links play like any modern seven. Probably the only true seven in Ireland at present capable of playing international rugby.

His international career has been frustrating. I can relate, it took me a long time to transfer my club form to a green jersey. Shane hasn't got the opportunities, for a number of reasons: Wally is a big factor, Sean O'Brien has become another more recent problem, but really it is a longstanding, embedded attitude to Irish backrow make-ups. We tend to go with a big, powerful seven who isn't really an openside in the strictest sense. Keith Gleeson broke the mould, but not for long.

I can relate to Jenno's plight, having always found it difficult, as an attacking fullback, to inject myself into the international game plan. Ireland has never really invested in an attacking fullback or a groundhog at seven.

Give Jenno a sustained run of games and you will get a player unlike most other loose forwards. I saw it first hand at Leicester for two years and Leinster reaped the benefits when he returned home.

He is on the plane but, as it stands, it's not clear how he's going to get on the pitch. Jamie Heaslip is the starting number eight, Stevie Ferris is fit again and so powerful (there is a kick of speed there too), and so Seanie gets the seven jersey. Then there is Denis Leamy's versatility, which makes him a good bet for the bench. Jenno and I could be spending a lot of time together in the stand.

The flight
It felt weird sitting on the plane. Two weeks ago I was utterly distraught after Deccie broke the bad news.

We flew Dublin to London, London to Dubai, Dubai to Sydney, then finally on to Queenstown.

Business class helped. We were told to stay awake until Dubai. Most of the lads did, and as it was an Airbus 380 there was a bar up the top where we all congregated. We put our committees together. This was Donncha O'Callaghan territory. I'm the second-oldest player after Rog so I hold a statesmanlike position on the Standards Committee. It is a true honour.

I also approached Deccie for a chat about tactics. I presume we are on the same wavelength: the other day in the post-match press conference he said there are some things that need to be introduced to the playbook.

To alter our current predictability, I drew up some new generic shapes we could adopt. I handed them to Deccie on the plane. Deccie took them but gave very little away about what he thought – nothing new there – so I started talking. We are too reliant on Stevie or Seanie running over someone – which they are well capable of doing – to open up the opposition. We are not creating space in other ways. Sure, the lineout is a valuable platform, but I'm talking about the backline. It is deeply worrying. We have a team and players capable of great things, but when it gets to the business end of this tournament we'll need to have worked on extra tactical stuff to expand our attacking style.

We have our patterns, but say we go to a wide breakdown, near the touchline, with a backs move. All we are doing thereafter is smashing it up. The forwards are too clumped together, the backs are out the line, and very quickly it becomes a pick-and-go situation. Any decent defence can withstand that all day.

On Saturday England simply numbered up and made their hits. We ran into the brick walls. We accepted slow ball. Quick hands to the other touchline, maybe a skip or a switch, and we are back to square one. It is only a matter of time before we get turned over, there is an error or we are forced to kick.

To simplify it: we are effectively running into defenders the whole time. We have a few weeks to ensure there are multiple attacking options for Jonny Sexton or Rog to implement when they get the ball. I'm talking about two or three forwards going on hard lines, inside and outside him, to fix defenders so that gaps are bound to appear in midfield or out the other wing. That would allow guys to read defences, create mismatches. Find the little defender and get a big guy at him or find a prop and get Drico coasting outside him. This is about players taking control of the attacking patterns, no matter what the situation. It's about always having options. Since I came back in from the cold I have been saying it non-stop to the coaches. Last week I was told, yeah, but not before the England game. I'm expecting the change Deccie spoke about in the coming days.

Week one

Queenstown is awesome. A panorama of snowy mountains, backpackers milling around the main street. Deccie brought an Ireland schools team here in 1992, so he knew most of us would love all the activities. That is Deccie's speciality – fostering a tight community.

In 2005 half the Lions squad went off tour up here before the third Test. They were raving about it afterwards, but I missed out because I'd been selected to play the All Blacks.

We arrived on a Thursday and had a few days off. On Friday I went jet-boating. After that we took a helicopter to a mountaintop restaurant, then we went luging down the mountain on a sled with wheels and a handlebar to steer. It's a miracle no one was injured or killed. Jenno flipped Bestie out of his cart and he was lying in the middle of the track as I came careering round the corner. Missed his head by inches. Great *craic*.

There was a good vibe in the camp, some training but also some really enjoyable downtime. This was the perfect start to the World Cup. My motto for this tournament was to get outside the hotel igloo at every opportunity, as I may never get to do this again.

We had a few beers Friday and mingled with the first wave of Irish supporters. Good night. On Saturday the whole squad went for a knees-up. Late one, but we didn't go crazy. Just a great bonding session of the sort that is good for a rugby team on tour.

My foot is feeling good. The New Zealand pitches are like mattresses: reasonably firm with a nice bit of give in them, both training and stadium surfaces are the best I have ever encountered. Just what you would expect from a World Cup in this rugby-obsessed nation.

Week two

Not much happening up in New Plymouth, venue for our first game against the USA, but we are constantly on the move over the next few weeks. Next we go to Auckland, then Taupo, then Rotorua. Mostly small towns. The travelling kills a fair bit of time and you change up room-mates as well. I had Jenno last week. This week it's Bestie; his chainsaw snoring is my punishment for rooming with a good skin. There is a rooming committee but I'm not sure how much influence they have. Deccie has the last say. There are no obvious divisions in the squad, but naturally a few guys are kept clear of each other in case they snap. Just the usual lunatics, never any harm to have a few in a rugby squad once their madness is harnessed correctly on the field.

The generic shapes I handed to Deccie are gathering dust somewhere. I drew up drills as well and offered other ideas that I feel should be in the playbook, but there seems to be a big fear of over-complication. Roughly ten moves are rolled out every game, but we can be better. At Leicester there are continuity plans for at least five phases; with Ireland three is the maximum before it becomes pick and jam.

I am not hearing much from the other experienced backs or young guys, plenty of whom are strong-minded individuals, so I feel the need to speak up. Again.

Creating space is what I know best in rugby. My thinking is that I am nearly done and probably not going to start against Australia, so it shouldn't sound like I'm trying to get the team to play around me. Let's play complicated attacking rugby – the skill set is there.

I see this week as a massive opportunity to improve our attacking approach. My ideas can be overruled and improved upon, but the debate should be happening. Our halfbacks should have a major say in all of this.

In France, an attacking style is bred into them from childhood. I've seen how they educate their youngest players. The ball is thrown in and they are just told to 'play'. After five minutes the whistle blows. They are shown the space that is not being used on the field. They are shown how the ball can be transferred into the wide-open prairies, coached how to pass and run lines from deep. Through repetition the approach to attacking the gainline becomes rapid and eventually magical to witness.

Once it clicks you can never forget that philosophy. A natural running game, God, that would be amazing. I'd love to coach that into Irish kids' psyche some day. And not just the skinny ones.

7. Geordan, not George

Around the year 2000, when I was starting to hit top form for Leicester, Dean Richards referred to me as 'the George Best of rugby'. It was a throwaway remark, Deano referencing some little piece of skill I had pulled off. And I was Irish – George Best!

I was no George Best, but it seemed like every journalist who typed my name during this period of time had to mention the comparison – and I'm not just talking about the lazy ones. It became nauseatingly ridiculous after a while, and it was all Deano's fault!

If I was to go along with the comparison, that would make Leicester the Manchester United of English rugby, which meant Dean Richards was our Matt Busby. We could keep going. Neil Back surely mirrors the influence of Denis Law and Austin would come looking for the Nobby Stiles comparison. At least there wouldn't be much debate about Martin Johnson being Bobby Charlton.

But in the summer of 2001 a comparison with another Irish footballer came to seem more apt. I very nearly became to Warren Gatland what David O'Leary was to Jack Charlton in the early years of Jack's reign as Republic of Ireland soccer manager: invisible. Back in 1986 O'Leary decided not to go to Iceland for a seemingly irrelevant summer tournament. Kevin Moran and Mick McCarthy became Charlton's resident centre backs for the next five years.

I almost made a similar mistake, reading a situation badly the week of the 2001 Heineken Cup final.

I had been asked to play for the Barbarians against Scotland and England five and eight days after the final, and accepted. This clashed with an Ireland camp in Limerick, in advance of a match against Romania in Bucharest the weekend after the Barbarians match. I had planned to go on holiday after Leicester's gruelling run-in had left me with a number of niggly injuries.

I phoned up Ireland manager Brian O'Brien to explain that I

intended to play for the Barbarians and then go on holiday, skipping the Ireland camp and the Romania match. It went down disastrously with Gatland. O'Brien was back on, telling me in no uncertain terms how unwise it would be to decline an international call-up, having played for the Baabaas the previous week. When I realized Warren's viewpoint I instantly changed my tune. I phoned him and said I would happily play against Romania if selected.

The incident made the papers:

The *Irish Times*, Wednesday, 16 May 2001

Murphy's volte face averts rift and keeps Ireland camp content
By GERRY THORNLEY

A potentially-damaging rift between Geordan Murphy and the Irish management was averted yesterday when the Leicester full back had a change of heart about making himself unavailable for next week's Irish get-together in Limerick and the subsequent June 2nd Test against Romania.

. . . Earlier yesterday, it was announced that Murphy had made himself unavailable, in part due to a niggling hamstring strain which had sidelined him for a couple of weeks before his return to action last Sunday, but also due to a preference for linking up with the Barbarians' squad for their matches against Scotland and England next week.

Not surprisingly this didn't go down too well with the Irish management, and coach Warren Gatland admitted they were 'disappointed that he's made himself unavailable.'

While acknowledging that Murphy's desire to rest his various knocks and bruises was 'understandable,' his decision to play for the Barbarians and not Ireland didn't 'stack up.'

Murphy had maintained that it hadn't been an easy decision, but his subsequent change of heart suggested that additional consultations had taken place during the day and that the advice he had received up until then had largely come from inside Leicester.

'I've had a think about it,' said Murphy later on, 'and if there was the slightest chance that it might be construed as me having turned my back on my country, it wouldn't be worth it and there would be no point in taking that risk. I am dedicated to playing for Ireland first and foremost . . . If I come through the game on Saturday and they decide it's good enough to carry on, then I may hook up with the Barbarians for their game in England [at Twickenham on Saturday week] and also play in the Romanian match. If they decide I should rest up for the Romanian game, then that comes first, and if they decide I should stop now I'll pull out of everything.'

Having been a bit miffed earlier on, Gatland was suitably forgiving after Murphy rang to apologise for his 'hasty' earlier decision. 'You've got to admire him for doing that and I definitely won't be holding this against him,' said Gatland. 'He does have a niggling hamstring and he might not come through Sunday anyway. There's no point in him training if it risks further injury.'

In short, though, it was the principle of playing for Ireland first that mattered. Having wondered aloud if the twice [sic] capped 23-year-old had been badly advised, Gatland commented:

'One of the things I felt when I first took over as Irish coach, with the team having 13 English-based players and two home-based, was that the players based abroad don't get a feel for what's happening here through reading newspapers, television, radio and talking to people, and so then sometimes you can make wrong decisions.'

Crisis averted – but the bruised pelvis I suffered in the Cup final was a fresh complication.

I explained my injury to the Baabaas management and they said I wouldn't have to train, just come up and play. That seemed fine, and playing for the Barbarians was a box every player wanted to tick, so I went to Edinburgh that week, met up with the squad and walked through our planned moves. The backline made it a once-in-a-lifetime opportunity. Lomu and Joeli Vidiri were my wingers, Paddy Howard and Jason Little the centres, and Jerry Guscott was coming off the bench in his last game before retirement. We beat Scotland 74–31. England were under-strength due to the Lions tour so we tore them apart, winning 43–29. Stimo and Leon didn't seem to enjoy the occasion as much as I did.

I got another whack on the hip at Twickenham, so the Leicester physios and Deano told me to go on holiday, but I knew I had to join up with Ireland and win my fourth cap in Bucharest first.

In the summer of 2001 I had an opportunity to join Leinster. Jim Glennon was in charge back then, and he phoned to see if I was interested in coming back to Ireland. It would have been a central contract because I had a few international caps, so I would have to deal with the IRFU directly.

Leicester had already said, 'Look, if you want to go home we understand but just give us some notice.' They tabled a new contract, more money, but not that good a deal. (I was on a salary of twenty-four grand sterling when we won the first European Cup in 2001.) I told Jim about the Leicester offer and asked to see an IRFU offer. They refused to give me one until I publicly expressed a desire to return. How does that work? Surely I can't say I'm coming home unless you make me an offer?

I told Jim that if the union were serious about me coming home they must put an offer on the table. He asked me not to sign anything with Leicester until after the weekend. 'I'll get you an offer by Monday.'

He came back and told me I had been graded as an Ireland 'A' team player, so a full international contract wasn't on the table. I wasn't interested – I just thought it was bad business. Even now my Irish teammates often don't believe the rough figure I tell them I earn playing in England – they assume I am on twice the amount – and at that time my Leicester salary was modest. But even so, the Leinster offer was not enticing. I didn't know a whole lot about money contracts, but a young Irish guy playing well in England, having just played fullback on the European Cup-winning side – make him a decent offer.

Off the back of my Heineken Cup displays and the Romanian outing, as it turned out, I was selected on the right wing against Scotland at Murrayfield in September 2001 for the rescheduled Six Nations game delayed by the foot-and-mouth-disease outbreak in Britain the previous spring. It was the first time Gatland tinkered with the winning formula he came across when hammering Scotland at Lansdowne

Road in 2000. I was on the right wing with Shane Horgan switched to inside centre, Peter Stringer made way for Guy Easterby, and Jeremy Davidson came in for Mick Galwey. It was my first-ever Six Nations outing, but it was September, the competition had been badly disrupted, and so it didn't feel as intense as it otherwise might have.

I had very little influence on the match because my hamstring exploded after twenty minutes. It feels like you have been shot in the back of your leg – that's why we call it the sniper's injury. You lose all power but still need two or three excruciating strides before you can stop. Your hands immediately go to the source of that pain but there is nothing to be done.

The whole experience was a horror show – we were torn apart, losing 32–10. It was the first time I'd ever torn a muscle, but Murrayfield had worse days in store for me.

The lads did a famous job on England in the concluding match of the championship in Dublin, which meant that the Scotland loss cost us a Grand Slam.

I was injured until November, when I got selected against Samoa. Jeremy Staunton was being tried at fullback – there was no room at outhalf due to the developing rivalry between Rog and David Humphreys – and so I was on the wing.

My list of Irish caps was ridiculous: USA, Canada, Japan, Romania, Scotland in the month of September for twenty minutes, and now Samoa.

I could understand why Peter Clohessy had no idea who I was when the Munster lads forced him to name everyone in the room after an Ireland training session. Hilariously, Claw struggled with half the lads' names. But he was the quintessential old-school rugby man, one of the last of a now extinct breed who played more amateur than professional rugby.

Because I was on the fringes, my player–coach relationship with Gatland never really developed, but he must be credited with trusting the young talent coming through, giving so many of us our first caps. I'm not sure why he got the sack at the end of 2001, but his assistant got promoted to the head coaching position: Eddie.

★

I was named in the 2002 Six Nations squad as a fullback. Eddie told the media it had a lot to do with my time wearing number fifteen at Leicester that season. But Girvan was his first choice and Shaggy was injured, so he picked me on the wing for my first Six Nations international at Lansdowne Road, which finally arrived on 3 February 2002 against Wales. It was also Eddie's first game as head coach. It was a dream start for both of us; we won 54–10. Now, this was more like it.

My two tries came from running decent support lines, one off a typical David Wallace rumble. It was freezing cold and I had very little to do, out hugging the touchline.

Paulie O'Connell won his first cap that day too, knocking himself clean out scoring a try. Of course Paulie wanted to play away without his marbles but the injury meant he avoided the media afterwards, so I spoke to them instead, admitting it was almost too easy: 'We seemed to be scoring two phases earlier than we should. Everything seemed to come to us on a plate. I looked at the clock a couple of times: at one stage it was 45 points and still twenty minutes to go. I thought, "This can't be right."'

Wales were shockingly bad, but it was still a Six Nations game in Dublin and I was involved. My seventh cap, but afterwards it felt like the first. The family were all there and I could see what it meant to my parents, my brothers and my sister Maeve. It was some scramble getting everyone tickets.

My father made a point of saying hello to a certain IRFU blazer at that evening's post-match function.

'Too slow, is he?'

You remember little things from a night like that. We were standing around the Berkeley Court lobby when former Ireland fullback Conor O'Shea came over to offer his congratulations. He was such a gentleman that I decided there and then, watching him speak to my father, that this was how an international should conduct himself.

Shaggy was still injured, so I kept my place for England at Twickenham two weeks later.

Unfortunately, a pattern was emerging. Seven minutes in, I had to chip the first ball I got, but Ben Cohen dived across and landed on my knee, which collapsed. I would miss almost two months with medial ligament damage. We got smashed 45–11 by an England squad that included Johnno, Backy, Ben Kay, Graham Rowntree, Dorian West and, unfortunately for me on return to Oval Park, Austin Healey. He wasn't able to say too much as England managed to blow a Grand Slam for the fourth season running, thrashing everyone, with scintillating attacking rugby, except for France in Paris.

Paddy Howard had been our resident playmaker at inside centre for the three seasons that culminated with the 2001 Heineken Cup victory; he also doubled up as backs coach, replacing Joel Stransky. Paddy was so influential that Will Greenwood had to leave Leicester for Harlequins in 2000 to guarantee game time and ensure he was selected again for the Lions.

Despite Deano and Wellsy having a blunt-force attitude to winning rugby matches, they could see the sparks of genius coming off Howard and gave him the necessary latitude. You know the cliché: our forwards won the matches and we decided by how much.

A lot of my own good play in those years was down to the way Paddy set us up. Regardless of the number on my back, when I came into possession it was at pace and attacking the opposition's outside channels.

After we won the 2001 Heineken Cup, Paddy returned home to Australia, taking up a playing contract with the ACT Brumbies. He had aspirations of breaking back into the Australian set-up before the 2003 World Cup, but surprisingly he didn't make the Wallabies squad. He ended up back at Leicester in 2004, via Montferrand, where he coached and played alongside Cockers, who had taken his own detour to France.

We scored some great tries straight out of Paddy's ACT playbook. A 'Brumbies Short' worked plenty of times – ten passes to twelve, thirteen comes short, ten loops around and hits the front runner, who was usually a trailing winger or flanker, who should have acres of space to gallop away.

Paddy ensured a progressive Australian attacking philosophy was kept alive at Leicester by recommending Rod Kafer to succeed him in the double role of inside centre and backs coach.

Rod is a complex thinker about how the game should be played, and he is widely credited as the mastermind behind the Brumbies' innovative approach in the late 1990s. His multi-phased attacking game was probably too advanced for us. Our forwards were of the old school: construct a dominant set-piece, hit rucks, get up and hit the next one, be hard, carry ball. Break the opposition and then hand us the loaded gun, usually at point blank range. 'Would you care to do the honours, ladies?'

Rod wanted us to use the tommy-gun approach: spray the opposition with so many bullets they had no chance of survival. Two valid schools of thought, but difficult to amalgamate. Much of the Brumbies' and Australian attack goes through the 'second five-eighth', inside centre in northern hemisphere dialect. Many southern hemisphere teams let their second-five call all the plays. We don't really have this position in Ireland or England, but it's a hugely important playmaking role in Australia and New Zealand, and Leicester embraced it by hiring Paddy and then Rod. The number twelve can take much of the creative pressure off the outhalf. It's a shame that this role has not really been recognized in the northern hemisphere, because a lot of natural twelves end up at outhalf and appear to be flawed tens, when really they are out of position.

Getting back to the European final in 2002 was a big achievement in itself: every team we came up against was trying to be the team that broke Leicester. It was an enormously difficult campaign that drew some of the best performances I have ever had the privilege to be involved in. Every time the opposition had us reeling, we came back at them. Be it via Tim Stimpson's place-kicking or Neil Back's control of the maul, we kept finding a way. Our way.

It was the Llanelli Scarlets that forced us to a level we didn't even realize existed. They were the first team in years to shake our feeling of invincibility at Welford Road. In our pool game in September 2001 we scraped through 12–9, but our forwards hadn't experienced such intensity against English opposition in the previous four years.

I was still injured from the rescheduled foot-and-mouth inter-national in Edinburgh, but I returned for the Calvisano trip and was involved again in the famous 31–30 nail-biter in Perpignan when Tim kicked the winning penalty two minutes into injury time to com-plete a comeback from 15–27 behind. It was not the first nor would it be the last time we relied on Stimo's boot to guide us home. France is the toughest place to go and win, especially the late-night kick-offs when the stadium takes on a carnival atmosphere, but in Perpignan we eventually silenced the Catalan drums.

That victory in France acted as a double blow. On the return leg in November, Perpignan had clearly lost interest in the competition, as French clubs tend to do after a home defeat. We thrashed them 54–15 to make it ten successive victories in Europe. Beating Calvisano at home guaranteed a home quarter-final.

Llanelli welcomed us to Stradey Park for our last pool game. It was our first taste of mortality for almost two years. They needed victory to progress. We went over the Severn Bridge with the wrong attitude and paid a heavy price. Up against Stephen Jones's control of the wind, a crowd comparable to a baying Welford Road, and a pack, including Wales and Lions number eight Scott Quinnell, that more than matched ours for intensity, we lost 24–14 as all the usually reli-able aspects of our play malfunctioned – like me catching high balls.

We assumed that was the last we would see of Llanelli.

The quarter-final paired us with Leinster at Welford Road. Tim was injured, so I was officially running at fullback against Girvan Dempsey, and I was handling the place-kicking. They took a surprise 10–0 lead through a Denis Hickie try that Austin swears he touched first. It didn't matter, as our response was to run in four tries before half-time. We simply blew them away. These were the days when Leinster could be punished up front.

I ran in our fourth try, off the back of a typically destructive break by Freddie Tuilagi, and my conversion made it 24–10 to kill off the contest. If I'd kicked better it would have got even uglier for Leinster, but we won 29–18, with five tries to two telling a better story.

Austin, just back from suspension and with a full head of hair after laser hair treatment, was superb at outhalf. The slagging was relentless but he loved every minute of it. Not only had he got hair plugs but he became a poster boy for the treatment. 'Money in my pocket, boys.' No idea how much he made but – and I say this as someone who is thinning pretty heavily myself – it's not worth it. I'll just have to embrace baldness when it is officially confirmed.

(Austin wasn't the only one to risk dressing-room ridicule for a full mop of hair. At the end of the 1999/2000 season, Neil Back turned up with a suspiciously thicker look than the previous week. Myself, Leon and Lewis noticed immediately, but it was a few hours before kick-off so we muffled our laughter. It became even more difficult during the game when Backy came out of a ruck, fixing his head. The chat afterwards was that his hair replacements had flapped up and he needed mud to stick them back on. We couldn't prove this as he was sin-binned for punching some guy almost immediately, returning ten minutes later with a scrum cap. He shaved his head after that.)

Sod's law meant we were drawn against Llanelli in the Heineken Cup semi-final. The match was played at the City Ground, home of Nottingham Forest Football Club, so 30,000 supporters could attend – Welford Road held only about 17,000 at that time. The Scar-lets were a strange proposition to us: unlike every other team we came up against, they were convinced they could beat us. Mainly because they already had. They carried that belief into England, and the City Ground very quickly became a neutral venue. Stephen Jones put them in front with his place-kicking before a try from Harry Ellis, our young scrumhalf, sparked a revival. It took a penalty off a scrum well inside our own half to settle it. Johnno was planning to go for an attacking lineout and engineer a drop goal but Tim had other ideas, immediately informing referee Dave McHugh of his intention to kick for goal from 57 metres. It bounced off post and crossbar before dropping over to secure a 13–12 victory that sent us into our second European final.

Munster would provide the opposition at the Millennium Stadium in Cardiff.

★

By that time we had captured our fourth consecutive Premiership title, beating Newcastle at home in April with three games to spare in the regular season. We lost just four games, all away and all on Sundays.

Bristol beat us in the opening round of the play-offs, but, seven days before the Heineken Cup final, it meant nothing. They had finished eighth in the table, thirty-three points adrift. Fewer than 5,000 people turned up, the lowest attendance at Welford Road since 1992 – another 20,000 supporters were understandably gearing up for a trip to Cardiff the following weekend. I wasn't picked, as Deano had been resting most of us to avoid a similar situation to the previous year when we creaked into the biggest game of our lives. Of course he had to pick some regulars, and sure enough Leon sustained a neck injury that ruled him out of the Munster game.

The 'Hand of Back' is not as hot a topic as it used to be with Munster folk, as they have had enough glory days of their own subsequently, but when I am feeling a little cheeky and the subject comes up I remind them about the other seventy-nine minutes they had to score more points than us.

For those who haven't heard about it, here's how the final minute of the 2002 Heineken Cup final unfolded. We were leading 15–9 and Munster had an attacking scrum five metres from our line, inches to the right of the posts. Peter Stringer went to feed the ball into the scrum but Backy slapped it from his hands into our side. Harry Ellis passed to Austin and he booted it into touch, forty metres upfield. The French referee Joël Jutge couldn't have seen it, as he was standing on the other side of the scrum, but the touch judge had no excuse. OK, it happened pretty quickly, but he missed it.

In such a demonic forwards battle, Munster were left with too many yards to grind out. (Just look at the match-ups: Quinlan, Wally and Axel against Lewis, Backy and Cozza in the backrow; Gaillimh and a young Paulie O'Connell brawling with Johnno and Ben Kay; the frontrow was gruesome stuff as Claw, Frankie Sheahan and Hayes met Rowntree, West and Garforth. Munster even brought on Jim Williams, Marcus Horan and Mick O'Driscoll. Carnage is the only word for it.) Munster won the lineout, but a turnover came when the man went to ground and Harry got his hands on it, allowing Austin, again, to kick the ball off the pitch.

Even if Neil's intervention hadn't occurred, I firmly believe Munster would never have got over our try-line that day. Yes, what Backy did was cheating, gamesmanship, whatever you want to call it. If you look at the scrum immediately before it, Lewis pawed at the ball in Strings' hand but missed his opportunity; Backy clearly noticed.

I felt sorry for Strings. I have a lot of time for him and what he has achieved in his career. It must hurt, but he never once carped about it. Not to me, anyway. He just took it like the man he is. I got no joy out of seeing the distraught look on his face or on the faces of so many guys I was playing alongside for Ireland. But I was happy Neil did what he did, because I wanted to win that game more than anything. I don't care how we did it, I just wanted to win.

What else can you say? If one of the Munster flankers, Alan Quinlan or David Wallace, had done the same thing they would for ever be known as a rogue – one of the most affectionate terms that can be bestowed on a Munster man. Neil's an introverted guy, so he never said much about it. One of the great openside flankers, his focus was extraordinary. He saw a chance to influence a European Cup final and he took it.

As I said, Munster people seem to have let it go, mainly because they won the tournament in 2006 and proved themselves a great team by regaining the trophy in 2008. It is a shame that men like Mick Galwey and Peter Clohessy never got there, but I believe we were the better team. We scored two tries that day and Stimo, of all people, missed a few kicks. Johnno also had a legitimate claim for a try when Frankie Sheahan overthrew a lineout, but Jutge called play back.

I crossed for our first after some quick hands by Austin, Rod Kafer and Freddie Tuilagi put Tim into space outside Rob Henderson. Stimo threw a cracking dummy to beat the first cover tackler, meaning all I had to do was trail him, take the offload and gallop over near the posts. Amazingly, Tim missed the conversion while Rog planted three penalties to put Munster 9–5 ahead early in the second-half.

Near the hour mark Austin stepped over Rog for a try, while ten minutes later Stimo nailed a massive penalty from the left to ensure Munster, just like Stade a year before them, needed a try to beat us.

Johnno, when leading us up to collect our medals, gave the trophy he had lifted twelve months earlier a little tap before walking straight past it. The honour of lifting it was bestowed on the original ABC club of my time at Leicester, as the departing Richard Cockerill was joined by Graham and Darren in the centre of the podium.

At the time we all knew that retaining the title of European champions was a great achievement, but it just seemed like a natural goal for us. Only now, looking back, can the scale of the achievement be fully comprehended. It was not until 2012 that Leinster became only the second club to have kept hold of the trophy.

A week after the Heineken Cup final against Munster I was back with my Irish teammates on a plane to New Zealand.

This really was a case of the one that got away. We so nearly caught the All Blacks cold. In a torrential downpour I was agonizingly close to getting the decisive try. Drico put in a nicely lofted cross-field kick which I caught, Gaelic style, over my head at full stretch, but Leon McDonald hit me as I was coming down near the corner flag. I grounded the ball but it was flagged for touch in goal. We lost 15–6 and blamed Adidas's new yellow ball, which Rog had a nightmare kicking. In fairness, the New Zealand outhalf, Andrew Mehrtens, ensured our complaints wouldn't be seen as sour grapes, describing the ball as a 'pig that doesn't fly'. There was no sweet spot.

It being my first time back in New Zealand since 1996, I visited Auckland Grammar. They remembered me and even had a space on the wall of internationals, beside Doug Howlett's picture, where they were going to put my mug. They had All Blacks, Tongans and Samoans, but I was the first from the northern hemisphere. I never did return to see if I'm up there. In fairness, I owe them more than they owe me.

The chastened All Blacks, having been booed off the paddock in Dunedin, wiped the floor with us 40–8 in the second Test.

★

The most glorious ever run by an English club side ended on the day Leicester beat Munster in Cardiff in May 2002. Very little was kept in reserve for the 2002–3 season. Gloucester topped the Premiership table. We finished a terrible sixth. Northampton took our five-year unbeaten regular-season home record away that November. We lost ten league matches in total – having lost fourteen in the previous four campaigns. Maybe, subconsciously, several players could be forgiven for switching their focus to the Six Nations and thereafter the World Cup. These men were always looking to the next challenge and we had wrung the club scene dry.

I was in the form of my life, constantly running at fullback as Tim was injured; he eventually moved to France at the end of the season, which meant I was poised to become the resident number fifteen at the club. But it was a shocking season by our standards.

Munster's revenge was swift as well. They knocked us out of Europe in a quarter-final at Welford Road, flailing us 20–7.

In order to qualify for the next season's Heineken Cup we needed to beat Saracens in a wildcard play-off in June. It took a hundred minutes but we eventually prevailed 27–20. Remarkably, less than two weeks later, Johnno, Backy and Wig were involved in the epic 15–13 defeat of the All Blacks in Wellington when England's defence held out with thirteen men after Neil and Lawrence Dallaglio were sin-binned.

By then I too had switched focus. I was long since established at club level; now, cementing my place in a young, talented Ireland side became my priority.

8. Ireland's Icarus Moment

The opportunity to properly stretch my legs for Ireland came at Murrayfield in 2003. Keith Wood was injured, so Eddie went with Brian O'Driscoll as captain for the Six Nations. The Lions tour in 2001 had established Brian as a world-class centre, and he had captained Ireland to victory over Australia at Lansdowne Road in November 2002. There were more experienced men in the squad, but it proved the correct decision. You want to follow Drico; it's the way he plays that makes him a leader. He gives every ounce of his exceptional ability every time he plays, and that is inspiring.

It was also clear that when everyone was fit Eddie's starting back three was Girv, Denis and Shaggy, so I was wearing number twenty-two in Murrayfield for the Six Nations opener.

When Shane's hamstring blew out I came off the bench and got a try. This wasn't the usual end-of-the-line Irish winger try, either. I came through a ruck just outside our 22 and the ball was just sitting there. A quick glance at the referee told me it was fine to grab it. I had to welly it down the field immediately, as four Scotsmen were on top of me. There was no cover, so I was in a straight sprint with twenty-nine other players. I liked those odds. Kenny Logan was my main competitor, but I knew I had him for pace so it was all about controlling the ball as it bobbled just outside the Scottish 22. I could have scooped it up Serevi-style, but I trusted my football skills, catching it perfectly with my left boot without breaking stride, so it skidded low. All I had to do was dive on it for an eighty-metre score. I leaped up, tongue lolling out like a greyhound, completely wrecked. Anthony Foley was the first to arrive with a bear hug. That's some running by Axel, in fairness. The buzz was extraordinary. David Humphreys had to get the ball for his conversion as I had flung it away, but still he gave me a high five.

Yeah, I enjoyed that one. I knew I had done something that probably only Denis and Drico, of the others out there, could replicate.

Girv joined Shaggy on the treatment table, so I was patrolling the backfield in Rome. It was pointed out before the game that I had nine tries in twelve games for Ireland. I made it ten in thirteen.

All of a sudden I had a profile at home. Dean Richards's 'George Best' comparison had embarrassingly followed me across the water. It was better than 'chicken legs' or 'pencil', I suppose.

Eddie made a comment before the French game that was meant to be complimentary. 'The problem we had was that he wasn't playing in Leicester at fullback but on the wing, and a couple of years ago when he was dropped in at fullback at Test level he did struggle, which is understandable. Now we recognize his future could be at fullback or on the wing. It's easy to go from fullback to wing. It's very hard to go from wing to fullback. Geordan is such a fine footballer you've got to find a place for him. He runs good lines, hits the line very well and has good hands. If he has to play fullback on Saturday so be it. I won't have any concern.'

My opinion on the fullback/wing question would be the opposite to Eddie's. Any fullback will tell you it's more difficult to go from fullback to wing because you are immediately constricted. My fear playing wing for Ireland was that a specialist winger would expose me at this level. I was a fullback! I started as a ten and evolved into a fullback. I played on the wing for club and country only due to my pace, and due to competition at fullback from Tim Stimpson and Girvan Dempsey. Fifteen is a specialist position in its own right. My strongest trait, I feel, is the ability to read situations. That can't really be done on the Irish wing. At fullback you have that freedom and that control.

Girv was still not right, so a decision between us didn't need to be made for France. My confidence levels had soared after a run of good performances. It seemed like the perfect moment to roll out the party piece.

It was a ridiculously windy day in Dublin when France came to visit. We got an attacking platform in the opening minute. I was switching from right to left in a pre-planned move when they wheeled our scrum. Dimitri Yachvili disrupted Strings's pass and it bobbled to my feet. A simple choice presented itself: drop goal or be smashed by two French backrowers. I smiled inside: I had to break my stride, but I knew it was on.

I had nailed a screamer a few months beforehand to see off Saracens. Then there was the one that made Bob Dwyer smile. The Naas and Newbridge boys will remember a few more. I gathered up the ball before delicately dropping it over from forty-five yards, turned and trotted back into position. Three–nil.

The conditions made it a game for the forwards to sort out among themselves. France had a grizzled pack, but several of our lads had beaten them in 2000 and 2001, and a good few of us had done them at underage, so there was no element of fear any more, while older guys like Kevin Maggs and Keith Gleeson probably hadn't experienced that emotion since their early childhood. I remember a lovely hit on Olivier Magne, the brilliant French flanker. I held him up, and Drico bowled him over. Humphs guided us home in the battle of the kickers, 15–12.

'Very unIrish-like. But there you go. Maybe we're changing traits,' I told the media. What I meant was that I had grown accustomed to winning every time I went out on the field, and now I was seeing that attitude beginning to grow in the Ireland camp. We had won ugly, in the sort of match we had often lost in the past.

The drama continued in Cardiff. Humphs had regained the number ten jersey, but Rog made a huge impact off the bench against Wales. I enjoyed playing with David because he always looked for me in attack. But this particular nail-biter at the Millennium Stadium was all about the boots of Rog and Stephen Jones, in an uncanny dress rehearsal for 2009.

Clearly sick of getting stuffed by us, the Welsh put up a hell of a fight, but Denis Hickie managed to block Jones's late drop goal after Rog's drop goal had put us 25–24 in front moments earlier. We rode our luck to go ten games undefeated. Unprecedented stuff for Ireland.

England were due at Lansdowne Road eight days later for a winner-takes-all Grand Slam showdown. I was coming up against England in the biggest Test match since 1948, having barely put a foot wrong all season. Girv was fit again but I was retained at fullback in a massive vote of confidence from Eddie. He made changes elsewhere, with Victor Costello and Gary Longwell coming into the pack while Paulie returned to the bench.

The England team picked itself – Lewsey, Robinson, Greenwood, Tindall, Cohen, Wilkinson, Dawson, Rowntree, Thompson, Leonard, Johnson, Kay, Hill, Back, Dallaglio. From this moment until the World Cup six months later, only the props changed. They had lost only one game in the previous four Six Nations campaigns, so to leave Dublin without the Grand Slam could have proved detrimental in their history-chasing World Cup year.

We had convinced ourselves that we were England's equal. How wrong we were.

When I saw my friend Martin Johnson's big stubborn head and that lip protruding out even further than usual, I could only smile. We were about to come up the steps at the old Lansdowne Road when a few lads noticed that England were on our side of the red carpet for the anthems. We were told that they were about to be moved. I could have told the officials not to bother trying. Johnno was only going to move if someone physically dragged him from that spot, and he wasn't alone. I could see Neil Back in his ear: 'We are not moving, Johnno!'

I used to get asked about this incident a lot, because I was Johnno's clubmate. I consider him a good friend and I genuinely believe he made a mistake when he came out of the tunnel and lined his team up on the wrong side. But in Johnno's mind the match always started once he laced up his boots so, once in position, he wasn't going to budge. A lot was made afterwards of his ignorance, but he is a man who bases rugby on physical domination. It was single-mindedness rather than ignorance.

None of that great English team were ever going to budge for anyone. I knew them well because other Tigers like Graham Rowntree and Ben Kay were in the pack. I knew they were incapable of backing down.

Some of our lads were pissed off. Most of them, in fairness, were looking for any additional reason to vent their hatred, and this was a decent one.

Drico led us behind the English line and on to the grass beyond the red carpet, so that President McAleese would shake their hands first, as per usual. Fair play to her for getting her heels mucky when shaking our hands. Don't know why, but she always stalled for a few words with me. 'Great to see you back, Geordan.' Maybe she felt I needed some encouragement, considering how slight I was compared to the rest of the lads. Or maybe she knew my father was an army man.

That was one of those rare days when I knew I would perform. I was playing at the peak of my powers, ultra-confident, and I promised myself I would make yardage every time I touched the ball.

The place is electric. A proper venomous Irish crowd.

Our pack starts like a freight train. England soak up most of the pressure, but it is immediately apparent that Anthony Foley and Victor Costello are bulling to get the ball in their hands. So are Drico and Maggsy. The rest of the lads just want to smash an Englishman. Mal O'Kelly and Gary Longwell get their massive frames into the action early. Marcus Horan, Shane Byrne and John Hayes are pounding into every ruck. Keith Gleeson is everywhere. He has to be because Neil Back is like two players. These opening exchanges are brutal.

I attack the line and throw a pass to Brian, but he knocks on. No matter. I know the ball will come my way again soon enough. They expect us to play for territory, but we are going wide early and regularly. Jonny Wilkinson wants to test my wingers. Sure enough, he fires a garryowen over to Justin Bishop's wing. This is my ball. Josh Lewsey and Cohen are thundering down the touchline but it is mine. I give Bis a little warning and then I'm up over his head and mark it in mid-air. I land and Josh bundles me into touch. He is trying to get the ball off me for a quick lineout, but I marked it. I give him the ball and dump-tackle him off the grass. Axel is pleased with this and gives me a little slap.

I'm up and away in the biggest game of my life.

But we are facing a team capable of scoring at any moment. We have a scrum on our 22. They wheel it, and before anybody reacts Richard Hill pounces, pops it up to Dawson who sprints clear. Strings catches him but the offload allows Dallaglio to flop under the posts untouched. Seven-nil.

The message in the huddle is clear: We must score next.

I catch another high ball and take off. The defence is lined up in front of me so I launch it into the heavens, but I overcook it and Jason Robinson marks it.

The initial surge of adrenalin wanes. They start to batter us. Greenwood grubbers through, Bis cleans up, allowing me to charge on to his offload, step Backy and Dawson and fly over halfway before Wilkinson puts me down. Everyone responds to the break. The forwards pile in. Drico gets on the ball and makes a few yards. Backy, first to every breakdown, is removed. Victor makes a big carry but is chopped down.

I pop up at fly-half and step inside three drifting Englishmen, straight into Backy and Johnno. They are waiting to crush me. Johnno wraps me up but Jonathan Kaplan penalizes him for not rolling away. Johnno argues with Kaplan. That's what he does, he makes referees know they have displeased him. He intimidates better than anyone I have ever seen.

Our big opportunity comes with the score at 3–7. Clean, first-phase ball is our strength. Foley off the top of the lineout, Strings to Humphreys, whose skip pass finds Drico. He draws the midfield defenders before flicking it wide, to me, at full speed. I go twenty metres into English territory in an instant. I'm moving so fast I can't see Denis haring up outside me. I know he is coming but I can't see him and all I can hear is the static of a radio turned up loud. What I can see is an indecisive Jason Robinson in front of me. But the English right wing is playing me. I step inside him, straight into a tracking Wilkinson, who hammers me. The English defence re-forms. The chance is gone. If I had offloaded or chipped it, would Denis have scored? (He told me afterwards it was a certain try, but I couldn't see or hear him.)

The dynamic of the game changes in that instant. We start going backwards in the collisions. Jonny dumps Bis. The English pack pile in and get the ball.

Humphreys nails a beauty from wide right: 6–7. We still think there is a game to be won. It is an illusion. England are only beginning to move through the gears. A Wilkinson drop goal makes it 6–10.

We keep coming. They have three men in the backfield, expecting us to kick, so the space is to move the ball wide, wide through the hands. If only we could play like this all the time.

I almost pull something out of the hat. Mal O'Kelly secures ball off the top of a lineout that allows us to get Victor running hard in a wide channel. Humphs gets it and steps Ben Kay, drawing in the English forwards. All pre-planned, we now attack the short side, where I am first receiver. I chip for Denis, but the bounce evades all the chasers, landing back in my hands. Kyran Bracken tackles me a yard short of the line. I get back up, Keith Gleeson flicks it to me so I try to burrow through the ruck. I get smashed.

Ireland scrum. I'm in bits. Drico is lying beside me, I pull him up.

Solid scrum, Humphs feeds Maggs, who charges head-down for the line, but Jonny tackles him and Backy shovels Keith off the ball as Dallaglio and Johnno secure the turnover.

We continue to batter into them, phase after phase, but England's defence is impregnable.

Wilkinson bangs over another drop goal, this time with his right foot, after Dallaglio charged up the blindside wing with only one man to beat – I went low. But it is 6–13 now. That's the difference: they take their chances.

England's maul breaks us in the second half. The killer blow comes when Greenwood sends Mike Tindall bullocking into our 22. I tackle him on the line but it is like being hit by a bus. His sheer force knocks me out cold for a few seconds.

When I come round I can see the game is over – all our lads are visibly shattered.

Greenwood suckers me at the end. We are 30–6 down and I'm trying to spark something from inside the 22. Will muffles his accent and calls for it on my inside so I let it go. He strolls into the corner, tips down and points into the crowd. It is a rout.

This Grand Slam decider came a little early for us. The scoreboard never lies and it said we got stuffed, 46–6, but there were opportunities in the early stages that might have planted seeds of doubt in English minds – we knew they were under tremendous pressure to finally complete the Slam. If we had taken just one of those chances we would have been ahead at half-time. The best of the lot fell to me.

Long term, they did us a favour. They showed us that the only way to defeat them was by pounding them into the dirt. That is the only way an England team will ever yield. You must break them. But there was no breaking that team.

Johnno became a hate figure in Ireland for a very long time. However, I think he healed the wounds in one midlands town. Many years later I asked him, as a favour to me, to speak at a fundraiser for Naas RFC.

'No problem, Geordie.'

I was a little nervous about how he would go down, especially from the reaction I tend to get at home towards him ever since the red carpet stance. The swear words are always particularly choice when Irish people are describing Johnno.

Typical of him, that night in my brother's club, he addressed the issue head on, explaining his thought process that day at Lansdowne Road, how he was hurting from previous failed tilts at the Grand Slam, and that he couldn't move when challenged as the game had already started in his mind. I stood in the wings and tried to gauge the Naas people's reaction. He walked off to a standing ovation.

England went to New Zealand that summer and won. They went to the World Cup in Australia and found a way to topple the hosts in the final. They did whatever it took.

I was rewarded for my performances with the Rugby Writers of Ireland player of the year award in May, before we went on tour of Australia and the Pacific Islands. Drico was injured so I played centre outside Maggsy against the Wallabies. Drained after a really productive but tough season, we got hammered 46–16 but I did fine in my temporary role. Mr Versatility. After Perth the dirt-trackers were sent to Tonga and Samoa, including Girvan, while I was sent home. It meant I was definitely going to the World Cup, and probably as Eddie's starting fullback.

How wrong I was. I thought some of my previous ankle sprains, hamstring tears and knee wobbles were bad, but pain from another universe was coming for me.

9. Murrayfield

Saturday, 6 September 2003
Ireland v. Scotland, Murrayfield, Edinburgh
I feel invincible. Every time I touch the ball these past few months something seems to happen. Gaps keep opening for me, passes keep sticking, tries keep coming.

Our final warm-up before the World Cup in Australia, and we are coasting. From a turnover in our 22, we sweep downfield.

Eric Miller takes my pass but runs laterally in my direction, forcing me on the switch. With a glance I can usually tell where the gaps are in a defence, so when I get the ball again I know the only option is to plough into the Scottish scrumhalf, Mike Blair, who is already crouched below me. All my weight is on my planted left leg as we collide. His knee hits my shin, bone on bone, just as someone nails me from behind. Squashed at the moment of impact, my leg snaps forward like a twig.

As I roll and land facing the Scottish try-line, the feeling of invincibility is replaced by a brand-new sensation coursing through my entire body.

A surfer who has been attacked by a Great White Shark will know this feeling. Something is dangling off the end of my leg.

Oh God no, please don't let this be happening to me.

The initial numbness is about to be replaced by excruciating pain but, instinctively, I place the ball back on our side. Small mercies: the ruck forms beside, and not over, my body. I reach down, feeling shattered bones in my sock. My bones.

Everything is reduced to a distant humming sound; the crowd, the ruck just inches from my head.

My fucking shin is gone.

Lying on my right side, foot popping up the wrong way, I apply pressure and straighten it, flopping my limp left leg over my right leg.

Waves of nausea washing over me now, I'm struggling to breathe, pain is flooding through my body. I must be screaming in agony because the referee Nigel Whitehouse halts the play. Scottish players look down at me, then quickly turn away.

If I was a racehorse there would be a screen around me. The jockey would be whispering in my ear, hand cupped over my eye so I couldn't see the syringe.

Instead, Dr Gary O'Driscoll is whispering in my ear. But there is no syringe. Not yet.

'Jesus, Doc . . .' I am spitting words, 'Jesus, Doc, my leg . . .'

'It's all right, Geordie . . .' Gary's tone is for a hysterical child.

Ailbe McCormack, our physio, does the necessary and asks me what's wrong.

'I've broken my leg.' My hands are blocking their view.

I'll always remember Gary's calmness. A heroic, amazing doctor who is stationed in the Arsenal dugout nowadays. One of the good guys in life, he is also Brian's cousin.

'Geordie, you don't know that. Let's just have a look.'

'No, Doc, I've broken my leg.'

I'm gasping for air.

'You might be all right. Take your hands away, Geordie.'

I comply. Seconds of silence follow as they stare at bone and blood spurting through my sock.

Somebody starts yelling: 'Stretcher! Stretcher!'

The choppers are circling overhead and there is sporadic gunfire as Mal O'Kelly strolls past, 'I love the smell of napalm in the morning . . .'

Gary is hunched over me, talking in his slow, soothing tone, 'You'll be all right, Geordie . . .'

My memory freezes. Probably a body's natural defence mechanism, shutting down due to trauma. Yet, other moments are etched in my brain for ever. Like being carried from the field with a television camera in my face.

'Get that away from me, please.' I don't even know if my words are audible but I say 'please'. My mother raised me well, I suppose.

We stall on the running track so they can put me on a trolley before wheeling me away – *Bye-bye, Geordan Murphy* – as the camera pans back to the action. The game always moves on.

Out of sight in the changing room, I am wailing in agony. Must have blacked out because next thing I know I'm in a smaller room. They moved me so the lads wouldn't come in for half-time and see me in this state. It would be impossible to give a team talk.

It happened after twenty-two minutes – the same time my hamstring exploded in this accursed stadium. There is a television up on the wall and the commentator says my injury might not be too bad.

'Could someone turn that off, please?'

I get a jab of morphine, but it doesn't kick in, and then I'm wheeled out to the ambulance, where I am given nitrous oxide. Ross appears. He was due to travel to Australia for the World Cup.

'I'm so sorry, Ross. You have booked your flights.'

The morphine is not working.

'So sorry, Ross . . .'

Am I apologizing for breaking my leg? I look down and groan. Hang on. Ross is at home in Naas, watching the game on television. Maybe the morphine *is* working. I look again and Ross is a paramedic. This guy isn't my brother and he hasn't booked flights to Australia.

A hazy drive to the Royal Edinburgh hospital, but the pain doesn't fade.

The orthopaedic surgeon, Charles Court-Brown, operates that evening. Double compound fracture of the lower left leg. Both the fibia and tibula snapped and came through the skin.

I wake up at 6 a.m. Everyone is gone off to prepare for the World Cup. Stuck in an unfamiliar hospital bed and coming off a raft of drugs, you can't help feeling sorry for yourself in such a situation. Lucie is there beside me.

I am distraught, assuming my life as a rugby player is over. Ireland fullback gig finished. Geordie Murphy of the Tigers no more.

Less than twenty-four hours ago I'd the confidence of a king. Now, nothing. Empty. Finished. Big fat lump in my throat.

Mr Court-Brown comes in and says plenty of reassuring words. The operation went well. They sliced me open, pushed back the kneecap and slid it down towards my foot, and buried a twelve-inch metal rod in my leg.

A doctor asks for my jersey. I hand it over but keep the Puma boot they cut off. Gory memorabilia. I'm not really bothered with that sort of thing, usually I give everything away, but a sick sense of humour makes me hold on to that particular item.

As soon as I'm alone, I cry like a baby. Gary O'Driscoll walks through the door at around 9 a.m. with some magazines. He sees the state of me and delays his flight back to Dublin for a second time. Like I said, that kind of guy. He talks me through everything and plants seeds of hope in my brain, but nothing registers for a few days. I am convinced it is over. I saw my leg. I know. He keeps reminding me that I was operated on by the same surgeon that got Henrik Larsson back playing top-class football after a similarly gruesome leg break.

I get out of hospital the following Thursday, fly home to Ireland, where friends and family are all there for me, but there is nothing anyone can say. You make this journey alone and it tells you a lot about yourself.

Initially, the road is too dark to see a way back.

Only if you're mentally strong can you find the motivation to mend your body. The process starts slowly, agonizingly so. Recovering from a bad fracture is a psychological battle as much as anything else.

Leicester's physiotherapist, Mark Geeson, having conferred with Gary O'Driscoll, set out a six-month rehabilitation timetable. On the first visit to a specialist in London I was told it would be an additional four weeks on crutches as the plate in my leg was loose. Only then could I start strength work in the pool, and only then would I be able to convince myself that I'd play rugby again.

Only then could I start aiming towards the 2004 Six Nations. That thought dragged me out of bed every morning.

Going training every day beats any other job in the world. Unless you are injured. I always arrive at Oval Park with a spring in my step and a smile on my face – how can this lifestyle not put you in good form? But when you're injured it is torture seeing all the healthy bodies heading out to pitches while you switch between the physio's table and the weights room.

It is a lonely personal battle, but I did have a rehab buddy. James Buckland, a hooker who is now with London Irish, had also broken his leg. Small words of encouragement passed between us during our mind-numbingly boring daily routines.

Rugby players get paid to wreck their bodies. My catalogue of injuries is actually pretty tame in comparison to others. Lewis Moody has had eleven operations, and counting, to repair several parts of his warrior frame. I'm only up to five invasive surgeries.

Of course, none of it compares to what happened to my Leicester club mate, Matt Hampson. Hambo became a quadriplegic, paralysed from the neck down, after a scrum collapsed at an England under-21 training session in 2005.

Matt is only five years younger than me so I knew him from around the club, but not well enough to go and see him in hospital. If I'm honest, I bottled it. Couldn't face into my own worst nightmare.

Thankfully, I grew out of that. I started going over to his house a few times and realized he is an unbelievable character. I'm involved with his foundation now as an ambassador. He got to a stage where he raised enough money to pay his carers, so he helps other people now. When he speaks in public there is never a dry eye in the house.

My first time under the knife was shoulder reconstruction in 2001. I'd been putting off joining the 'zipper club' (named after the scar) since dislocating it at the start of the 1998/9 season against Wasps at Loftus Road, a football ground with a really tight in-goal area. After Austin's miscued drop goal I was following up the scraps and the bounce spun up nicely, so I launched myself through the air, grounding the ball for a try but wrecking my shoulder in the process. It went back in handily enough (don't mind Mel Gibson in *Lethal Weapon*) but it kept popping out over the next two years whenever I creased it badly in contact or along the turf.

The serious injury was the hamstring at Murrayfield in 2001, then medial knee ligaments at Twickenham in 2002, then my leg snapping again at Murrayfield.

I've also had three cases of scratched retinas, the third of which meant the Leicester medics missed a double hernia as I wasn't active ahead of a particularly big game. I needed double bilateral inguinal repair surgery as a result, but we will get to that in due course.

I did the shoulder in the exact same manner in the 2009/10 season, only this time I didn't get the try. I was putting pressure on Bath's Joe Maddock in the in-goal when I smashed it into the dirt.

That was particularly bad because I also put a hole in my head at the same time. Ten stitches – I think I went into the advertising board. My shoulder wouldn't pop back in straight away so the doctor had to have a few goes at it. There is no fine art to this process. It is just another man trying to force your shoulder back into its socket, a violent and uncompromising experience which was made worse by somebody forgetting to lock the wheels of the physio bed. The first time he yoinked at my arm all three of us – me, doctor and bed – flew across the room. They say grown men shouldn't cry, but there are exceptions to the rule. There is a nice picture somewhere of my head pissing blood and my arm dangling off.

But that's what we do for a living. And the older we get, the slower we get and the creakier our joints become. I guess Deano had my best interests at heart all those years ago when he slashed my wages in an attempt to fatten me up. He wanted me to be able to take the hits further down the road. I never did fatten up, but still took the hits.

Rugby injuries, in general, are becoming increasingly problematic. Statistics released in 2009 showed that a quarter of players in the Premiership are injured at any one time. Leicester use the injury dispensation rule to sign a guy mid-season every season. When a frontliner is crocked, the second string or academy strength in depth has to be trusted – but lose two players in a specific position and a club has to look outside.

A successful example was Leicester bringing in Lote Tuqiri when I did my shoulder in 2009. One of the best ever wingers to play either Rugby League or Union, Tuqiri made a genuine, albeit brief, impact at Leicester.

There'd been a few problems with the Australian Rugby Union, who tore up his contract without a public explanation. A world-class player was suddenly on the market, and our board did some smart business by snapping him up on a six-month contract. I had a preconceived notion that he might be a bit up himself and prove a disruption to the dressing room, but he was very quick to blend into our well-established culture. No airs or graces, just straight down to work. His wife, Becks, is the nicest woman you could meet. She is a sports psychologist, and I found her interesting to chat to about mental preparation. I have no doubt the two Tuqiri boys have a future in the game if they want it. Samson, the elder, was just as valuable to the Tigers under-sevens and under-eights as his dad was to the senior team. Chip off the old block, big curly hair – going out smashing kids two, three years older than him.

The real shame was: Lote departed when his deal expired. I think his return to League with the Wests Tigers in Australia was already in place for the following season. I think he had a tinge of regret, as Leicester seemed to suit him at that point in his career and life. Young family, living in a small, leafy village with little to do but play rugby. I was disappointed that I only got to play with him a few times.

'I think this World Cup was tailor-made for Geordan Murphy,' Eddie kindly said immediately after Murrayfield. 'His speed, agility, his football skills would have thrived on the hard ground of Australia and he could have been one of the stars of the tournament.'

What might have been, I suppose.

The Irish backline had gelled during the previous Six Nations. I had a good feel for what Drico was going to do, same for David

Humphreys or Rog at outhalf. With Brian all you have to do is trail him, because ninety-nine times out of a hundred he'll free his hands out of the tackle or pop it up after going to ground.

After Murrayfield, I was quickly forgotten. That's what happens when you get injured: you become useless to those preparing for the next challenge.

I visited the squad before they departed for Australia. It was a difficult moment, walking into the team room on leaving day, but I put on the bravest of faces, wishing my friends well on their adventure. David Wallace and Rob Henderson had also missed out through injury.

That was a tough night. A few days later the lads were in Australia as some make-up artist dabbed foundation on my face. I was making my first foray into television as a panellist for both ITV and RTÉ, hobbling from London to Dublin and back again without realizing I probably shouldn't be working for both at the same time. In studio you don't need to be as knowledgeable as pundits get credit for, simply because there isn't enough time. Whenever I tried to expand on the usual guff, somebody interrupted me. So I kept it simple, which is a skill in itself, I suppose. I also enjoyed mixing with the likes of François Pienaar and Will Carling on the ITV panel.

Watching Ireland's narrow pool defeat to Australia in studio was tough, especially when Humphs came so close with a late drop goal attempt. Brian's try was brilliant and yet again he was one of the few Irish players to come away from the tournament with an enhanced reputation.

The Wallaby defeat meant a quarter-final against France. We were full of aggressive intent, but the game was gone after twenty-five minutes when France pounced on a loose pass and Christophe Dominici finished off a typically brilliant counter-attacking try. Despite the eventual manner of that defeat (43–21), the team clearly had a promising future. Only Keith Wood, having battled back from several chronic injuries to regain the captaincy, was heading off into the sunset. A young and talented group remained. I was desperate to be part of it all again.

★

The rehab period ensured I became an eyewitness to much of England's post-World Cup celebrations. Seven of my Leicester teammates were in the England squad. Should have been eight, but Austin was surprisingly overlooked and never played for his country again.

Johnno, along with Ben Kay and Neil Back, started the final against Australia while Lewis came on as a sub, and Martin Corry and Dorian West were on the bench. The seventh, Julian White, picked up a bad knee injury during the tournament.

On their return I seemed to be invited to every celebratory dinner with the magnificent seven. It was the sympathy vote – a case of 'Geordan's injured so we better bring him too'. Everyone wanted a piece of them, so we were out a couple of nights of the week for a few months.

It usually went something like this: 'Ladies and Gentlemen, Leicester Tigers seven World Cup winners . . . and, eh [*barely audible*] Geordan Murphy who got injured the day before the Ireland squad was picked so he never got to go to Australia.' I was the terms-and-conditions part of the night. People didn't care once they saw the William Webb Ellis Trophy.

Anyway, I was sick of people feeling sorry for me. You get over the worst setbacks in sport quite quickly because they are nothing compared to the worst things in life. Perspective comes easily enough. OK, I was an ogre for a few weeks, but once the tournament was over I could joke away. The seven heroes noticed and started to take the piss.

By the end of November they were all playing for the club again, but my recovery began to accelerate only in January when I started running again. It wasn't long before I was on bag-holding duties. Mobility wasn't a problem and I knew my speed would return once I stopped running with a bloody limp, yet I didn't feel ready to play rugby again. My head wasn't right. I had done all the hard graft, but how do you test your tibia without banging it off something? That never really happened in training.

The Six Nations got underway in February, with Ireland losing 35–17 in Paris despite a promising start. Paul O'Connell, already an established leader in the group, led the team out for the first time as

Brian was injured. The next game against Wales in Cardiff also came too soon for me, but the new Leicester coach, John Wells (Deano having departed in January when the board tried to move him 'upstairs' after some poor results), decided it was time to accelerate my rehabilitation. That Saturday I was named on the bench for the Premiership game against London Irish at the Madejski Stadium. I was still moving like Long John Silver, but Wellsy made me an offer I couldn't refuse.

'Just ten minutes, Geordie, at the end of the game.'

'Are you sure, because I might need . . .'

'Yeah, Geordie,' Wellsy insisted, 'no matter what the score is, you are coming on for the last ten.'

I eventually got my head around that. Ten minutes.

All my bravado and determination to return dissipated when I woke that morning. Petrified. Rubbed my fingers along the scar on my leg. The first game after *that* game. Felt like I was starting all over again.

We had signed the South African Jaco van der Weizhuizen as full-back cover, but he was more effective as an attacking ten, so Andy Goode, recently signed from Saracens, switched to fullback to ensure a goal-kicker was in the side.

After kick-off myself and another South African, Glenn Gelder-bloom, jogged down behind the goal to do some stretching. The last ten minutes. No problem.

Dan Hipkiss went down injured after eight minutes.

'You better get up there, Glenn.'

Glenn is a centre, but they could switch Ollie Smith to the wing.

The physio mic crackled beside us.

'Get on the field, Geordie.'

Must be some mistake.

'No, you're all right. I'm only doing ten minutes today.'

I felt worse than before the 2001 Heineken Cup final at Parc des Princes. They had to practically shove me out there.

'Go!'

Fuck.

Straight away, London Irish outhalf Mark Mapletoft launched the ball into the heavens. There was plenty of traffic around ground zero, but Goodey had a direct line to it. As fullback he must go up and catch it. I eased off the wing to cover in behind. Goodey is a quality outhalf, but he had no interest in high balls.

'Geordie, that's yours!'

A golden rule of rugby broken right there.

I was forty metres away. With no time to argue, I charged over, leaped up and took it over a few bodies before crashing to earth. The ruck swallowed me whole before spitting me out its backside.

Afterwards, Goodey tried to defend himself, claiming he was trying to get me into the game.

'So, you were thinking of my best interests, Andy.'

'Of course, Geordie.'

'Did you want to catch it, Andy?'

'No, Geordie.'

Still, it worked. Exactly what I needed. One cleanly taken garry-owen and I was a rugby player again. My opposite winger that day was Justin Bishop who, along with Bob Casey, sought me out afterwards to welcome me back.

We won, as did Ireland the next day at Lansdowne Road. Drico, sporting his mid-decade blond mane, returned from an injury lay-off with two tries as Wales were ripped apart yet again. This was the beginning of the O'Driscoll/D'Arcy midfield axis. Denis Hickie was recovering from a snapped Achilles tendon, so Tyrone Howe had the left-wing spot.

Ten days later I got another run for Leicester as we hammered the Barbarians at Welford Road. There was no weekend match as England were playing Ireland at Twickenham, and I went down there to watch our first victory in London since Simon Geoghegan's famous try in 1994. With England 6 points down and twenty minutes left, Mal O'Kelly made a famous corner-flag tackle on Mark Regan. It was the newly crowned world champions' first competitive defeat in a very long time.

The Triple Crown was on the table.

Having missed out on the championship and Grand Slam the previous season, this was a huge opportunity for Ireland to finally win something. The Triple Crown hadn't been done since 1985. I half watched most of that famous Mick Doyle team on telly, but I would be drawn out to the back garden before the finish. Yeah, I knew of Dean, Kiernan, Mullin, Crossan, Ringland and MacNeill, but I couldn't help myself: Camberabero to Sella to Lagisquet . . . Blanco!

I was ecstatic when recalled for the training camp. The Italy match was a fortnight away, so I flew back to Leicester for a friendly against Northampton the following Saturday. A perfect tune-up, which I needed. I knew there was a chance of selection when Declan Kidney appeared in the Franklin's Gardens crowd.

Appointing Deccie as Eddie O'Sullivan's assistant coach, along with Niall O'Donovan, in 2002 was not the IRFU's wisest ever decision. Eddie wasn't prepared to hand over his backline so Deccie was marginalized, and everyone knew it. There was already plenty of speculation about his next job, as he was due to leave the Ireland coaching ticket after the championship. Ulster and even Leicester were mentioned before he took the Dragons job.

It was only after playing eighty minutes against Northampton that I finally made peace with myself about the injury: it was a freak occurrence that probably won't ever happen again.

I returned to the Ireland camp in Citywest that Sunday night, six days before Italy came to Dublin. On Monday morning Eddie was running me on the left wing. When the team was announced that afternoon, I was in, with Tyrone dropped from the twenty-two. He took it like a gentleman, wishing me well. I felt a responsibility to show my pre-World Cup standards, as another player had been discarded to make room for my return.

The contestants on that week's version of *The Weakest Link* were all rugby people. I wasn't overly keen about being interrogated by Anne Robinson, but I was involved with the charity Sparks, as my nephew has cerebral palsy, so I had good motivation.

My dismissal came swiftly enough.

Anne glared at me: 'In the children's TV series *Trumpton* the fire team, led by Captain Flack, comprised Pugh, Pugh, Barney McGrew, Cuthbert, Dibble and who?'

I looked at Will Greenwood who dramatically shrugged his shoulders.

'Eh, Spew?' I eventually replied.

'No, Geordan,' chided Robinson, 'Grubb!'

As a result, Brian Moore, Martin Bayfield, Will and Thomas Castaignède all voted me off.

'I was just shocked he didn't know the name of the firemen,' said Bayfield. 'A schoolboy error.'

Inevitably, with Moore and Robinson staring each other down, it got a little tetchy.

'If you were prime minister,' Robinson asked the former English hooker turned pundit, 'what would you like to see happen?'

'I'd like to ban ginger people from being on television,' Moore replied.

Italy can ruin any Test match when they put their minds to it. We eventually prevailed in a messy game, 19–3, but it was no outing for a winger. O'Driscoll went ahead of Denis Hickie as Ireland's all-time top try-scorer, and while the game represented a significant milestone for me, it was a dress rehearsal for Scotland's visit to Lansdowne Road a week later, when the Triple Crown would be at stake.

Matt Williams had left Leinster to take up the Scottish coaching job but it wasn't going well; they had even lost in Rome. Still, Matt's knowledge of our players meant that the media turned him into the pantomime villain returning to spoil the Triple Crown coronation. Besides the 2001 nightmare, we had generally beaten Scotland with plenty to spare in recent years, and we were expected to win comfortably. Always dangerous territory for an Ireland team.

We started well with a try off a pre-planned move, as usual for us, off clean lineout ball. The forwards rumbled into Scottish territory, Rog fed Brian in midfield, and his perfectly floated left-handed skip pass to Girv opened up the wide channel. A switch inside brought Shaggy charging off his wing. I trailed Darce in midfield, knowing the ball would be in his hands soon enough, but Gordon was having a magnificent year in his new position and didn't need me.

My try came just before half-time when Shaggy, again, came in from the blindside wing to commit three backs. Axel and Mal secured quick ball as first Rog then Drico threw skip passes that allowed me to swan dive over at the Havelock Square end.

The celebrations were temporarily quietened by Ali Hogg's try early in the second half, and Chris Patterson's conversion made it 16-all. Our response was ruthless, with Wally muscling through three tacklers for a third touchdown before Strings sniped over. I had a quick hand in Darce's second try near the end. When he changed the point of attack to my wing, I took his pass but, seeing he'd maintained his running line, I gave it straight back.

That try sealed Darce as Six Nations player of the tournament, and a few moments later we were able to join an already raucous party. It lasted a few days.

Less than seven months earlier I'd been lying in an Edinburgh hospital bed, convinced that my horribly broken leg would prove the end of my career. Yet here I was in the thick of what was becoming the greatest time to be an Irish rugby player.

Eddie was down amongst us as we rounded the south terrace, arm in arm with his captain, just in case anyone had any doubt about whose team it was.

10. Mr Positivity

Friday, 9 September 2011
New Plymouth, New Zealand
The Irish fullback's hamstring made a familiar popping sound this morning. My hamstring.

I've been selected for the opening game of the World Cup against the USA and, two days out, this happens.

At least it didn't explode, but I know from the pain that I am in trouble. We were doing some four-on-three attack drills at New Plymouth Boys High School and I was sprinting flat out when it tightened. You could almost hear the alarm bells sounding in the coaches' heads as one of their older models spluttered to a halt.

And I felt every one of my thirty-three years as Irish physio Cameron Steele rubbed my biceps femoris.

'Yep, right there,' I winced.

'I think you'll be all right, Geordie,' he said, meaning no obvious tear, as a lean-looking Rob Kearney eased into the backfield while I tenderly crept outside the white line.

I'm staying positive. It's not sore to stand, which is a good sign. It aches now because I got massaged after lunch by our masseur Willie Bennett, and he put acupuncture needles in the troublesome area tonight. I got an injection as well, so I can run tomorrow. I'll stretch it out to see if it's a bad strain or not.

No matter what, I'm playing Sunday. This is my one and only chance to stake a claim for inclusion in the Australia game.

Up to then it had been a great bloody week. I felt sharp for the first time since January. Deccie named the team Tuesday. I was confident of being selected, having run from fullback over the weekend, but you're never certain. He does make occasional tweaks.

Rob is probably going to return against the Wallabies anyway, and it also looks like Andrew Trimble's form will get him on to the bench for that match.

All I crave is an opportunity. Yeah, my hamstring is just fine. I'm going to play. I need to play. Mr Positivity is now in charge of my body and my brain.

Drico is back for his first game since the Magners League final against Munster in May. It has been glossed over, but he's been the biggest worry of all with a trapped nerve in his shoulder/neck area that has plagued him for several months. Shane Jennings is also getting a chance at openside, as Seanie O'Brien's still recovering from a knee problem. Conor Murray is a form selection at scrumhalf. This is very close to being the strongest Irish team and, pending tomorrow's session, I'm in it.

Other matters have been shelved. Again.

My generic shapes and drills are not going to be introduced. I have pushed it as far as I can with the coaches. We have introduced a couple of variations on moves, but I'd like to see more. The time to do this was a week – or a month – ago, but Deccie has his masterplan and it is to retain a simplistic approach. From speaking to the Munster boys who've been with him through most of his professional coaching career, he likes keeping the playbook concise. I feel like a jackass, constantly trying to suggest new stuff as each specialist coach seems restricted in what he can do.

This is a flaw in the system.

At Leicester there is an open forum. Matty O'Connor will tell us how it is going to be done, but those with a constructive opinion can help shape the process.

I thought Mervyn Murphy would be the best guy to approach. Merv's got a good rugby brain, he played centre for Connacht for several years, very intense, but I get on well with him, and his video analysis is always on the money. He sees stuff others miss and has no problems disagreeing with my theories on attacking strategies.

During the Grand Slam season in 2009 Merv was the brains behind several moves. The try against Wales, when Tommy Bowe gathered Rog's cross-field kick and burst through Shane Williams and Gavin Henson, was his idea. He knew that Rog had it in his kicking arsenal and that Tommy's height would be a huge advantage over Williams.

So, I went to Merv. No joy. He is confined to his specific task – video analyst.

At least I can work with Keith Earls and Tommy on a few back-three patterns, structuring where we want to go when the ball is kicked to us. There are options, but the way Ireland plays it's tougher to rove freely around the park. If we get quick ball we'll be fine but the forecast is for rain, and the Americans – with Eddie as coach – will attempt to spoil every breakdown.

After training I've been taking skills sessions. Drico and Paddy Wallace along with four or five other guys do pad drills that myself and Daryl Gibson used to work on a few years back at Leicester. Daryl was the next in the impressive line of imported second-five-eighths at the Tigers who ensured our backline continued its progressive southern hemisphere approach, whenever the forwards let us have the ball. The former All Black seamlessly filled the role of Paddy Howard and Rod Kafer before him. Such was his impact that he was made club vice-captain before returning to coach the Canterbury Crusaders.

Paddy Wallace has been taking the piss, calling me 'Coach Murphy', but, as a natural number twelve himself, he seemed to enjoy the different techniques used to put a man into a hole. Kissy even started holding a pad, putting a defensive slant on it.

Saturday, 10 September
Captain's Run at Yarrow Stadium, New Plymouth
The game plan for the USA? Play what's in front of you, I suppose. We saw from Merv's clips that there's space in the wide channels. We'll look to expose that. We don't want to run into them all day. We don't want to get into an arm-wrestle. We want to move them around.

We've looked at their key players. Todd Clever, the openside, has proven himself in South African and New Zealand provincial sides, while everyone knows the Biarritz winger, Takudzwa Ngwenya, is rapid. Just check him out on YouTube smoking Bryan Habana and Shane Williams.

Eddie will have them prepared for how he thinks Ireland will set up. Additional pressure has been created by the four warm-up defeats, our confidence levels are low as a result of those defeats, and we face America on the tenth anniversary of 9/11. The opening half-hour will be tough.

Tuesday, 13 September
Waipuna Hotel outside Auckland

The 22–10 victory over the USA was a disaster. I took some anti-inflammatories and paracetamols the morning of the game, stressing about the hamstring. Adrenalin got me through the warm-up, but first time I got the ball it tightened as I tried to accelerate. Not that there were many opportunities to sprint in the conditions, unless you were Paul Emerick picking off Darce's pass at the death and wheeling away for the American try that meant we didn't have time to secure a fourth-try bonus point.

Eddie must have done a rain dance. We were welcomed at the ground by puddles on the halfway line, and it bucketed down for much of the game.

We won the toss and decided to face a strong, gusty gale so I had plenty of early meteors fired down my throat. With a dominant set-piece, we had most of the possession and should have crossed for a few more tries, but our decision-making was poor. We took way too much out of the ball.

The Eagles smashed everything in green. They piled into the breakdown. We knew they would be like this, what with Eddie and the day that was in it, but we just couldn't find any rhythm.

They wanted to drag everything down into the mud. And they were right to. There was a load of shit work to be done. In the second half their centre, Andrew Suniula, had me in a throat hold. 'What the fuck are you doing, you prick.' I shoved him away. Yeah, it became a scrappy dog-fight. Still. We should have won by at least 30 points.

I didn't feel right, so around the hour mark I came clean, telling Cameron about my concerns if I had to go flat out.

'But don't tell them,' I pleaded, knowing they would immediately pull me off. Damaged goods.

Cameron was apologetic. 'I have to tell them, Geordie. I don't want you to do further damage.' I lasted sixty-seven minutes.

Eddie came up afterwards and congratulated me, but I didn't actually speak to him because I thought there would be a post-match reception. In fact we went straight back to the hotel, but I've been on too many tours down here where the team plays badly and I've sulked in my room, so I went out for a beer with Rory Best, Jenno and Paddy. We got bicycles from the hotel and rode the kilometre into town. A couple of fans were shocked to see us cycling through New Plymouth a few hours after the match. We found a bar, went in and talked about the game for about ten minutes before putting it out of our minds.

On Monday we flew up to Auckland, where I went for a scan on the hamstring. I have a grade-one strain: seven to ten days' recovery. Phil Morrow, our fitness coach, said I was lucky not to have torn it. It means I'll definitely not be involved in the Australia match.

We are staying at the Waipuna Hotel, which is comfortable but isolated. Deccie said on the way down that he turned down hotels in Auckland as the boys would have been on the top floor with a casino below us, then down another floor to the team room. He just felt there would be too many distractions, but distractions are what some guys crave. These decisions are always tricky. This place is quiet, but it is definitely better than the Bordeaux situation in 2007. A bit of isolation is no harm as we'll be on the move again in a few days. I'm fine either way, because I have a couple of friends to catch up with in Auckland.

The English seem to have got it wrong with their Dunedin base. They have moved to Queenstown this week, so I think they will enjoy themselves. I've kept in touch with Crofty and Lewis. I told them not to worry, wait until you get to the adventure capital of the southern hemisphere. They can do all the things we got up to – choppers, bungee jumping, rafting. They are doing it the opposite way around to us, but I don't see what could possibly go wrong for them in Queenstown . . .

★

Deccie came to see me today before naming the team. He had on that same look I saw in Carton House a few weeks ago.

'Geordie, you know you are not going to train tomorrow . . .'

I made it easy for him.

'I'm not expecting to play against Australia, Deccie. I wouldn't pick myself, if I'm honest. I am nearly there but I'm not fit to play a Test match. Thanks for coming to speak to me.'

He's put Eoin Reddan at scrumhalf, with Conor Murray on the bench ahead of Isaac Boss. Seanie is in for Jenno, with Leams covering backrow. Cian Healy returns as well. It's a strong side.

Rog came up to me after the meeting to commiserate, and I told him about the hammy. He was close to dislodging Jonny Sexton from the team. Jonny missed a few kicks against the USA, but I know from his demeanour that he is OK. Just one of those things, he said when I asked him. He was happy that the coaches showed faith in him.

The Russia match comes six days after Australia, and the physios told me to take a week off to get myself right. Be selfish. There are certain things I can do, like running at 70 or 80 per cent, below the pain threshold, to keep ticking away. I called to Bobby Sourbutts, the Leicester physio, and he said the same.

I should be right for the Russia match, but it is always about the coaches' perception and to them I am a lame old stallion.

Myself and Jenno are both outside the 22 now. As leaders in our club environments and senior players here, we both feel we had another role to play.

Watching the boys train this morning, we both saw it, there appears to be a serious problem: they all looked tight and were cranky with one another.

There is an honesty policy in the Ireland set-up. It has been an important part of the team culture for several years. Stab you in the belly instead of the back. If someone makes a mistake, tell him to his face. There were lots of mistakes today and people were telling each other about them. The honesty policy has become a means for people to vent their frustrations.

At 6 p.m. we had a review of the USA game. Lads were tetchy watching it back. There is a hangover here that must be addressed; everyone is disappointed with the recent results and performance levels, especially last Sunday's showing. We seem stressed, under immense pressure. Everyone wanted to explode out of the blocks, but it hasn't happened. Our energy needs to be channelled better before it is too late.

After the meeting the coaches left, but the players stayed seated. Myself and Jenno stood up and addressed the group. This was our contribution to the Australia game. Not being involved directly gave us perspective. Jenno spoke very well about the non-starting fifteen pulling their weight in training to ensure no negative vibes seep into the group.

I had spoken to a couple of the England lads about the Wallabies. Playing Australia is to them what playing England is to us. They never have any problem reaching those high-voltage levels because they can tap into this huge hatred for Australia. The English boys think it is strange that we don't beat the Aussies more often, considering what we've done to England over the past eight years or so.

I said as much to the group.

My other point was that we are too hard on each other when things go wrong. From what I've read about sports psychology, when you get overly stressed you under-perform. I don't want to belittle the opposition, but I want to alleviate pressure so the guys produce their best performance.

I was speaking as someone who has spent much of his rugby life outside Ireland. I said it is a typically Irish trait to be down on ourselves. But why should we do that? We should look to what's coming. We have nothing to be down about. We don't compliment ourselves enough. I said that we have some of the best players in the world in this room, and that we have to be confident, bring the mentality that we bring to games against England in Dublin.

I felt it was now or never for us to make a statement in this part of the world, something this team has yet to do. Raise our game like we know we can. We have been on the verge of winning in the southern hemisphere against Australia on plenty of occasions. Maybe it was down to belief that it hasn't happened. And belief shouldn't be a problem with the men in that room.

I left it at that.

The lack of new attacking ploys is frustrating. I know some players want something bigger and better to catch out the Wallabies, something creative, but it is not going to happen now. Instead, we have returned to older stuff from the playbook, tweaking moves that are simplistic enough. There will be two or three players catapulted into channels where Australia have numbers with the intention of breaking through. Basically, a repeat of how we went about gutting England last March. Just tear into them. Old-fashioned Irish blood-and-guts stuff with good set-piece play.

Tomorrow is our last session. I just hope the lads can relax. Donncha will keep everyone entertained on the team bus as only he can, relieving some of that unbearable tension. Everyone knows this is the moment. If we lose at Eden Park the Italian game will bring stifling pressure just to qualify second in the pool. This is the biggest challenge for us since the Grand Slam match in Cardiff two years ago.

God, I'd do anything to be playing, but the World Cup is not about me any more.

11. Wasp Stings

In my middle years at Leicester, London Wasps arrived as the major force in English rugby. Not only did they climb up alongside us, they overwhelmed us in the really important meetings – finals, basically – dominating in much the same way as we had before them. The pain of each new defeat to them was always worse than the one before.

The best thing I can say about this time is that we refused to accept it as our permanent reality.

Many things changed at Leicester. Five head coaches in five years (six, including Richard Cockerill's temporary stints) sounds like a club in turmoil. But we were nothing of the sort. We didn't win as many titles as before, but whoever became champions – and it was usually Wasps – had to pummel us into submission before climbing the winner's podium. Yet, while all these changes took place around me, and new faces came and went with their new ideas (some brilliant, others ridiculous), the culture within the club never faltered. Because of this we were able to remain a respected force in both the Premiership and Europe.

It's good to have a nemesis in professional sport. Wasps against Tigers really became London against Leicester. Or to simplify it further: Lawrence Dallaglio against Martin Johnson.

A huge factor in England being a global force up to 2003 was the combination of Dallaglio and Johnno in the same team. You could see them practically scrapping each other to make that massive tackle on the gainline in England's Grand Slam game at Lansdowne Road or during their epic victory in New Zealand and throughout the 2003 World Cup. What usually happened was that they both got there at the same time, crushing the poor unfortunate ball carrier. Teammates would follow either man into an unbreakable ruck or fight alongside him to the bitter end of an unwinnable match. There is a great picture from the 2005 Premiership final when both men, blatantly offside and off their feet, are glaring up at referee Chris White in search of a favourable decision.

That said, they are very different men. Johnno is a quiet, humble guy with simple values: get your work done, don't say a whole lot and never take a backward step in combat. Dallaglio was perceived, in Leicester anyway, as someone always pushing himself on television and the press, talking about other players or about himself in the third person. But he never took a backward step on the field.

A major advantage for Wasps was Dallaglio remaining on the scene for a full three seasons after Johnno retired. It was a great time to be a Wasp, under the guidance of Warren Gatland and Shaun Edwards. In contrast, there were a string of upheavals in our coaching set-up, starting in February 2004 when Dean Richards and Leicester parted ways after a twenty-two-year relationship.

Everybody knows it wasn't an amicable split. Poor results had been streaming in since the previous season, and the returning World Cup winners were simply too late bedding back in to save Deano. Out of Europe and struggling in the league, the board culled several back-room people, offering him a role 'upstairs' in the realigned club structure. He interpreted that as nothing at all and walked. It was a sore point at the time. Deano's Bar at Welford Road was stripped and emptied.

The promotion of John Wells to head coach mid-season was fairly seamless, as he was already on the training pitch with us every day. The Six Nations brought further disruption, but when the old heads really needed to produce something special we hammered Wasps down in Adams Park 48–17. (They were poised to retain the league title, confirming a new era of dominance, but whenever either of us was even one per cent off top form, a heavy beating followed.) Further victories over Harlequins and Sale in a wildcard final secured European qualification.

Wasps dusted themselves down to announce their arrival as a northern hemisphere superpower by winning both the Premiership final and the European Cup, beating Munster in a thrilling semi-final at Lansdowne Road and then Toulouse in the final.

We had won four league titles on the trot, so they made it their stated intention to equal and surpass the milestone. They were typically brash Londoners and that bothered us. The tension between the clubs led to some of our games blowing up, like the November 2004 draw down in Adams Park, when there was a massive punch-up with Corry and Harry Ellis scrapping with Dallaglio.

In the 2004/5 season Wasps came in search of a third successive league title. This was Tigers territory and everybody knew it. Our plan was to send Johnno and Backy into retirement from the club game in the same manner as their international careers finished. Victoriously.

It didn't go to the planned script, but there were some amazing dying kicks from Johnno's Tigers. We were drawn in the same European pool as Wasps, so we were able to deny them the opportunity to retain their title as we had, beating them 37–31 and 35–27 in rounds three and four.

Around this time Stephen Jones was strongly considering signing for the Tigers. Our chief executive, Peter Wheeler, somehow believed it would be a good idea to let myself and Lewis Moody show him around. So, with the club credit card in our possession, we gave the Welsh outhalf our version of the Leicester guided tour. We duly poured as many sambucas down his throat as we could purchase before dumping him at the entrance to his hotel and disappearing before the sun came up. The Wednesday Club rides again!

Many years later Stephen wrote in our testimonial brochure that he woke up the next day on the floor of his hotel room, not knowing where he was or why he was there. His pounding head wasn't helped by the incessant ringing of a telephone. Then he remembered. He got up, dressed and limped in to the club, where Wellsy sat him for two hours in front of a screen of the Tigers in action. I'm sure our two faces popped up a few times. We may, on reflection, have been responsible for his decision to join Clermont instead.

It seemed like a season didn't pass without a defining showdown against an Irish province. In 2003/4 we were chastised by Ulster at Ravenhill 33–0, before gaining immediate revenge at home 49–7, and in 2005 the reward for dethroning Wasps was a Heineken Cup quarter-final against Leinster, coached by Deccie for that one year, at Lansdowne Road.

When I first played for Leicester against an Irish team I was just happy to be involved, oblivious to perceptions of me back at home; but after beating Munster in a European final and winning a few caps, my profile increased significantly. When I was home or out in Dublin with friends, people would recognize me. Some would feel it was their (usually drunken) obligation to hand over some abuse. So when I came back to face my native province, the need to perform, and be rated in my own land, became a major motivation. There had been a long build-up to this particular game, and I'd just spent the past two months in the Ireland camp with the likes of Drico, Shaggy and Reggie Corrigan.

The eventual result had very little to do with me – it was all about Johnno and Backy raging against the dying of the light, one last time, in Europe. I was getting worried until we upped our intensity in the second half and Daryl Gibson ran in a try after some brilliant play by Lewis. I was nearby, gently encouraging Daryl to chip on so I could grab the glory at Lansdowne Road, but the 29–13 result meant more to me than scoring a try.

We got smoked by a sensational Toulouse side in the semi-final at the Walkers Stadium in Leicester, our new home for big European matches. That result increased the importance of sending our two greatest warriors into the sunset with another Premiership medal.

Playing Wasps around this time usually became a case of who was quickest on the draw. Some days it was us, other times it was them. First off the mark usually won, as you had to take risks to claw the deficit back, and the defences were so good. When we had to chase the game, their blitz would punish us severely. With us, a turnover usually meant a massive Pacific Islander being catapulted into a one-on-one scenario. That usually guaranteed five points.

Despite the strong defences, the games were always high scoring, at least for the winners. Henry Tuilagi, a monstrous ball-carrying backrower, was invincible in Backy and Johnno's last ever game at Welford Road when we hammered Wasps 45–10. We scored early and repeatedly, but after Henry bumped Dallaglio and Worsley he got tangled in Tom Voyce's legs, breaking his tibia and fibula. My injury. Even the giant Samoan struggled with the pain. It meant Wasps were waiting for us in the Premiership final at Twickenham two weeks later while our wrecking ball was gathering dust in the stand.

Having done them three times that season, we were favourites, but they reversed the result when it mattered the most. It also marked the end of John Wells's time at the club as he took up a position with the RFU Academy.

That's how the great lock and flanker went out at the end of the 2004/5 campaign: merciless beatings to end our interest in major competitions. We felt terrible to have let them down, but neither of them is a fairytale type of guy. In sport most people lose more than they win. That's just the way it is. Those two won a helluva lot more than they lost.

At that summer's pre-season training I was delighted with the duo signed as their replacements, and not just because they were Irish.

Having played either with or against Leo Cullen since we were teenagers, I was able to tell the club about his natural leadership attributes.

Shane Jennings was hand-picked by Neil Back. Jenno made such a sustained impact that he practically turned Lewis into a six. His natural game suited the creative style we were developing under Paddy Howard, and he was on fire during those two seasons at the club; the locals were confounded by Ireland's continued failure to recognize as much. He wasn't capped until June 2007 against Argentina.

Paddy returned to replace John Wells. We knew we were getting an innovative, attacking coach, but none of us imagined how impressive a head coach he would become. Training became more enjoyable as we started to notice how certain drills impacted on our match-day performances.

I don't think it was a conscious plan, but the Irish contingent at the club grew significantly during this period. We needed fresh blood in certain positions – scrumhalf, outhalf and hooker – and the Tigers'

1. The 1996 Leinster Senior Schools Cup semi-final against Clongowes at Lansdowne Road was when I announced my existence to the Irish rugby world. We won that day, and I scored a try and made the touchline conversion, but we lost to an awesome Blackrock College team in the final (*Irish Times*)

2. (*left*) In the back garden in Naas, wearing my Ireland strip for the Under-19 World Cup in 1997

3. (*above*) With my brother Ross and my brother Nick's wife Leyman in Boston in 2000: the tour when I won my first senior Ireland cap

4. (*right*) With my family in 2003: my sister Maeve, my father and my mother in the front row; my brother Nick, myself and brother Etienne in the middle row, brothers Ross and Brian at the back

5. (*below*) I fly past my grounded Leicester team-mate Ben Kay and Mike Tindall as we make an electric start against England in the 2003 Grand Slam decider at Lansdowne Road. But they were a brutally efficient machine, and beat us 42–6 (*Matt Browne / Sportsfile*)

6. (*above*) September 2003: I'm in agony with a shattered leg as Dr Gary O'Driscoll and the medics gently roll me on to the stretcher at Murrayfield. My World Cup is over before it starts (*Brendan Moran / Sportsfile*)

7. (*below*) Six months later, having made a full recovery, I outsprinted Simon Danielli for a try in the match that clinched Ireland's first Triple Crown in nineteen years. Drico, behind me, was in his long blond mane phase (*Brendan Moran / Sportsfile*)

8. (*above*) October 2004: Myself and Johnno, playing his last campaign, commiserate with our former teammate Will Greenwood after a 15–9 victory at The Stoop (*Getty Images*)

9. (*right*) Making a point to Eddie O'Sullivan in March 2005. The two of us never really saw eye to eye (*Getty Images*)

10. I got this kick away before Rodney So'oialo hit me in the third 2005 Lions test at Eden Park, but the All Blacks were too good for us, winning the match 38–19 and the series 3–0 (*Brendan Moran / Sportsfile*)

11. Girvan Dempsey, my friendly rival for the Ireland number 15 shirt, 'interviews' me during kicking practice at the Stade de France before the 2006 Six Nations opener (*Brendan Moran / Sportsfile*)

12. In the first rugby match ever played at Croke Park, against France in 2007, I broke away for what would have been an end-to-end try – but Steve Walsh ruined my shot at redemption by blowing up for a French knock-on (*Ray McManus / Sportsfile*)

13. Shaggy went ballistic after I dived over for our second try against the Pumas at Parc des Princes in the 2007 World Cup. That made it 15–21 on forty-seven minutes, but the boots of Contepomi and Hernández concluded the slowest, most painful of World Cup deaths (*Getty Images*)

14. The irony was not lost on me. Having been discarded, yet again, I returned to the Ireland camp at the eleventh hour for an injured Girvan Dempsey and won man of the match in the 34–13 defeat of Scotland in February 2008 (*Matt Browne / Sportsfile*)

15. I wore sunglasses and a brave face for the press conference before the 2009 Heineken Cup final against Leinster; but my eye was badly injured and I struggled to see properly during the match, which we narrowly lost (*Brendan Moran / Sportsfile*)

16. I filled in for the injured Martin Corry as Tigers captain for the 2009 Premiership final at Twickenham; after we beat London Irish, Coz handed me the trophy (*Getty Images*)

17. (*left*) September 2009: Jay Pancholi and Harj Sing do running repairs after I split open my head and dislocated my shoulder trying to score against Bath at The Rec. No try (*Getty Images*)

18. (*below*) Leading the Tigers out, with my nephew Josh as mascot beside me, before the 2010 Premiership final; we beat Saracens to take our third title in four years

19. February 2012: Saracens players desperately attempt to put me off nailing the winning score at Vicarage Road. It was the worst drop goal ever …

20. … but they all count. One of our boys busted my nose open in the full-time celebrations that immediately followed. The 20–19 victory ignited our season (*Both photos Getty Images*)

scouting system noticed the bottleneck in Ireland created by just three provincial teams competing in the Heineken Cup. A raft of aspiring pros were being starved of minutes. We signed Frank Murphy, Gavin Hickie, Johne Murphy and Ian Humphreys around this time, and Paul Burke also signed as outhalf cover in 2007. Burkey remains at the club today as an assistant coach. I have a neat little routine before most matches, just after the warm-up, when he fires a few garryowens my way.

I had a direct hand in Johne's arrival to Leicester after his older brother, Billy, who had been in Newbridge with me, made contact. I knew he was good enough, despite missing out on the Leinster Academy after sustaining a bad knee injury. The Murphys, no relation, are from Rathangan, which is about fifteen miles from Naas. Johne was playing for Lansdowne RFC but the opportunity arose for our scout (and club legend) Dusty Hare to run the rule over him when my brother Ross was involved in hosting the Leicester Academy game against a Leinster selection at Naas RFC. Johne played well enough to be brought over on trial. He was signed up after a few months, and lived with me in town for the first year or so.

I enjoyed having a sizeable Irish contingent at the club, but the coaches weren't best pleased one Monday morning when I arrived at Oval Park unable to see out of my left eye. Considering we hadn't played a game that weekend I had some explaining to do. It happened on an 'Irish' night out, must have been around Paddy's Day, which was basically a pub crawl through Leicester, ending up at a place I knew well.

By the early hours it was just myself, Gav and Jenno holding the line. One of us stepped in when a guy pushed a girl but, on mature reflection, we misjudged the situation, failing to notice how badly outnumbered we were. True to form, I barely contributed to the ensuing brawl as I was instantly blindsided by a dig, hence the eye injury, and went down like a sack of spuds, leaving Jenno and Gav to fend for themselves. I knew the bar owners, so I was sheepish when I returned a few days later. To my relief, they said it was simply a case of bad timing. A group of lads from abroad had come in, looking for trouble, and their golden opportunity arrived with our act of drunken chivalry. Luckily I only missed a few days' training, but this was the start of my scratched retina problems.

Paddy rotated the squad cleverly. He told players on the fringes when they would get their opportunity. Simple, clear man-management. Inevitably in team sports some guys will always feel hard done by, like Leon Lloyd. Paddy had a lot to do with Leon being capped for England, having spent three years putting him into gaps that didn't initially seem to exist. But when Leon tried talking to the head coach as a mate, he quickly found himself training with the seconds. He eventually moved to Gloucester, but had to retire in 2007 after wrecking his knee. Leon then became Foundation Director at Oakham School, a big, private, rugby nursery in Leicestershire, not unlike Blackrock or Clongowes, that has produced Lewis, Tom Croft and Matt Smith. Leon is actually from Coventry, which means he's as tough as old boots – other examples being Adam Balding, Neil Back, Danny Grewcock and Jim Hamilton. We probably should have made Leon an honorary Irishman for our pub crawl.

Despite the Irish influx and Paddy's exciting new methods, it was another season that ended in disappointment.

Sale Sharks (with Charlie Hodgson, Sebastien Chabal, Jason White and Jason Robinson in their ranks) beat Wasps in the Premiership semi-final as we overcame London Irish. Off to Twickenham we went for our second successive final, only to be well beaten again, 45–20. You tend to remember only your mistakes in defeat. Mine came early on as Hodgson's cross-field kick slipped through my hands on a horribly wet day. I was so close to the touchline that I presumed it would bobble into touch, but it bounced back into play, hit my foot and dribbled into the in-goal area, allowing Mark Cueto to crawl after it for the try.

In Europe we qualified from a pool that included the Ospreys, Clermont and Stade, only to lose our quarter-final, to Bath again, across town at the Walkers. They beat us 15–12 despite having two men sin-binned. We didn't turn up, and we knew it was an opportunity missed to take on Biarritz in a semi-final down in San Sebastian, the heart of the Basque country. Munster – thanks to some moments of inspiration by Peter Stringer and Rog – saw off Biarritz to win that elusive Heineken Cup.

The 2006/7 season finally saw us reclaim our place at the pinnacle of the English game. Only problem was that Wasps came back at us stronger than ever. An incessant run of epic encounters began with Munster's visit to Welford Road in October. I missed this one because I scratched my retina again when Seru Rabeni, our monstrous Fijian winger, threw an innocuous reverse pass in a game of touch which I wasn't expecting. Splat. When the laughter died down, the lads realized I wasn't in good shape.

The English media's build-up to the Munster game was all about Ronan O'Gara. In an interview with Donald McRae of the *Guardian*, Rog stated that Irish teams don't expect to lose when travelling to England or France any more because they had a back catalogue of results that instilled confidence. He also suggested that Sky Sports hyped up average English players. His comments sparked a lively debate and were used as a stick to beat him.

The stick would have been all the bigger if he hadn't followed up his words with a performance. We were leading 19–18 towards the end when Nigel Owens awarded Munster a penalty sixty-two metres out. Jenno rolled the ball away so Owens – harshly, in my one-eyed view from the dugout – walked it ten as punishment, a decision that just about brought the place-kick inside Rog's radar.

He lined up the kick, faced with a scenario he knows so well: hero or villain, depending on how it went. Nail the penalty, end our twenty-one-month unbeaten streak in all competitions at home, and silence the critics; or miss and have egg on his face for saying what he had said.

On a damp, windy day, horrid for place-kicking, Rog nailed the kick before going on Sky Sports and apologizing if anyone took offence at what he had said. 'I'm probably a big name in Ireland but I didn't think the reaction would be as big as it was [in England]. I suppose lesson learnt. Keep the head down . . . I have huge respect for Leicester. Munster have tried to model Leicester for the last six, seven years.' His stock immediately soared among English rugby people. It is easy to take Rog the wrong way if you don't know him. The man gives it straight when he talks, and sometimes that upsets people. I got to know him from an early stage in our careers and we remain friends today. Like I've said, not your usual rugby man, but a special rugby man all the same.

After that defeat a stream of Irish people rang and texted to commiserate. It was assumed, after just one pool round, that our European campaign was over. We beat Cardiff and Bourgoin twice, but the same stuff kept coming my way: 'You won't win in Thomond Park, Geordan. Nobody wins there but Munster.'

Three months of this, non-stop; I relayed each and every comment to my teammates. I loved seeing men like Corry and Lewis bristle in silence. *Yeah, this is working.*

Until then, I hadn't fully appreciated the magnitude of Munster's unblemished twenty-six-game European home record which spanned twelve years, but our logic was simple: we have Welford Road, they have Thomond Park. They came to our sacred patch of grass and beat us, so our response must be to return the favour. We at Leicester understand the surge of energy that comes from fanatical home support. We also know that on very rare occasions that energy can be harnessed against the host.

Everything that had gone before in the history between us and Munster counted for nothing. I knew we were one of the few clubs in Europe equipped to win in Limerick. We would attack Munster's weaknesses but, more importantly, we'd target their strengths as well. That meant Leo had his head buried in a laptop, making special plans for the lineout.

They had already secured safe passage to the quarter-finals by winning in Bourgoin, but defeat for us meant elimination from the tournament. So we needed it more than they did.

The other motivational tool we twisted to our advantage was the fact that this would be the last ever game at the old Thomond Park before the bulldozers rolled in. The last chance to beat Munster in their ancient cathedral had our boys giddy with excitement.

There was more. On the week of the game a Munster official

contacted a Leicester official with a request that we get off the field as quick as possible afterwards as there was going to be a fireworks display to say farewell to the old stand. Of course, it was relayed to the players as: 'We have been instructed to leave the pitch immediately after so Munster could celebrate another famous victory with a fireworks display.'

Putting it like that to men like Martin Castrogiovanni, Julian White, Shane Jennings and Alex Tuilagi was the same as turning each Munster forward into a burglar they stumbled across in their living room in the middle of the night. I spent that week stoking already rampant internal flames with well-timed yet seemingly throwaway remarks. You glance at the boys and see it registering.

Yeah, this is definitely working.

Paddy Howard said in the media that Thomond Park was 'just a field', but we were more of the mindset that people said it couldn't be done, and we had to prove them wrong. In Leicester it is always said that you must earn everything you get. I know the Munster mindset is similar.

We liked the fact we were playing the ultimate villain's role in this story. Even the Irish subplots were building nicely. Andy Goode was injured, so Ian Humphreys was given a start at outhalf. The best compliment I can give Ian is that he plays in an uncannily similar attacking fashion to elder brother David. Seru and Alex were tasked with providing defensive cover in the ten channel so when the Munster loose forwards came looking to run at Humphs, one of the Island boys would be waiting.

A sign up on our dressing-room wall that season read: 'Dominate mentally, physically and verbally.' It was one of those rare games where I knew from the warm-up onwards that all three would be the case. Leo and Jenno spoke passionately about how important this was to them. I talked about the need to silence the crowd. I always said something when we were facing an Irish province. I think it helped when the boys heard how much I wanted to beat my fellow countrymen.

After twenty minutes or so I finished off a very good try; Lewis attacked the short side, got his hands free and I took the offload.

There is a picture of me racing over the line in my folks' house in Naas.

We still needed to use that famed Thomond Park energy against itself. Munster had a kickable penalty that would've made it 9–8, but they went for the jugular. Scrum down. The crowd went berserk. Julian White's twisting technique silenced them. The momentum shifted so violently that Ollie Smith crossed for a try up the other end soon after to make it 6–13. It stayed that way.

Humphs had a Rolls-Royce of a night in difficult conditions, smoothly kicking us into their 22 at crucial moments. Everything clicked, from Shane's spoiling on the ground to Leo's brilliance in the air, while Martin Corry and Lewis behaved like the senior English duo who had preceded them in the Tigers pack.

We went out to make Munster prove they were better than us. Like they had been on their two previous visits to Welford Road. I suppose we needed to win to prove it was a great rivalry.

I've played against friends on many occasions for both Leicester and Ireland. You don't get any enjoyment from the look on their faces if you win, but you do have a greater desire to beat them all the same.

That night the Tigers squad celebrated a historic victory at a pub in Limerick city owned by Tom Tierney's father-in-law. Tom is a former Ireland, Munster and Tigers scrumhalf. All my family were down as well, so it went on into the small hours. One of those great gatherings when, for just a few hours, we forgot about the gruelling season that still lay ahead.

After the 2007 Six Nations, our run-in was insane as we were at war on three separate fronts, including the EDF Anglo/Welsh Cup. Talk of the treble kept building as seven of our last eight matches became do-or-die scenarios.

If everything went to plan we would be collecting all three trophies at Twickenham – an achievement to rank alongside retaining the Heineken Cup in 2001.

The reward for our win at Thomond Park was another home quarter-final against Stade Français. (Munster, meanwhile, had to go to Llanelli, where they lost, so we avoided the Ali–Frazier scenario in the semi-final.) We beat Stade 21–20, thanks to a late try from Tom Varndell and an even later block-down by Lewis as the brilliant Argentinian, Juan Martín Hernández, tried to kill us with a drop goal.

Next up was the Ospreys in the EDF final. Paddy's rotational policy meant fringe players got game time in this competition, so I was on the bench as we bagged the first of a planned three-trophy sweep.

I have been sin-binned three times in my career; twice in European semi-finals and once against Munster in a pre-season game (when Leamy pleaded my case with the local ref!). The European yellows both came from the pocket of Irish referee Alain Rolland; and Rolland was the referee for the Llanelli match.

Early on I made a tackle about ten metres outside our 22. Noticing that no one was at fullback, scrumhalf Dwayne Peel went to snipe from the base so I jumped through the ruck and hauled him down. Whistle blows.

'Rawlers, what the fuck . . .'

The card was in the air so I had to stop talking and walk. Thankfully Jenno ran in a cracking try from thirty metres and we went on to win 33–17, finally ending the Walkers hoodoo.

Wasps overcame Northampton to join us in an all-England European final.

Defeat to Bristol in a regular season game was followed by handing Wasps a 40–26 licking at Welford Road. It proved an ideal tune-up for Bristol in the Premiership semi-final a week later. We duly progressed to our third league final in succession, where we smashed Gloucester. Alex and Seru came off their wings to attack Gloucester's weak point at every opportunity, with Alex galloping over for two of our seven tries. Martin Corry made a typically selfless gesture by having Jenno and Leo lift the trophy. We knew they were going home and understood the reasons why: they wanted to bring their new-found knowledge and a winning habit back to Leinster. It is always difficult to replace iconic figures like Martin Johnson and Neil Back, but Leo and Shane let nobody down when filling the number four and seven jerseys.

More change was coming, with Paddy Howard also returning home, to Australia, after the Heineken Cup final.

We found ourselves on the cusp of monumental success. But while we were playing non-stop every week on live television, Wasps had been watching studiously from the shadows.

Sky Sports couldn't be accused of over-hyping this one. It was a massive occasion, understandably billed as the definitive meeting between the two dominant clubs in England on the European stage.

Wasps certainly did their homework. They exposed an obvious weakness of ours in ruthless fashion. Frank Murphy was our only remaining fit scrumhalf. Wasps knew this and right from the first ruck Joe Worsley clattered into him with a shoulder charge. It should have been a penalty and yellow card, but Alan Lewis, the referee, missed it. Frank was clearly dazed until half-time, and by then most of the damage had already been done. I'm not criticizing Joe; you do whatever it takes to win cup finals. We had a weakness in our armour, so Wasps went directly for it.

Their two tries were concocted in the video room. Watching our games leading up to the final, they saw Julian White was positioned at hooker on defensive lineouts and exposed his lack of mobility. For the first try, Raphäel Ibañez threw a quick lineout to Eoin Reddan at the front and he dashed over untouched. For the second, Ibañez played a one–two with Simon Shaw, again exposing a defensive flaw at the front of the lineout; our blind winger, Alex, was covering the ten channel, so the French hooker was able to brush off Frank to touch down.

Once Wasps were ahead, their defensive system and physicality guided them home. It finished 25–9.

That was the most difficult of all the defeats to swallow in this period, because we knew we were good enough to win that treble. But as much as it grates to say it, Wasps were the better side. They had a great set-up with other seriously good players like Josh Lewsey, Phil Vickery and Mark van Gisbergen, as well as Ibañez, Shaw, Worsley and others. Some days we thrashed them, others times they flogged us. Unfortunately, a pattern developed in which they had our number on the biggest days of all.

Vince Lombardi said it best: Winning isn't everything. It is the only thing. We live by that at Leicester. We would have to come again.

The Leicester–Wasps rivalry followed me halfway round the world, to a South American nightclub.

Just six days after we lost the final, I came off the bench for Ireland, at outhalf, against Argentina in Santa Fe. Felipe Contepomi's dropped goal had put the Pumas into a 22–20 lead. Sure enough, it fell to me in the dying seconds to win the Test match, but my drop goal was blocked. Terrible way to end an already depressing week. At least the post-match function promised to be fairly special. We were welcomed at the entrance to the disco by drop-dead-gorgeous Latin American girls doing beer promotions. All very informal and great fun.

Eoin Reddan was demented, drinking tequila and still celebrating his success as the scrumhalf for the European champions. He started winding me up about the final.

'What happened to you last week, Geordie?!' he was roaring. I nearly smashed him there and then at the bar. David Wallace tried to step between us, so we both turned on him. It was fairly late in the evening. Redser insisted I drink my tequila shot. I declined.

'Look, if you won't drink it, I'll drink it!'

Down it went, but seconds later he went pale.

So, to recap, I'd just lost a Heineken Cup final, skewed a drop goal that could have won a Test match for Ireland, and there's Eoin Reddan puking on my shoes. We are able to laugh about it now. Ah, we probably laughed about it then.

In response to enquiries from Ireland, France and other English clubs I had occasionally considered my options, but I simply didn't believe any other club would hold me in the regard I was held in at Leicester.

Also, I was now part of a tradition that didn't just sprout out of the ground one day.

If a player is fortunate enough to play twenty games for Leicester he is awarded a green tie. On that night the senior players will take him out for a few beers. He dips the tie in the other players' beers until the tie solidifies, symbolizing your connection to the club for life.

Blue ties were introduced a few years ago for anyone who reaches the hundred-game milestone, but the green tie means more to me. I figured this out the hard way after some typically subtle prompting by the great David Matthews. David, a wing forward who joined as a teenager in 1955, became only the third life-member of the club in 2005; he had certainly earned the recognition after 502 games, 119 tries, fifteen conversions and twenty penalties. He also coached the club, and when I first met him he was a member of the board, as he still is today.

One night after a game David paused in the members' bar and, leaning on my arm, said out of the side of his mouth, 'Nice blue tie, Geordie,' as he patted his green one before ambling on. Message received. A lot of men worked damn hard to play twenty-odd games for the club. Since that night, I always wear my green tie unless it's hard as rock from a recent dipping ceremony, regardless of the fact that I am knocking on 300 games.

The great Irish and Lions winger, Tony O'Reilly, got a green tie despite being a game or two shy of twenty appearances for Leicester. The story goes that he was guest speaker at a big club function a few years back when they presented it to him, but only after the board of directors were so divided that it went to a vote, which went three to two in favour of awarding O'Reilly the tie. I have my suspicions about who voted nay.

It was the principle of it. No club thrives like the Tigers have done without their diehards. I'd like to consider myself one some day.

12. Choking, Strangled

What should have been a truly golden period for Irish rugby started in 2004, when we won the Triple Crown. Having recovered from my leg break, I was playing well again and was rewarded with the number fifteen jersey for the 2005 Six Nations.

When we got it right, we were a very good side and, besides New Zealand and France, we beat every major rugby nation in the following three years.

England came to Dublin seeking to avenge the previous season's defeat at Twickenham. The difference between the teams was a Brian O'Driscoll try that I had a small hand in. I was constantly throwing dummy passes as a teenager, but the Rugby League defensive alignments in the professional game have made this old trick practically extinct. A feint to pass can result in the man in front of you drifting just as another defender arrives in his place. There are always exceptions to rules, of course. Fast ruck ball and a rapid change of direction makes anything possible. We were trailing 13–12 in the second half when I took a pass from Strings on the short side. I saw Charlie Hodgson was stuck in two minds about whether to tackle or drift, so I sold him a dummy that would have made Waisale Serevi smile. Split-second territory now. Drico was screaming on the outside but I couldn't see him. Against England two years previously I didn't offload blind to Denis Hickie, but at least I could hear Drico this time. I let the ball go, but as I did Hodgson's fingertip deflected its flight path. Shit, I just butchered a chance I had created from nothing – but Drico brilliantly gathered at full speed and tip-toed along the sideline. We were both pretty pleased with that one.

It was only my second time playing against Lewis Moody – for one reason or another we kept missing each other over the years. He absolutely detests anyone pawing at his face on the ground. It drives him insane and he was always sufficiently riled up in a game without needing to find another level of aggression. But I couldn't resist giving him a few pokes at the bottom of a ruck. He couldn't retaliate because I had him in a headlock. He went absolutely berserk as I leaped up and sped away.

It was a pretty stupid move as Lewis was never going to just let it lie. Later, as a high ball was dropping, I knew he was charging towards me. I was already down on my hunkers so I decided to Top Gun him – hit the deck so he'd fly right over my head, not being able to hit the brakes. What I didn't consider was the possibility that Lewis would do a double knee drop into my kidneys to halt his momentum. As I writhed in pain he slumped over me with that crazed smile.

The championship ended badly with defeats at home to France and in Cardiff, as the Welsh came from nowhere, playing some thrilling rugby, to capture a Grand Slam at our expense.

Still, I had done enough to be selected for the Lions tour to New Zealand. In fairness, it wasn't the greatest-ever achievement as Clive Woodward brought about two hundred players. OK, fifty-one in total were selected or called out – far too many to create the essential unity needed for a squad made up of four nations.

Our first gathering at the Vale of Glamorgan outside Cardiff was for a bonding day. Clive had brought in some guy called Sir Humphrey Walters to tell us about sailing around the world. To be honest, his story did nothing to motivate me. Then we did a painting exercise. Ridiculously childish stuff that straight away had me thinking it was going to be a very long tour.

And so it proved, although I ended up playing more minutes than any other player, starting with the Argentina Test at the Millennium Stadium.

Not only were there too many players, but a twenty-seven-strong management team meant there wasn't enough time to get to know certain coaches. Dave Alred was an example. I was out kicking from hand during the warm-up when Dave approached me.

'Oh, you kick?'

He started giving me some pointers about my technique fifteen minutes before kick-off. I was thinking: where have you been for the past ten days, mate? Obviously off with Jonny Wilkinson, who has a great relationship with the man, as do a number of top golfers in more recent times.

'I think I will do my own thing for this game, mate.'

The Argentina fixture was a mistake in itself, as nobody wanted to get injured the day before departure on the actual tour. The Pumas had no such concerns and duly tore into us Lions. We were lucky to salvage a draw when Jonny, who had not played a Test match since the 2003 World Cup final due to injury, landed an injury-time penalty.

On arrival in New Zealand, I immediately noticed a different reception by the natives from previous tours: they seemed to consider everyone to be part of the English team that had won there two years before. The usual condescending attitude I'd experienced when touring with Ireland was replaced by a torrent of abuse. This was an All Blacks revenge mission and their adoring public weren't shy in letting us know. Same went for the local media, who lashed into us at every opportunity. It got very personal.

Most days we'd split into small groups to visit four or five different venues – schools, rugby clubs or hospitals – but the next day's headline would still read 'Lions no show at school', with a picture of little Timmy crying.

Going for a walk in our tracksuits one day, an elderly woman stopped us. Ah, a nice little old lady.

'Hello.'

'Tana and the boys are gonna smash you!'

She piled on the abuse, but it was nothing compared to some of the disgraceful comments in the stand during games. I'd know, because that's where I was for the first two Tests. Selection seemed almost preordained. I was a fixture on Ian McGeechan's Wednesday side, which turned into a successful and enjoyable yet completely separate entity from Clive Woodward's Test team.

We'd play a match on the Tuesday or Wednesday, train Thursday and maybe Friday from 6 a.m. until 9 a.m., while the Saturday team would train after us. We'd travel at different times as well. Two tours really.

The Drico spear tackle? It looked horrendous, but Tana Umaga and Keven Mealamu are not dirty, they're just hard and they were so fired up that a split-second action got out of hand. When two power-ful men combine with that much force it was always going to end badly. They should have come out straight away and apologized.

The way it was handled meant the New Zealand media got an opportunity to hammer on about Alastair Campbell, our resident spin doctor, who had worked for Tony Blair in 10 Downing Street. Campbell is actually very easy to get on with, a smart man who said all the right things, but he still shouldn't have been out there.

I assumed my tour was over on the Tuesday before the third Test when we beat Auckland 17–13 in Eden Park. The ever-growing number of dirt-trackers had planned a trip to Queenstown, but I had to pull out as Clive asked me in the changing room not to go 'off tour' as I might be required for the weekend.

Team selection was postponed for twenty-four hours owing to multiple injuries. My own shoulder was killing me, but I wanted a proper Test cap for the Lions so I kept quiet. Sure enough, at break-fast the next morning Clive told me I was at fullback, with Josh Lewsey switched to wing.

The game was a dead rubber, but the All Blacks were only think-ing one thing: whitewash. They destroyed us. All I remember is the black jerseys flooding through our lines very early on.

They were a great team, while we were no team at all.

Four months later New Zealand were back to haunt us again, giving Ireland an almighty beating, 45–7, at Lansdowne Road. When Aus-tralia also did a job on us a week later and before we stuttered to victory over Romania, the media started questioning Eddie's role as head coach.

I got a shedload of criticism for kicking turnover ball against Aus-tralia when we had an overlap deep in our own 22. Afterwards, people said I wouldn't have done that for Leicester – but I would have. I could have drawn the man and put our winger in space, but the cover was drifting hard and they would have got to him by the 10-metre line, where we would have been scrapping to retain possession. If the kick stayed in play, the pressure would automatically switch to Australia in their own territory.

Eddie's less than ringing endorsement of his fullback was more a defence of mounting criticism that his coaching methods were shackling our natural instincts: 'Like, there was talk of Geordan Murphy being told to do X, Y, Z, and it's nonsense. His strength is playing what's in front of him. Against Australia, he kicked a ball and there was an overlap. I was shouting, "It's on." It was his decision. You have to let fellas go and play, but you have to give them a road map they can work around. I think the players would verify that. The fly-by-the-seat-of-the-pants approach only works once out of ten.'

Our plan for the opening game of the 2006 Six Nations in Paris was to blitz the French right out the gate. The defensive line was to rush up and shut them down.

After two minutes I missed a tackle that allowed Aurélien Rougerie in for their first try. It came from a French scrum on our 10-metre line. Everyone, besides me holding in the backfield, blitzed up as planned. Tommy Bowe came off the left wing to hit Carl Heymans, only to slip, allowing the French to pour through. I was faced with a two-on-one against Christophe Dominici and Rougerie. Drico did amazingly well to spin around and tackle Dominici just as he offloaded. I had been trying to buy time between both men, but Rougerie took it and blasted up the wing. He power-stepped off his left foot, and I wasn't near enough to grab him.

We thundered back at them. I came into the line, throwing a reverse pass that nearly created a try, but it eventually ended up as a French 22 drop-out. They hacked it down the pitch and towards our 22, but I had it covered. Freddie Michalak was tearing after Leamy, but I was coming across from midfield and knew I could slide in and gather, and Leams would be over me to secure possession. But Leams put on a burst of pace, and dived in hope of grabbing the ball himself. Seeing this, I altered my path slightly, but the three of us — myself, Leams, and the ball — met at the same time. Smashing into my teammate's massive frame wasn't enjoyable, nor was seeing the ball squirt to Michalak, who scooped it up and put Olivier Magne under the posts.

Gifting the French two early tries in Paris is like leaving a trail of blood to your tent for a pack of starving wolves. The stadium band cranked up the volume, the crowd bellowed 'La Marseillaise' as Les Bleus tried to give them tries off every attack. There is no tougher opponent than the French in this mood. Moments later, David Marty blocked and gathered a Rog kick to race clear for the third try. 19–0 became 29–3 by half-time, thanks to another disastrous moment by yours truly.

Gathering a kick near the left touchline on halfway, faced by a line of blue jerseys, I wasn't giving their back three any free ball. Well, that was the plan. I saw Drico and Shaggy were behind me so I flung a long, looping pass infield that Heymans gratefully anticipated to sprint away for their fourth try. Heymans and Marty got two more before our remarkable four-try comeback as the French tired. A crazy game ended 43–31.

I had played poorly, and admitted as much into several dicta-phones afterwards. The former Irish international Neil Francis was having great fun hammering lads with his player ratings in the *Sunday Tribune*. He gave myself and Rog two, but the zero out of ten for Tommy was unnecessary. It can take months and sometimes years for a young player to rebuild his confidence after an experience like Paris, especially when the slagging starts up. A few older players took the piss out of him, as is their way, but it didn't sit well with him. Tommy was discarded after Paris, fuelling speculation that he was out of his depth. He deserved better treatment. Despite a few meaningless Tests in 2007, Tommy wasn't seen again in a green jersey until the 2008 Six Nations. We all know the type of player he has become.

I gave an interview a week or so later: 'After the France game it was probably the worst I have felt after an international; my chest hurt and I sprained a rib [a combination of colliding with Leamy and being smashed late by Marty], but really I was hurting from the feel-ing of having let my teammates down. I think I was certainly to blame for the first try.

'Some people seem to think I have become a bad player after two games, but there is nothing I can do about the French game now, so it's a case of onwards and upwards, both in terms of my own performance and for the team.'

The theory that I performed better for Leicester than for Ireland gained plenty of momentum after the Stade de France. I thought it was bullshit, and I criticized reporters who were spouting the idea. This wasn't a wise move, as they merely propagated the idea on the back of my comments.

We recovered from Paris, beating Wales and Scotland to set up a trip to Twickenham, where another Triple Crown was on offer. Thousands of Irish people had won a bundle of cash the previous afternoon, St Patrick's Day, when War of Attrition romped home in the Gold Cup, followed by two other Irish-trained horses, Hedgehunter and Forget the Past. This was the peak of the Celtic Tiger, so many of these delirious punters merely transferred the party from Cheltenham to London.

An English team stacked with my fellow Tigers – Andy Goode, Harry Ellis, Julian White, Cozza and Lewis – looked to have spoiled the party when Goodey's penalty put them 24–21 ahead with five minutes remaining.

We had a scrum on our own 22. There was no plan for this situation, so Rog tried something we had never practised.

'Look, Geordie, you go left, Drico, you go right, and I'll chip into space for one of ye to go get it and run the length . . .'

Fair enough!

Before the ball came out Rog decided to attack the narrower right side, quickly chipping their defensive line. The bounce fooled full-back Tom Voyce, allowing Brian to grab possession just on halfway, where he was tackled – but not before he sent Shaggy tearing up the touchline. Lewis caught him five metres out with Rog, of all people, first to arch his body over the ball, then Simon Easterby arrived, before Strings talked referee Nigel Whitehouse into giving us an advantage due to all the offside white jerseys. But none of us were thinking draw. Strings fed Drico, who was immediately enveloped by Cozza. I was standing as first receiver on the open side but Strings went blind again, throwing a ballsy looping pass that missed Rog and Easterby. Like any good winger, Shaggy was hugging the touchline.

Like any good flanker, Lewis was on his feet and looking to bury him. From a standing start, Shane had to fully stretch his six-foot-four-inch frame for the corner while Lewis dragged him by the legs into touch.

Whitehouse called time off with 78.21 on the clock. Touch judge Nigel Owens said the grounding was good, but Lewis was over to make sure they went to the TMO. It was a try, and Rog's touchline conversion glanced the left upright on its way over to make it 28–24, meaning England needed a try. But first they needed the ball.

Goodey put the restart up as high as possible between the 10-metre line and the 22, but Easterby grabbed it over his head. Rog kicked to touch on halfway. Paulie fecked up their lineout enough to force a turnover and Rog booted it into the stand, again, only for Whitehouse to tell us there was another fifteen seconds to go. Borthwick grabbed the lineout, Dawson dummied and attempted to snipe just like he did in the 2003 World Cup final, but Easterby hammered him. They attacked right, we turned it over, but it wasn't finished yet as Strings had his kick blocked down by a kamikaze dive from Lewis. The ball spilled loose for Rog to shin it into touch. Triple Crown secured. Easy.

Going training that Monday morning in Oval Park was pretty sweet.

In the summer of 2006 things fell apart between myself and Eddie. We went to New Zealand for a two-Test series, yet again coming desperately close to finally beating the All Blacks. We had chances in both matches. With seven minutes remaining in the first Test we trailed 24–23 when I caught the ball inside our half, chipped and regathered, before offloading to Drico. The attack went into their 22 but Luke McAlister, in for an injured Dan Carter, intercepted and the pendulum swung the full distance for Troy Flavell to steam over down the other end.

We lost the second Test 27–17. An incident early in the second half brought an end to my fifteen-game streak as Ireland fullback. Joe Rokocoko was flying down the left wing towards me. I heard Darce say he had my inside and, after Rougerie a few months earlier, I wasn't getting stepped on the outside again. Rokocoko glided inside, where Darce put him down. Watching the video in Perth that Monday before the team to play Australia was picked, Eddie insisted I should have smashed him into the stand.

I disagreed: 'If I commit to that tackle and miss it, he's going the length. With Darce there saying he has my inside, I am more than happy with what I did.'

Eddie freaked out. 'No, you want to put him into the stand!'

In my head I replied, 'Well, you try putting a sixteen-stone winger who moves like a fucking conger eel into the stand, Eddie.' Rokocoko has the rare ability to step off his right then immediately off his left at astonishing pace. You are doing well not to fall over.

I reiterated my argument: Darce had the inside covered!

Eddie disagreed, and I was dropped for Australia with the explanation that 'Girv is a better defender, we are going to go with him.'

That was it. I knew I was goosed. I got the last five minutes off the bench as we were well beaten by the Wallabies.

During the years when Girvan Dempsey and I competed for the Ireland fullback jersey, both of us got pigeonholed. Girv was praised for his steadiness and excellent positional sense, but the perception was that he lacked flair. In contrast, I was constantly labelled as a classy attacking player with bouts of flakiness. That was both of us nice and compartmentalized.

Sure, there were aspects to Girvan's game that I lacked, and vice versa, but in many respects we were similar. At fifteen, you mind the shop when everyone else is away and you endeavour to bring a different dimension to the attack.

Ironically enough, in Leicester these past five years or so, I have come to be viewed as the solid, dependable fullback.

After that summer of 2006, more often than not Eddie picked Girv at fullback; I'd get into the side on the wing only if one of the backs was injured. I would be playing fullback for Leicester on such a regular basis that when called up to play wing I didn't feel comfortable. If I came up against a specialist winger I was in trouble. In footballing terms, it is like a central midfielder playing wide right. A good player can play anywhere, the saying goes, but an excellent midfielder won't necessarily be an excellent right-sided player.

That November I came off the bench for the victory over South Africa and played fullback in our win over Australia. Eddie told the media he wanted to look at me there because I was playing wing for Leicester. Yes, on occasion I had number fourteen on my back, with Sam Vesty at fifteen, but I was running from fullback off nearly every play.

Against Australia I wanted to get the ball, pull some moves, put people in for tries, but it was a day when you just needed to do the basics correctly. It was lashing down at Lansdowne Road, but we still played well. I scored a try off a pre-planned move when Shaggy's inside pass had me running around under the sticks. I nearly got another in the right corner, but Chris Latham tackled me into touch.

My relationship with Eddie was pretty well over. We didn't really speak much after the row on the previous summer's tour. If you were in Eddie's good books or he was in a good mood, he'd be your best mate. If you weren't, he wouldn't bother with you.

In February, when Eddie picked Girv at fullback for the Wales match, a journalist mentioned my performance in Leicester's recent defeat of Munster at Thomond Park. Eddie said: 'But I've always been careful about reading too much into one performance. He played very well in that game, and didn't play badly in other games, but you have to balance it over a period of weeks. It's a tough call because his form is right up there again.'

This was a World Cup year. I was bench-warming but desperate to make an impact if given the chance.

I made two brief cameos in Cardiff, creating a try with perhaps my best ever thirty seconds in a green jersey, but Eddie was more interested in what happened near the end of the match.

On twenty-seven minutes Ireland were trailing 9–5 as a bloodied Denis Hickie came off to be stitched up, and I replaced him on the left wing. Hickie arrived back on the touchline eight minutes later, just as Dwayne Peel fired up a box kick. I gathered before relaunching a garryowen, which I climbed over everyone to catch. Wally took it on, allowing me to regain my feet and slip into outhalf, where I zipped a long pass out to Darce, before Rog found O'Driscoll with another skip pass and our captain stepped the cover for another cracking try.

As Rog was knocking over the conversion, Hickie returned and I sat back down. With twenty minutes left, word came down from upon high.

'Warm up, Geordie.'

I eventually returned to the field for the last five minutes, but only owing to Drico tweaking his hamstring. The game was all over the place, Wild West stuff, but we had a 19–9 lead. Their winger, Aled Brew, ran over me before someone hauled him down.

I am a small rugby player, so I'll always be targeted and occasionally the Brews of this world will expose my size, but generally I'm a good defender. My statistics at Leicester prove as much. They won't be memorable tackles, but the guy is stopped.

Eddie highlighted the Brew incident and made it very clear to me that he didn't want to see it happen again. We both knew he didn't want to pick me but Drico's hamstring was gone, so Shane Horgan went to centre and I was on the wing again – under strict instructions NOT to miss another tackle. I can take tough love, but I carried a terribly jittery mindset into that game.

And this was no normal Six Nations outing. It was the first ever rugby match at Croke Park.

It was a bitterly cold Sunday lunchtime kick-off. We started poorly, allowing them into a two-score lead after one shocking moment. It remains the low point of my career. Not only for the missed tackle but due to the amount of criticism I was subjected to in the aftermath by former players – men who had played the game for long enough to know better.

I remember it clearly. We were defending close to our line. John Hayes was inside me. They were lining up, with Vincent Clerc and Raphäel Ibañez coming cross-field. The ball was skipped out to Clerc, ten metres from our line, so I was thinking I must get close to Hayes as Clerc could wheel him. Hayes is actually a very good defender, but I don't believe in the 'look after your own department'

theory; at Leicester it is drilled into us to stay close to your props as
they have enough to be worrying about. All I was thinking was Clerc
is going to go. He didn't, though. He passed to Ibañez, who ran a
screamer of a tight line . . .

The previous week I had been doing tackle drills with Neil Back at
Oval Park.

'Drop your hips and hit low, Geordie.' We did it at least twenty
times. Drop hips, hit low – like you would teach a six-year-old.

Yet when Ibañez went at my inside shoulder, instead of dropping
my hips and hitting low I stuck my hand up and did an impression of
a well-oiled turnstile. I was never going to stop him with that technique. Inexcusable.

My thought process after it happened was clear and simple: I have
to fix this immediately. Get the ball. Attack.

My first chance to make a difference came just before half-time.
Rog's try and penalty had put us back in the game, but I could see
Yannick Jauzion was poised to put the outside man away for a certain
try. I sprinted up, hitting man and ball.

Coming off at half-time I still needed to atone for the missed
tackle, and that meant I needed the ball in my hands. The golden
opportunity arrived fifteen minutes into the second half. Even before
Pieter de Villiers threw the pass I knew I would intercept and score a
try. We would win the game and all would be forgiven. I was a stride
or two off warp speed when I heard the whistle.

'I'm sorry, I'm sorry, I blew a second early,' Walsh said immediately looking at me in the distance.

'Not much fucking use, pal, with 80,000 people blaming me for
handing France seven fucking points in the first ever game of rugby
in this fucking stadium!' (As usual, I said this more with a glare than
actual words.)

Walsh had been playing advantage for a French knock-on. Instead
of my try it was an Irish scrum. The ball fell limply from my grasp.
People make mistakes. Some are remembered, some aren't.

My hamstrings started cramping soon after, so I needed our physio
to remove the lactic acid. While I was down his mic crackled.

'You are coming off, Geordie.'

'But I'm OK!' we had just gone 14–13 ahead with twenty minutes remaining.

'You are coming off, I'm told.'

Oh shit, this is bad. Trimble came on. A brilliant driving maul shunted France into Rog's range and his penalty seemed to have saved us. We led 17–13 entering the final moments, but I watched on helplessly as Jauzion won the restart before Clerc wriggled over for his infamous late try.

Everyone was desperate to atone against England a fortnight later. With Drico returning I reckoned I would have to be satisfied with the bench. Eddie named the team Tuesday morning without speaking to anyone, and I was dropped from the squad entirely.

'Any problem, come talk to me,' he said, so I went to him before training. By the side of the pitch at St Gerard's School in Bray, we had a proper falling out. I told him what I thought and he gave his opinion right back. It probably wasn't the most productive conversation with regard to the procurement of future caps, but I felt I didn't deserve this treatment. I was so desperate to play against England that I lost it, stating that he should have defended me publicly when I got hammered in the media for missing the tackle on Ibañez. Instead, he'd justified the criticism by excluding me entirely.

That evening I phoned Paddy Howard.

'Geordie, you sound depressed.'

'I am in a horrible place – what will I do?'

'Take a break, Geordie. Get away.'

Enter Jimmy Ferris and David 'Magic' Johnson, who I played against in the '96 Leinster Schools Cup final. They suggested a weekend sojourn far away from the world of rugby, in Riga. When times are bad, you know who your true friends are: they will drop whatever they are doing and take you to Latvia. Seriously, though, they realized I needed to get out of Ireland, and there would be nowhere to hide in Leicester that weekend either.

Paddy also did what a coach should do for his player: he stood by me publicly. 'Geordan has the aerial skills and an eye for space, his fullback link role is good and he's a good footballing brain,' he said. 'He also brings some balance to the back three.

'Because the two provinces [Leinster and Munster] dominate the style of play with Ireland, most players coming in have to adjust. At fullback it is not as hard, and in Ireland he'd be better at fullback in that system. Wingers appear to be under more pressure in the Leinster and Ireland system. As wingers they may have the sense that people are coming at them more.

'I'm absolutely sure there is always more than one person who makes a mistake. If Geordan Murphy was beaten in the inside, perhaps there should have been someone covering the inside.'

Paddy was wrong, it was my mistake alone, but he defended his player regardless and that's all that mattered.

I watched Ireland's dismantling of England in a Latvian pub. I wasn't sober. That Ireland team had that England team's number. It was very simple: you front up to them physically. And on that historic occasion, the first Ireland–England match at Croke Park, every Irish man was going to front up.

I presumed my Six Nations was over, but I was called back into the squad for the trips to Edinburgh and Rome as Denis Hickie was struggling with a back spasm. I ended up as twenty-third man both times.

Ireland landed in Rome with a chance of winning the championship if we got a rake of tries and Scotland did us a favour in Paris, but I didn't need to be there. Denis told me as much as we walked off the plane. This was confirmed by the management a few hours later, so I asked Eddie, would it be OK to return to Leicester as they had a game on the Sunday. I rang Paddy and he said they were all set, so instead I joined Paul O'Connell, who was injured, for a few beers in the Hard Rock Café.

I was a little dusty the next day when awoken by a knock on my door.

'Team meeting is about to start and Eddie wants you to do the warm-up before the game just in case.'

Hundreds of Irish supporters would have seen me drinking bottles of Heineken at the bar the night before, and there I was on the Stadio Flaminio pitch in my gear.

I watched from the stand as we racked up a huge score, only for a late Italian try to deny us the championship on points difference.

The starting XV that beat England at Croke Park became irreplaceable in Eddie's eyes. He continued to talk about the squad and 'form' selections in public, but everything revolved around the untouchables. Regardless of how well someone like Stevie Ferris or Alan Quinlan or young guys like Luke Fitzgerald, Jamie Heaslip, Tommy Bowe or Rob Kearney performed in training or at European level, the XV were cast in stone. The sense of competition for places, so crucial in any side, was missing. No one got a go, a real opportunity to break into the starting XV.

This bred a completely unnecessary division between 'them' and 'us' within the one group. The chosen XV went into cold storage that summer, with none of them touring Argentina. They had earned the right to be deemed the best players in their positions, but with a World Cup coming up it was a mistake to isolate them from the rest and wrap them so tightly in cotton wool.

Irish rugby would pay a dear price for it.

After touring and losing in Argentina came a week in the most mind-numbing place on planet Earth: Spala. The cryotherapy facility at the Polish 'Olympic sports centre' allows athletes to recover and train for longer each day; it was a favourite of Warren Gatland, and continues to be for Wales. There is nothing else to do there and, inevitably, grown men begin to behave like children. Myself and Rog almost killed each other on one of our earlier trips to Poland for no reasons other than stir-craziness.

The World Cup warm-up games in August had me running out at Murrayfield almost four years to the day after my leg break. I was nervous – could lightning strike twice? It didn't, but after the match something really strange did happen in the changing room. Eddie sat down beside me and started talking like we were old war buddies. I was in shock – he hadn't spoken to me in eighteen months, apart from instructions not to miss tackles or to 'get back on the wing' whenever I wandered infield for the ball at training – and here he was, chatting away. I took this to mean I was going to the World Cup; until then I'd had a nagging fear that he might find a reason not to bring me.

The thirty-man squad had some surprise exclusions. Luke Fitzgerald was overlooked for rugby league convert Brian Carney, while Leams was the only number eight included – Jamie Heaslip didn't make it. There were three fullbacks – myself, Girv and Gavin Duffy.

One of the filthiest matches I've ever played in was the hastily arranged warm-up against Bayonne. It was obvious that we were under-cooked, especially the frontliners, so we went off to face a French club team on their own patch. Neil Best got chinned in the first breakdown, but the really serious incident came when the big Kiwi lock, Makeera Tewhata, attempted to crush Drico's face with a haymaker. Brian didn't see it coming as he was breaking up a row. Alan Quinlan, Donncha and Paulie came rushing in, but what could they do? If they started unloading they could have been suspended on the eve of the World Cup.

We should have seen it coming. It was the equivalent of France coming to play an Irish province before the World Cup started in Ireland: a few boys wouldn't be able to resist hoying into them. From their perspective, it made sense. Richard Dourthe was even quoted in *L'Équipe* before the game saying that it would be better for France if O'Driscoll wasn't playing in the World Cup. Dourthe had been smoked by Drico at Lansdowne Road back in 2001 and was never selected for France again.

I came on as Brian went to hospital for an X-ray for what turned out to be a fractured sinus. Of course, he recovered to be Ireland's stand-out player for the third successive World Cup. A week later, after beating Italy in another warm-up (thanks only to a poor refereeing decision) and on the eve of departure to our base camp in Bordeaux, Eddie informed the squad that the IRFU had extended his own contract until after the 2012 Six Nations. I'm sure a few boys were doing sums in their head. I know I was. Christ, I'll be thirty-three by then.

The room was silent. What did he expect, spontaneous applause?

Here's what I was thinking: four more years of his autocratic style of coaching. Four more years of those ridiculous expressions ('You can't unring a bell . . . Ashtray on a motorbike . . . You want to go out there and set your hair on fire.') Four more years of him roaring abuse at lads. Multi-pattern phases were his thing. There would be a drill with a designated ball-carrier and if an unsanctioned hand touched it he would go spare.

Our hotel was in an industrial estate a half-hour outside Bordeaux – i.e. in the middle of nowhere. The food was terrible. Our menus had been sent over in advance, but the French chefs didn't understand our dietician's instructions.

I shared a small room with Simon Easterby, two single beds – fine for a night, maybe, but for two rugby players sharing for several weeks it was too small.

The tactics employed in August were unchanged for the first two games, against Namibia and Georgia. The plan was to beat them up, don't show our hand until the France and Argentina matches. I remember thinking at the time that it was a dangerous approach; World Cups are about discovering form, getting used to our patterns, generating momentum – not exploding out of the blocks in game three. The Namibians were mainly big Afrikaners, raised on Currie Cup rugby. This sort of physicality was all they knew. Eddie put out the same team that had demolished England six months beforehand, with the exception of Andrew Trimble replacing the injured Shane Horgan at right wing.

I was on the subs bench. Mervyn Murphy told me to warm up with twenty-five minutes to go. We were ahead, but the performance was terrible. I was very keen to get involved. I could see the lines of attack that we could exploit, I knew exactly how I could make a difference.

'I'm ready, Merv.'

Ten minutes later, nothing had happened but there was still time to make an impact.

'I'm ready, Merv!'

Merv put a finger to his ear.

'You are not going in yet, Geordie.'

Seven minutes remaining: 'Warm up, Geordie.'

'I'm ready, Merv.'

Hand to earpiece.

'Not yet, Geordie.'

As injury time approached, I got the call.

'Go, Geordie! Go do your thing!'

Merv didn't actually say that. I jogged into the line, watched a few miserable phases and then walked off the pitch, knowing I'd expend more energy in the shower.

It was even more excruciating against Georgia, six days later. Standing in the dugout again, I could see how we could shred this third-rate defence, although I probably had a better chance of touching the ball in the stand than on the field. It was lost in the forwards all night long. But the Georgians were massive and their pack, based primarily with French clubs, had the time of their lives. They couldn't believe we were playing right into their hands.

I all but begged to be put on. Eventually word came down to the bench.

'Warm up, Geordie.'

Until that night I never knew what it felt like to be the last kid to be picked. Jerry Flannery, Simon Best, Isaac Boss and Neil Best went in as subs, but the nod from Eddie never came, so I stood, like everyone else, watching those final moments in horror as we defended our try-line. It was so close to being the worst ever result in the history of Irish team sports. We escaped with a scarily close 14–10 victory after Leamy got under the ball-carrier over our line. Referee Wayne Barnes and the TMO couldn't see if the ball had been grounded. No try. Imagine the consequences if Leams hadn't got his ample frame under that Georgian drive?

Still doesn't bear thinking about.

Now, we were in the middle of the World Cup and the form we'd shown when thrashing England, the performance that had everyone (players especially) stating we were contenders to win the tournament, was completely absent.

Training became more intense, players were nervous, and we were trapped in a vicious circle. The attitude was: we need to work harder, train harder.

I remember sitting in the gloomiest team room imaginable. We were travelling the next morning from Bordeaux to Paris by TGV for the next pool match, against France. I was to be a mere passenger on the high-speed train and at the game, having been dropped from the twenty-two.

I had been omitted, seemingly, for my half-minute performance against Namibia.

As we trudged out of the selection meeting, my dropping allowed those with a more acerbic sense of humour to keep themselves entertained.

'Geordie was dropped for not warming up correctly.'

Yeah, we had ventured on to the dark side of the moon. The lads needed something to cheer them up, let it be at my expense. My smile was their cue to continue.

'The way Geordie sat on the bench was a disgrace.'

Not making the starting XV was no longer a surprise. Girv was the first-choice fullback, while Andrew Trimble was preferred to both Denis Hickie and myself on the left wing. But this was a new low – dropped off the bench for no reason at all. I didn't think it could ever get worse than being discarded the week before the historic England match at Croke Park during the previous Six Nations, but at least there was some clear rationale for that decision.

With respect to Gavin Duffy, a decent fullback in his own right, his selection as number twenty-two had the media smelling a rat. I was not given a heads-up in Bordeaux about being dropped. Eddie no longer even recognized my presence as we passed each other in the corridor, so, like everyone else, I read his explanation in the newspapers.

'I think historically Geordan's last two games [against France] haven't been a hunting ground for him. He [Duffy] also fills the centre for us and it's a bench that gives us more options.'

This had reporters scratching their heads, given that I'd played fullback, wing, centre and outhalf in fifty-one Tests over the previous seven years. Also, in Andrew and Shaggy we had converted centres on the wings. The 'options' theory didn't stack up, and Eddie conceded as much in his next breath: 'It's part of it as well – and it's not a major part, it's a minor part, I threw it in at the end – is that he [Gavin] covers centre as well as back-three. The underpinning issue is the last couple of occasions he's played against France have not been good days for him all right. That's my decision, I stand over that and someone has to make that decision. You might disagree with it, as you possibly do, but that's the way it is.'

The idea that I had a problem against France because of two recent poor performances against them was ridiculous. It felt like a spiteful decision rather than a rugby decision. Not only to me but to my club colleagues in Leicester and to my family in Naas.

Peter Stringer had also been demoted from starting scrumhalf to dirt-tracker, unfairly shouldering the majority of the blame for the performance for throwing an intercept pass that led to Georgia's try. Fla came in for Rory Best at hooker.

I was in the team room eating dinner when my mobile vibrated. It was a journalist with a bizarre question.

'No, I'm not on my way to Mexico!'

'That's what I heard . . .'

'Well, I am in the hotel having my dinner.'

Another call came almost immediately, from a friend asking a similar question.

'No, I'm not at the airport. I'm in the hotel eating my dinner!'

'Please don't leave, Geordie. It would be so bad for everyone if you walked out.'

'What? Eh, OK. I won't leave the squad.'

All the lads were staring at me now. Another call, another journalist. Then another friend. And on it went.

I was an outlaw, en route to my secret Mexican villa having walked out of camp after a blazing row with Eddie. For that evening no number of denials could stop that rumour spreading like the plague. There was nothing to it, of course. No matter how hard it gets, I'd never walk out on any team, especially not my country.

Still, it went on all night.

'No, I didn't have a row with Eddie. Not recently, anyway.'

'Don't do it, Geordie. Don't leave.'

'OK, I won't.'

'Geordan, stick with it.'

'OK, I will.'

The whole situation was not helped by the veil of secrecy draped over the squad. We should have let the reporters in more and had a bit of *craic* with them, but the attitude was, 'Oh no, we can only give them what we want to give them.' When a siege mentality is fostered, human nature will inevitably lead to conjecture and the incessant fuelling of rumours.

Our emperor's rigid control of everything meant that when one thing failed it created a domino effect into all parts of the system. I did wish to be on a Mexican beach, as it felt like we couldn't hold out much longer. The French and Argentinians were at the gates now.

Having lost to Argentina in the opening pool game and as tournament hosts, the French simply could not afford to lose to us, and it showed once they got over early nerves. They won 25–3. It meant that to qualify we needed four tries against the Pumas while also denying them a losing bonus point.

Miracle territory.

My tournament was just beginning, though. Girv picked up an injury against France so I was recalled as starting fullback.

Eddie was asked if he had any faith in me.

'I wouldn't say I have no faith in Geordan. If I had no faith in Geordan he wouldn't be in the squad. I have plenty of faith in him. As I said, France had been a team Geordan had struggled against. This is a different game and a different team.'

That's OK, then. Not that I was complaining. I'm convinced he wouldn't have picked me if the media hadn't been piling on the pressure for him to do so.

On the Wednesday before we played Argentina, Simon Best was walking around downtown Bordeaux with Paddy Wallace when he lost sensation down his right side and found he had difficulty speaking. There was a taxi strike in Bordeaux, so our liaison officer drove him back to the hotel, where Dr Gary O'Driscoll examined him before accompanying him to hospital. Simon, elder brother of Rory and someone I have played rugby with since Ireland under-21s, had to leave the squad and eventually announced his retirement a few months later due to an irregular heartbeat.

The players were not informed of the facts straight away – it was only over coffee a few days later that Rory and Paddy told me what had happened. Maybe the management didn't have the full facts over what was happening to Simon, but we should have been sat down immediately as a group and been told what they did know. It felt as though we were being treated like children.

That week I remember sitting with Simon Easterby in our room, two seven-year Test veterans agreeing that this was as bad as it could possibly get. We just didn't feel in any way like a team.

The management should have encouraged methods of developing camaraderie, so essential for a group of men living in each other's pockets for several months. You knew it was happening in other camps. A social event should have been arranged for the players and management the day the World Cup squad was announced – a meal somewhere or just a rake of pints – but it never really happened.

Everyone was in ultra-serious mode from day one and individuals put an enormous amount of pressure on themselves.

Since 2007, I have become a student of sports psychology.

In his book *Bounce*, Matthew Syed, who represented Great Britain in table tennis, has a chapter on how and why people choke. Syed wrote about being trounced in his first match at the Sydney Olympics by a mediocre opponent. He choked.

Syed uses the example of driving to explain what happens when someone chokes or crumbles under pressure. A learner driver must focus on the mechanics of driving – keeping the steering wheel straight, pushing the clutch and watching the road when changing gears. After several months, hundreds of hours, these actions are performed effortlessly, without conscious control. Your driving skills are no longer explicit, they become implicit.

For a top-level athlete, whose skills are implicit, choking arises not from a lack of focus, but from too much focus. If you find yourself concentrating on the mechanics of a complex task in rugby, error tends to creep in. The expert performer, someone who has practised long enough to automate a skill, has the capacity to choke in the most dramatic manner.

Syed wrote about a speed skater named Sarah Lindsay and how she avoided choking under immense pressure by constantly telling herself that it was just speed skating. No big deal. It worked. In the Olympic final she went out completely relaxed, finding her own personal release-valve for the pressure. She trusted her talent and her preparation, and she exceeded all expectation placed on her by achieving that deep sense of relaxation which is required before entering the arena.

We were never going to find that zen-like calm before the Argentina match. Our collective mindset had spiralled too far out of control by that stage. We, as a team, had become the athlete that is too focused on performing tasks that should come naturally, implicitly. We had created such an intense environment that we couldn't loosen up enough to perform.

Personally, I felt very relaxed. I was just so happy to have an opportunity to play in a major World Cup game, made even more special by being at the Parc des Princes – the arena Didier Camberabero, Patrice Lagisquet, Serge Blanco and Philippe Sella turned into their playground, and where I had won the European Cup in 2001. I planned to attack, every chance I got.

Argentina had been the feel-good story of the tournament, beating France in the opening game and playing an aggressive brand of territorial rugby concocted by the newly appointed Leicester Tigers coach, Marcelo Loffreda.

They scored first, but Drico barged over for a try to keep us alive. Argentina responded with Juan Martín Hernández launching crazy high balls as his teammates flooded into the backfield. I played well that day but, again, it's the things that go wrong that stay with you the longest. My future Leicester teammate, Horacio Agulla, raced in for their second try before half-time after Hernández leaped like a kangaroo over my head to catch his own skyscraper, before offloading, one-handed, for prop Martin Scelzo to rumble into our 22.

Felipe Contepomi's touchline conversion made it 18–10 at the interval. He kicked another penalty before we responded with a well-worked try that I finished off. It was the standard fast, clean, first-phase Irish score. Off-the-top lineout ball saw Drico brilliantly fade outside Manuel Contepomi before Wally's excellent pass allowed me to dive over. But that was it. Felipe landed two more penalties, followed by another Hernández drop goal, off his left boot this time, to end our World Cup in ruthless fashion.

They deserved their victory, but I still believe if we hadn't been forced by the pool situation to chase four tries we would have won. Hernández was majestic in a team that was eventually strangled to death by South Africa in the semi-final.

The post-mortem for Ireland stated: death by choking. It was true, and we must live with that, but we were strangled by our circumstances as well.

I was incredibly disappointed when Eddie dug his heels in and refused to resign. I strongly considered retiring from international rugby myself, despite being only twenty-nine. But the Six Nations rolled around again and I hoped it might be different.

13. The Assassins

Something happened this evening that needed no words and will stay with everyone in the room for ever. Jerry Flannery handed out the jerseys for tomorrow's game against Australia.

Fla tore his calf, yet again, at training last Tuesday. The medics' facial expressions told their own story. Everyone knew about the eighteen-month battle Fla had fought to make it back, but now the World Cup is over for him. He'll fly home soon, with his rugby future clouded in uncertainty. Sean Cronin sits on the bench behind Rory Best, while Damien Varley has been flown out as cover.

It's always that straightforward in the trenches. Ship out the wounded and call up the reserves.

Morale in the squad took a dip when the injury was confirmed Tuesday evening. Everyone loves Fla. I was one of the first to know for certain as I needed an injection in my shoulder, because of a sore A/C joint, so I went with him to the hospital. Nothing was said in the car there or on the way back. He knew before the scan that it was gone. He was inconsolable.

But Fla stuck around for one last duty. Deccie asked him to do it. Only when Jerry started handing out the shirts did it hit home just how much it meant to him. The twenty-two sat in a circle with the rest of us on the periphery. He was in floods of tears. It was tough seeing an old teammate so visibly upset. Each man going up to face him had a lump in his throat as well. You were taking a jersey off a man with forty-one Irish caps, a man who would die to be out on the field alongside you.

Nothing was said except each player's name and number. Nothing else was needed. He looked each man dead in their eyes as he handed them a green jersey. Even watching it from the periphery, the hairs stood up on the back of my neck.

Afterwards, Deccie thanked Jerry, saying he showed what it means to wear the jersey, before we all stood and shuffled silently out of the room. This wasn't a mere gimmick by Deccie, but it was a masterstroke none the less. A genuinely good idea which had a profound effect on us all. For the starting players, it gave an already special game that extra bit of spice. Nobody wants to let Fla down.

The Ireland rugby team must become that speed skater Matthew Syed wrote about in *Bounce*. If we do that, the performance will definitely follow. It is just a rugby match; it is what we are all good at doing. As six-time world snooker champion Steve Davis said: play as if it means nothing when it means everything. Do that and we cannot fall into the mental hole we dug for ourselves in 2007. That so many guys on the field tomorrow went through that brutal experience four years ago has to count for something.

The blueprint for beating Australia was presented by the All Blacks, also at Eden Park, back in the summer. We will focus on nullifying the influence of their core men – seven, eight, nine and ten. David Pocock is a world-class openside, but I don't think he will be an issue. The lads will look after him, and our backrow will be queuing up to nail their big ball-carrying number eight, Radike Samo. Will Genia is a special player, so is Quade Cooper. But Jamie, Seanie and Stevie are coming for them as well.

We had the evening off last night. I took the lads to a restaurant I know in Auckland called Wildfire. I asked everyone, but most people had plans – Redzer and Drico were staying in the hotel, and another gang were going up the Sky Tower, so I only booked a table for eight. Just before the bus was to leave lads started wandering into the lobby.

'Ah, yeah I'll go.'

'Ah, sure if you are going . . .'

Typical rugby fellas on tour: making their minds up at the last possible minute. Most things they do are so regimented that the ability to be breezy is something they cling to whenever possible. Anyway,

I walked into the restaurant with nineteen hungry men. The booking was in my name so I ended up having to quarterback the situation. The restaurant were good about it. The boys loved it – what's not to love about an All You Can Eat meat-fest – ensuring my street cred was pretty high on the trip home.

Monday, 26 September 2011
Rotorua

Before the game last Saturday night I needed something to do out on the pitch. I was in my tracksuit so I acted as a foil for Redzer, who fired some bullets my way. When he was happy and jogged away, I stood in the middle of Eden Park, soaking it all up. It was amazing to see so much green in the stadium. Plenty of gold as well. The final is back here in a few weeks.

The energy in those moments before kick-off is very hard to describe. After all my years with Johnno and the Leicester boys before some massive games, I can't remember anything like the silent ferocity of our boys in the changing room.

Having clapped them on to the field, we went to our seats in the stand. We, the dirt-trackers, had self-christened ourselves 'The Assassins' since beating Connacht at Donnybrook. We had to do better than 'The Muppets'. I was joined by Shane Jennings, Leo Cullen, Isaac Boss, Fergus McFadden, Paddy Wallace, Tony Buckley and Damien Varley (who immediately blended into our camp, mainly because he is a cracking guitar player). Even among the non-chosen eight sitting in the stand, the mood was edgy. Rugby players usually watch games in silence, but not that night.

It very nearly got out of hand. Australia made a half break and some guy in a gold jersey, sitting in front of myself and Shane, leaped up when nobody else did. He decided to remain standing.

Jenno politely asked him to sit down.

The guy ignored him. There were evidently a few beers on board. Jenno leaned over, gently tugging his jersey to put him back in the seat. He turned and started spitting abuse. I was so wound up that I came out with some fairly nasty replies. I couldn't help myself.

All the boys got a kick out of it afterwards. Donncha presented

Shane with an award for 'assaulting an Australian supporter' on the bus later that night.

Moments from the game stand out. Stephen Ferris's mauling of Genia in the second half as the other seven forwards busted a gut to pile in on top of the little scrumhalf; Cooper at fifteen trying to run the ball from his own line, only to be smashed and held up by Drico. We could see the Wallabies were rattled, but they have so much pace I knew they were capable of turning it around with a try from eighty metres out.

Throwing Rog on after forty-nine minutes for Darce, with Jonny having just put us 9–6 ahead, was a great move. Sexto switched to inside centre, something Deccie had tried in August, so it meant he stayed on the field as Rog was put in a position to do what he does better than most: close out a tight game.

Maybe Australia felt we were a speed bump on the road to bigger and better challenges. We choked them in the tackle – one man high, another low, holding the ball-carrier up until a turnover is awarded. We've been doing that for two and half years, but the Australians seemed surprised by it. They hadn't done their homework properly, or maybe they didn't respect us enough. We were a speed bump all right, one that tore off the back fender of their finely tuned machine.

We tore into them physically, getting to their key players – eight, nine and ten. It helped that Pocock ended up missing the match through injury, because he is world class at the breakdown, and they also missed hooker Stephen Moore. Everything worked out perfectly for us on the night.

Afterwards, Paulie made a speech in the changing room where he referred to Jenno's and my words earlier in the week, when we took control of a pre-game players' meeting in an attempt to assist the match-day squad's preparation. Paulie said that helped get him up for the game. He was talking about the importance of the collective. The thirty. It is quite an honour when Paulie names you as a motivational figure, because there are few greater than himself.

The atmosphere within the squad has been fantastic ever since.

It took a few hours to leave Eden Park that night and return to our hotel, where there was a meal prepared for us. But the process was very enjoyable. The lads were on some buzz. The centre of Auckland had been pandemonium the night before when I went down to the Viaduct Harbour to watch the second half of New Zealand versus Japan. A mate of mine who lives locally suggested we go to a bar down on Parnell Road that wouldn't be as busy so we could enjoy a few beers. It was a release that was definitely needed.

Next morning we were up early to fly down to Taupo. On the road again.

Monday we were off, but I felt good training Tuesday. Deccie named the team for Russia but I wasn't in the squad. I knew that would probably change as Tommy had a sore calf. Sure enough, by Thursday I was on the bench.

New Zealand television anchors are calling it 'The Green Tide'.

We tried to warn the people of Rotorua what was coming behind us. They had no idea. The hype around the team is unreal now. Sports shops all along the path of destruction are sold out of Ireland jerseys. This would be heaven for the street merchants who ply their trade around the Aviva on big match days. There are so many Irish people in this part of the world these days, and it seems like all of them have downed tools to follow us. People back home, thinking ahead optimistically, are already talking about flying down for the semi-final. They are everywhere we go, and you can't miss them because of the gear. The normally conservative Irish rugby fans with jersey and pint in hand are now face-painted, green-wigged and guzzling from beer bongs.

Sure enough, Rotorua was nuts last night after we beat Russia 62–12. Actually, it was more like a big Irish session than a Test match. I didn't enjoy the game, to be quite honest. I came on ten minutes into the second half (at least Deccie has addressed the flaw of under-using his bench) but there was no structure at that stage, and I hadn't played on the wing in ages. The game already won, I hugged the touchline in the vain hope of creating space inside me if the lads would ever let the ball come wide.

That was never going to happen. Everyone was looking to charge upfield, trying things they would never consider against a higher calibre of opposition. We got a little greedy, but that happens when the score gets out of control.

Vasily Artemiev's try came off a move Merv had flagged in advance. We had rehearsed how to counteract it earlier in the week. Artemiev just ran a really good line, came off his left then right foot. Rob slipped awkwardly. When I saw him on the ground I thought he might have twisted his ankle. He was still down after the conversion so I asked if he wanted to swap positions, but he was fine. False alarm.

That night out was too stressful to enjoy, especially after the roasting Mike Tindall has been getting in the UK media after a bouncer in a Queenstown bar released CCTV footage of him on a night out. We went to a restaurant called The Lonestar, a steakhouse where we got a booth, but a few quiet beers quickly turned into the Irish support-ers devouring us. Lads were getting dragged away for pictures. At closing time we went into the restaurant bar and asked for a few bot-tles of Corona. Sold out. Well, what have you got? All their tequila, whiskey, vodka and international beers were emptied too. The choice was Steinlager or wine. When that place closed at about 12.30 we went on to another pub. Same situation again. Empty kegs. Rotorua had been drunk dry by the green wave. We found another late place, but it was even crazier. Supporters on the drink for ten, twelve hours just drunkenly snapping away. I was camera blind before I got to the bar counter with Leo. The owner put us in a corner for safety rea-sons. I bailed before the drinks came. I felt bad for married guys in the squad who were just standing there talking to their teammates when girls draped themselves on them for a picture.

I will be disappointed not to feature against Italy, but you can't really fault Deccie for sticking with the twenty-two that beat Aus-tralia. In my head I feel I am not going to get a run again. So, that might be all from me in a green jersey.

Russia was a missed opportunity to keep the opposition coaches, who are analysing us, guessing a little bit more. We should have rolled out a few wide moves even if just as future decoys.

Deccie talks about playing cup rugby a lot. Like most of us, his roots are the schools game, with Pres Cork. That's where he became a coach. The mentality of schools cup rugby used to be about pressure, making the opposition lose rather than going out positively to win. The cornerstone of our attack is the unleashing of two tremendous athletes, the big ball-carrying Stevie and Seanie.

Ironically, neither grew out of the schools system. Both are rough diamonds unearthed in junior clubs.

Monday, 3 October 2011
Dunedin
I met the enemy for coffee on Friday. Martin Castrogiovanni and I own an Italian restaurant called Timo in Market Harborough, just out the road from Leicester. He had made no secret of this being the game Italy were targeting from months out. He had a sore groin but had been passed fit to start.

Castro's importance to Italy has been discussed in team meetings. The plan is to wear him out. Keep their pack on the move. We didn't talk about the match because Castro rarely gets around to having serious conversations. That's why I enjoy his company so much.

The Otago Stadium is only a 30,000-seater, but it is a greenhouse – fully enclosed by a transparent roof – and you really feel like the crowd is on top of you. Great atmosphere. It hit me only at the captain's run on Saturday how much of a sickener it was not to be involved.

On game day I went for a late-morning walk down to Courtenay Place in Dunedin. It was heaving with the Irish, all on the drink already. I couldn't help thinking many of them would struggle to remember the game if they even made it into the ground. On the bus ride down Donners referred to the scenes as Lansdowne Road on crack cocaine.

I had never seen such an excited gathering before. Forget Heineken Cup finals and Grand Slam deciders, this was another level. Maybe it was because the game was on so late or that we are all so far away from home, but it was a carnival.

Losing Castro so early to a hamstring injury hurt Italy. At half-time the boys promised to increase the speed of ruck ball and up the tempo. They immediately did as much, Earlsey got in for two, Drico

another as we tore them asunder, winning 36–6. Seanie and Stevie
were immense again. 'Where is their weakness?' was Nick Mallet's
rhetorical summation of Ireland's potential.

We move on to Wellington next for a quarter-final against Wales
and a shot at going where no Irish team has ever gone before. I know
I'm just one injury away from the bench, but that makes it even more
agonizing not being involved. It looks like my last ever game for Ireland was on the bloody wing against Russia. Starting with USA,
Canada and Japan, leaving with USA and Russia. At least there were
some amazing days in between.

14. Bulletproof

After the 2007 World Cup, the healing process began the moment I pulled a Leicester jersey over my head again. We had enough problems of our own to refocus the mind.

Go get the ball, Geordie. Make things happen.

Along with Castro, I was playing Premiership rugby a full three weeks before most of our internationals returned. Seru Rabeni was next to clock in (Fiji beat Wales to reach the quarter-finals) but the absence of five Englishmen, Argentinian prop Marcos Ayerza, Alex Tuilagi and new signing Aaron Mauger – the All Black being the latest in our royal line of inside centres – meant we didn't field a full-strength XV until early November.

The last man to arrive was Marcelo Loffreda. After eight years in charge of his native Argentina, the club's newly appointed head coach showed up at Oval Park two days before our opening Heineken Cup match against Leinster.

The return of Martin Corry, Lewis Moody, George Chuter, Ben Kay and Dan Hipkiss took longer than any of us expected, especially after seeing England pounded 36–0 by South Africa in the opening game. Astonishingly, they recovered to beat Tonga, Samoa, Australia and France, before pushing the Springboks close in the final, losing an old-fashioned arm-wrestle 15–6.

Their odyssey seemed like the polar opposite to my depressing sojourn in Bordeaux. They reached the final by adopting a bullish, player-power stance, seizing control of their own destiny mid-tournament when it became apparent that the coaches weren't going to provide the necessary clarity of leadership. It must have helped that so many players were already in possession of World Cup winner's medals – and that something similar had apparently happened in 2003, when Martin Johnson reportedly ended up running the England training sessions and calling a halt when he was satisfied. After being thrashed by the 'Boks, the squad and coaches gathered in a room where everyone was encouraged to speak freely. This I can relate to, having seen it happen at Leicester. It can be a gruesome, even a cruel process, but it is the only way to halt a downward spiral. Another option is a massive drinking session – and the English boys did that too, after the meeting, under the protection of armed police, to release the tension that had been building. It had the desired effect on morale.

Martin Johnson calling a halt to training must be a memory worth keeping – I've never heard any other player to have such authority.

Men like Lawrence Dallaglio, Mike Catt, Phil Vickery, Jonny Wilkinson and Martin Corry recognized they were on a path to failure and had the bravery to alter their course, and by doing so they wrote an international legacy they could always be proud of: two World Cup finals. Some achievement for a team Ireland had beaten in our four previous Six Nations encounters.

Viewed in that light, Ireland's failure hurt even more. The only tonic for this kind of pain is the game itself.

The board had appointed Marcelo knowing he would not arrive until Argentina's tournament was finished. Maybe they, like almost everyone else, figured Los Pumas wouldn't make it as far as the semi-finals.

It was his first northern hemisphere job, so the initial plan was for him to shadow Richard Cockerill until mid-December when, it was expected, he would have settled in and improved his English enough to start conveying the master plan.

But the Premiership and the European Cup wait for no man. Following a World Cup, those months up to Christmas are notoriously difficult for a club like ours. Loffreda probably wasn't aware that the Welford Road faithful were already running out of patience, having sat through a Gloucester tanking, 30–17, on 6 October. That was Castro's and my first game back. It was swiftly followed by defeats away to Saracens and Bath.

It got worse. With our playing resources already stretched, the injury count climbed to double figures (I played half-crocked for most of this campaign). The club was on the brink of crisis.

Looking for positives, the absence of Alex and Seru gave my fellow Kildare man, Johne Murphy, a sustained run in the team, and he proved himself a more than capable performer at this level. He had to be, as we were under constant pressure in the backfield.

Another silver lining was Cockers getting to sit in the head coach's seat without a bunsen burner under him. This gave him scope to learn on the job. Cockers had just spent two years as forwards coach under Paddy Howard, for whom he was a perfect foil – a Tiger since 1992, a forward and, well, passionate is too soft a description. He is a zealot. Spend eighty minutes within spitting distance of Cockers during a Tigers game and you will see how deep the well goes. Another bit of free advice I'd give is to steer clear the morning of a match. He gets a little tetchy.

Players respect Richard Cockerill. Sure, plenty have fallen out with him, but he did a great job keeping a leaking ship afloat before and after Loffreda arrived.

The plan was simple: we would jump-start the 2007/8 campaign by beating Leinster at the RDS on 10 November.

There were welcome additions to the line-up for the EDF Cup match against Cardiff a week before we went to Dublin. I was at fullback with Varndell and Alex on the wings, Seru and Danny Hipkiss in midfield. Marcos and Julian White were the props with Castro as cover, Ben Kay joined Louis Deacon in the second row, while Cozza and Lewis flanked Jordan Crane. A very strong side. We thrashed them 42–20.

Marcelo arrived a few days later. The squad met their new coach for the first time that Thursday. Two days later we had a potentially season-defining game in Dublin.

I wasn't right and shouldn't have played, having strained medial ligaments in my knee. Generally in Leicester the rule of thumb is if you cannot train by Wednesday, you cannot play Saturday; but these weren't normal times at the club. I couldn't even do the Friday captain's run, but Cockers wanted me out there. It was to be my fiftieth European appearance, it was in Dublin against Leinster, and my family were coming up en masse from Naas, so I agreed with him. It wasn't a long discussion.

'Can you play, Geordie?'

'Yeah, I can play.'

I got heavily strapped up and ran out there, duly producing an absolute stinker of a performance. My bushy biker handlebar moustache – grown to help raise funds for the Matt Hampson Movember appeal – meant any chance of being inconspicuous was impossible.

The worst moment came when Shane Horgan, my Ireland roommate when we both started out, chased me down after I had a decent head start. In that situation you can't use injury as an excuse; I was away and he caught me. I had to suck it up. Shaggy was delighted as scragging my collar denied Leicester the losing bonus point.

In a viciously tough pool that also included Edinburgh and the mighty Toulouse, our margin for error was all used up. To reach the quarter-finals we needed to be perfect at home, win in Edinburgh and get at least a bonus point in the south of France.

Marcelo Loffreda's plan to 'shadow' Cockers was immediately scrapped after the defeat. He said something along the lines of, 'We were very poor, I coach now.'

That first Monday morning session, unfortunately, was the beginning of the end. His style worked wonders for Argentina, but the kick–chase approach was practically obsolete within months of France '07. It was too predictable. He lost the boys from the very first drill. And when a coach loses a rugby team, or any professional group for that matter, it is nearly impossible to win them back.

There was a language barrier, but it was clear he wanted us to replicate Argentina. The depressing realization was that we were going to be chasing balls and running straight into people until next May.

The theory that We Are Leicester, so therefore we should be able to out-muscle opponents, is bullshit. Despite what many think, it is not that simplistic in the Premiership. The season is a slog all right, so if the primary tactic is to physically dominate every team, it eventually takes a costly toll.

After two years of the innovative and constantly progressive, Paddy Howard approach, our new coach transported us in a time machine back to the 1980s. Marcelo's tactics were heaven sent for our opponents, who quickly figured us out.

I can't say I enjoyed having to catch bomb after bomb every day in training, either. Don't get me wrong, I love being the guy under them – it's a fullback's primary duty – but multiple times in training with Alex, Lewis and Seru chasing? Nightmare.

Andy Goode was having a grand old time. He'd sit there on the 10-metre line giggling as I got up from underneath the torso of a grinning Tuilagi.

'Put this one on the 22, Goodey.'

'I'll try my best, Geordie,' as Lewis, stamping his hoof on the half-way line and breathing like an unfed bull, came next. I'd have a split second to catch the ball and swerve before my best mate smashed me to pieces.

'The 22, Goodey.'

'I'll do my best, Geordie.'

There were other drills, but it was the same principle. We'd pair up, I'd fire up a garryowen so my buddy could chase it down and vice versa. We were just launching everything into the sky.

God, I missed Paddy.

Marcelo was a lovely man, but there was a communications issue. He could speak English, but not fluently. The team talk would be peppered with phrases like, 'We must *terrorate* the opposition.' Every pre-match speech in the changing room was signed off with, 'Good game, enjoy.' You are steeling yourself for war and guys are sniggering.

I know it can't be easy to walk into such a massive club where so many established, world-class players have strong opinions, but a coach must be able to command instant respect. He doesn't need to be liked, but he must be respected.

We reacted to the Leinster defeat by crushing Edinburgh a week later, 39–0. An Achilles problem meant I sat out our impressive victory at home to Toulouse, in which Aaron made his debut. He was miles from full fitness, but I was confident we'd signed the best number twelve in the world.

The return leg in Toulouse cruelly exposed the shortcomings of the Loffreda approach. Kicking to a backfield of Poitrenaud, Clerc and Heymans is like playing Russian roulette with three bullets in a six-shooter. It was a see-saw game until Clerc's late try denied us a bonus point, all but ending our European campaign with two rounds remaining.

Things had already started to unravel at training, and it was becoming increasingly evident in our performances. I could see it in players' body language and little comments when Marcelo was out of ear-shot, not that he would have understood.

In January, Edinburgh beat us 17–12 at Murrayfield. It may have been a tough pool but we had never been consistently this poor on the road. We followed the coach's instructions to the letter: up went the ball, yielding a few penalties, but we were making life very difficult for ourselves. You expect trench warfare in games against Northampton or Wasps on winter surfaces, but some days the smart play is to vary the attack. All we did was kick and chase.

That was, until the boys eventually took matters into their own hands.

It wasn't a players' revolt as such, but when it became blatantly obvious that aerial bombardment was not leading to points we would play from memory. We had a team overflowing with brilliant strike runners: Tom Varndell was a try-scoring machine, and as soon as Alex or Seru broke the defensive line five points could usually be chalked up.

There are moments that tell you everything you need to know about a club. The last pool game at home to Leinster was one of them. There was a slight mathematical chance that both teams could still qualify, but Toulouse hammering Edinburgh at home would render any calculations irrelevant. We didn't care about that. This had nothing to do with the season ahead or the tactical approach of our coach. This was Leinster, with Jenno and Leo, now repatriated to their home province, returning to Welford Road. The boys were keen to roll out the bloodiest of red carpets.

It became one of those feral encounters we usually save for a do-or-die local derby or European knockout fixture. That's the best compliment we could have paid Leinster – it meant nothing, yet it meant everything. Julian White was lucky to only see yellow for clocking Mal O'Kelly; six minutes later, Goodey sparked a mini-riot in the mud when he almost decapitated Drico. Everyone piled in as our outhalf took a ten-minute break. Of course, the crowd interpreted two perfectly legitimate sin-binnings as high treason against their beloved Tigers. We opened the hurt locker and welcomed our opponents inside. It finished 25–9, just to even up the ledger in our latest Irish rivalry.

That same week I was named in the Six Nations squad. Denis Hickie had retired and Shane Horgan was injured, so I was picked on the left wing for a typical scrappy 16–11 defeat of Italy. I was switched to the right for Stade de France as Rob Kearney's selection on the left made it a trio of fullbacks in the back three.

It was a familiar Parisian experience. A Clerc hat-trick and another try by Heymans had us trailing 26–6 early in the second half. I was hammered in the press for going 'Awol', as Clerc's tries were a result of the French pouring down my wing. For his first try I was in the line, having just climbed out of a ruck. Still, my wing, my fault is the easy reasoning. Second try, faced with Skrela and Clerc, I had no chance. Third, same again, but in that case it was Heymans and Clerc.

I was amazed to be sent back out for the second half, but equally certain I would be discarded, come the Scottish game. The French, as is the norm after an electric start, faded badly as our pack minced them, pulling it back to 26–21. We had been battering away well into injury time when the ball came to me in the right corner. I made a decision to grubber in behind for Girv to chase, but Heymans got there first, hoofing it into the stand. Game over. I was disappointed it didn't come off but glad I had the balls to attempt the do-or-die play. In times gone by for Ireland, so gripped by the fear of being dropped, I'd have taken the safe option. This time, knowing I would be dropped regardless, I flung all my chips on the table and awaited the river card. It didn't come off, we lost, but at least I no longer felt constrained in a green jersey. Drop me all you like. I was long past being distraught.

Sure enough, on the Tuesday before we played Scotland at Croke Park I was sent packing. Tommy Bowe came on to the right wing, with Kearns holding his place and Shaggy in reserve. I wasn't even needed when Drico hurt himself, as Eddie turned to young Luke Fitzgerald.

'He wasn't particularly happy with his own game in Paris,' said O'Sullivan without ever hearing me say as much. 'He went out and gave it his best shot but it didn't work out for him and I've got to take cognizance of that and make a selection decision which is tough, but Geordan has bounced back before and that's the test for him again. There are tests within tests for players here at the end of the day.'

At no point in the day was that how I saw it.

I had no problem with young quality players like Lukey, Rob and Tommy getting their opportunity, but I assumed my Test career was over. It wasn't a case of bouncing back, as my form at club level was consistently above the average and had been for many years. It was a case of someone else getting injured. Different year, same old story.

Since I'd scored that try from fullback against Australia in November 2006, Ireland had played seventeen Test matches. I had been dropped from the squad six times, on the bench four times, picked on the wing four times, and had three runs at fullback.

The comedian Risteard Cooper had already written several satirical columns in the *Irish Times* about imaginary Eddie and Geordan conversations. That week gave him another under the headline: 'Murphy to blame but it's not Eddie's fault.'

The Irish rugby team hotel. E O'Sullivan breaks the bad news to G Murphy once again.

5.14 a.m.: EOS knocks on GM's door

EOS: Geordan, are you up? Open the door!

GM [*groan from within*]: Ah, Jeez what time is . . . Hold on a sec! [*door opens*] Sorry about that. Everything OK?

EOS: You having a bit of a lie-in are you?

GM: What time is it?

EOS: It's 5.15 in the morning.

GM: Right!

EOS: I wanted to have a word about the team for Saturday. You know me, Geordan, I'd give a berry to a badger, but sometimes you gotta move the ladder and change the light bulb, you understand me?

GM: Think so, yeah. Think it means you're blaming me for everything that went wrong in France, you're giving Tommy my place, dropping me from the squad and you're never going to pick me again?

EOS: There's no need for melodrama, Geordan. You can't stuff a marshmallow into a parking meter.

GM: OK, sorry I don't get that one.

EOS: You're a confidence player, Geordan. Everything that you do on a rugby field emanates from that. It's a brittle confidence and it needs to be nurtured sensitively and managed skilfully. What you need is someone you can go to when the chips are down, who you can talk to openly and honestly, who you rely on and trust. So will you ever go and f***ing find someone and give me a buzz when you come back.

Eddie closes door on G Murphy.

The Tigers had a big game at home to Sale that same Saturday, so I told myself that was where I belonged.

But there was one more twist.

Girv damaged his hip in training. I was recalled, legging it to East Midlands airport Thursday night without any clear indication whether I would be starting, on the bench or playing the familiar twenty-third-man gig. On Friday morning I was parachuted straight into the side at fifteen. My Achilles was sore but I dared not complain.

Eddie insisted, in real not imaginary comments, that this was all just a temporary inconvenience: 'Obviously Girvan is our starting fullback, there's no question about that, and Geordan is our number two fullback. I know he's very happy to be back.'

Imagine the dent in confidence for a guy reading those comments from his coach before a Test match? It was a disgraceful way to treat anyone. Thankfully, I was bulletproof by then.

★

There is a fine line between an outstanding performance and no performance at all. It is in the lap of the gods. When Rory Lamont burst through in the early stages that day, I could have been swatted aside, but I hit him hard and he went to ground. Soon after, I put a neat kick into Scottish territory that led to Wally going over off a scrum. I was involved in two more tries, plucking the ball from the sky and running a clean line off my old mucker at outside centre. Drico always knows the perfect moment to release others in better positions.

I thought it desperately pitiful that Eddie, in the immediate aftermath, felt the need to say: 'I'm delighted for Geordan but Girvan has been outstanding for Ireland at fullback.' It was true, Girv had been outstanding, but to say this after the performance I had just produced seemed very petty. 'He's a different type of player to Geordan and he's often maligned unfairly. But his strike rate is extraordinary. He's scored many key tries – against Georgia at the World Cup and against Italy in our first Six Nations match.'

After reading this, a friend of mine summed it up with a one-word text: 'Wow.'

The reporters asked about my unique build-up to the game. I said: 'Injured on a Monday, couldn't train. Left out of the twenty-two on Tuesday. Back to Leicester Tuesday night. Fitness test for Leicester on Wednesday. Got myself right. A bit of physio Thursday. Got a phone call. Back on a flight. Back over. In Thursday night. Possibility I'm going to be involved. Get up Friday morning and I'm in the team. Team run. Bit of homework last night. Thankfully things went all right today.'

I admit I enjoyed the Man of the Match announcement before the finish, yet I meant it when I said, 'The forwards probably wouldn't have heard it – they were all grafting away. We were busy doing our hair out the back. It probably should have gone to one of the forwards [Wally being the leading candidate with his try, twenty tackles and numerous carries] but, sure, it makes a better story for you guys. I thought it went OK. I made a few mistakes. I dropped the first high ball that was kicked in to me.'

I did. It's always the mistakes that you dwell on. Always harder to remember moments of excellence because they happen without consciousness. For the really special acts you are almost staring down at yourself wondering, *Is that really me?* It's not quite an out-of-body experience, but there is a calmness that seeps to your core. I've only ever felt it out on the grass.

Still, I knew what had just happened. I could play this sport for another twenty years and there would be no better way of giving Eddie the two fingers in response to how he'd treated me.

My Achilles wobbled against Leeds the next week, ruling me out of the Welsh game and allowing Rob his first run at fifteen. The match was hyped as Eddie versus Warren Gatland, the two having worked together with Ireland. Gatland not only won the coaching duel but captured a Grand Slam in his first season as an international coach. Wales had now pocketed two slams in what was supposedly our golden era.

I declared myself fit for England at Twickenham but pulled up after twenty minutes. I couldn't even struggle on until half-time to get some treatment – the Achilles was gone. The game remains notable for Danny Cipriani kicking the lights out as we were pummelled 33–10. Cipriani was hailed as the new messiah, but Johnno arrived in as England manager and saw it differently. Danny hasn't been capped since 2008.

Ranked third in the world just over a year before, we finished fourth in the Six Nations. The clamour for Eddie to resign came from even his most loyal supporters. Driving home from training that Wednesday, I switched on the radio to hear Eddie had fallen on his sword. Wonder how much that cost the IRFU.

I'm no trouble-maker, but I never felt comfortable under his leadership. At times, he seemed to be strategizing for his own self-preservation rather than focusing on the team's best interests. His contribution to Irish rugby must be recognized as valuable but, in so many ways, he stunted the growth of a unique generation of players.

Just as in the aftermaths of the two previous World Cups, the loss of players had prevented Leicester from making an impact in Europe in 2007/8, but we were determined to retain our Premiership title. We scrapped into fourth spot in the table, thanks to a typically dramatic

31–28 defeat of Dean Richards's Harlequins at Welford Road in our last game of the regular season. Qualification for next season's Heineken Cup and progress to an away semi-final in Gloucester were secured by Tom Varndell's late try, coupled with Sale losing to London Irish.

It was one of those Welford days that Deano himself used to orchestrate from the back of the scrum. It must have been tough for him to see the pandemonium unfold from the opposite side of the fence.

Having started the season so poorly, we were faced with the task of becoming the first Premiership club to win a play-off match on the road. Gloucester were still seething from the smashing we gave them in the previous year's final. Tries from Alex and Aaron kept us alive, but we were still two points adrift entering the seventy-eighth minute and were stuck down the wrong end of the field.

We have a move that unlocked the Gloucester defence in 2006 and sent me strolling under the posts. I insisted we run it a few times in training that week, but with a slight variation. I was trying to second-guess Leon, as I knew their coaches would tap into his knowledge of our playbook. Basically, I hoped they believed I was desperate enough to call a move on myself that had worked against them before.

It was a simple double skip pass by our twelve, missing the arriving blindside winger and thirteen, straight into my hands at full speed. I told Aaron my plan, which was to use my arrival as a decoy.

There we were, entrenched in our 22, when I roared the play as loud as I could. I ran a flat line, and when Tom came off the blindside wing James Simpson-Daniel was forced to split into the wide channel, but Aaron hit Danny Hipkiss, whose break carried us miles up the pitch. After two more phases Goodey slipped into the pocket and coolly dropped the goal. I got huge satisfaction from the manner of victory, as I had promised the lads that the move would work.

Now we had a chance to do to Dallaglio what Wasps had done to Johnno and Backy in 2005: send him into retirement with a final defeat. Of course we had to go and beat Wasps in the EDF semi-final (losing the final to the Ospreys), a result that maintained the established routine of the past five seasons. We do them in semis, they beat us in finals. The 26–16 loss turned out to be the dying sting of Wasps' greatest era.

I think the board would have sacked Marcelo even if we had retained the Premiership and EDF Cup. The relationship was doomed to fail from the outset. I was a senior player so, as in any good set-up, my opinion was sought. It was very difficult, because Marcelo was a decent man and an impressive rugby manager, but the language barrier, the outdated tactics and the lack of any established relationship with senior players meant he was not the right man for the Leicester job.

Around this time I was also asked by someone in the IRFU about Paddy Howard. I told them he was the best coach I had ever encountered, but the Ireland job eventually went to another man I held in high regard.

On my return from Ireland's summer tour of New Zealand and Australia, led by interim coach Michael Bradley, I was greeted by the South African, Heyneke Meyer, and his new coaching team, which included Cockers and a former Australian outhalf named Matt O'Connor. Matty's first session was slightly different from Marcelo's. I was impressed, and immediately confident that a new period of trophy-gathering was about to commence.

I was equally enthusiastic about my international career entering an Indian summer under Deccie. Same old problem: I just needed to get into the team. I knew I was running out of time.

15. Captain Murphy

The possibility of going back to play my club rugby in Ireland kept cropping up every time I negotiated a new Leicester contract.

Before signing my last deal in 2010, I spoke to Ulster or, more accurately, to David Humphreys. I've always respected Humphs and now he was director of rugby I was willing to hear his vision for Ulster rugby. I knew that up in Ravenhill they were sick of watching Munster, and then Leinster, winning European titles while Ulster got knocked out in the pool stages every season. They wanted to bridge the ever-widening gap. They were offering a two-year deal that was financially better than Leicester's three-year offer.

I had given ten long years to the Tigers and had just had a testimonial season, so this seemed like my last chance to leave. Ulster wanted an Irish fullback to go with their new foreign recruits, mainly from South Africa.

But I stayed at Leicester for one main reason: I love winning. It is the most addictive feeling I've ever experienced. While it looked like the building blocks were in place for Ulster to become a successful club, playing for Leicester is a guaranteed way of being in the shake-up for honours every season. Even in transitional seasons we are always there or thereabouts come April and May.

Moving to England as a teenager had made me a better player than I would have become staying in Ireland. This was because of the faith placed in me by the Leicester management, not to mention the talent of the players I worked alongside. I developed a loyalty to this place and a passion for the jersey. It's my club and I care about its present and future success.

Richard Cockerill told me once that before Leicester sign a player they try to get a handle on his personality. You can make any player with the right attitude better, but a tosser will always be a tosser.

Leicester is about the people in the club. We shy away from the flashier personalities that crop up on the market. It's no coincidence, I think, that the Hensons and the Ciprianis of this world are looking for a new club every couple of years.

We don't always get it right, but more often than not we nail it.

I suppose it was the captaincy that locked me into Leicester for life. You can't simply turn and walk away from that kind of responsibility, once it's been bestowed.

The first time I led the Tigers on to the field was 4 April 2009 against the Sale Sharks at Welford Road.

It was the business end of the season, and we were in a bit of turmoil. Heyneke Meyer had been forced to return to South Africa over Christmas due to a family illness, officially resigning at the end of January. Yet again, Richard Cockerill took over on a temporary basis. With club captain Martin Corry and vice captain Aaron Mauger both injured, along with Lewis, who was the longest-serving member of the squad, Cockers decided to put my experience to some formal use.

'Really?'

'Yeah, Geordie – captain. Do you want it or not?'

There was sniggering from my fellow messers down the back of the classroom when it was announced to the group.

That game against Sale is notorious for Julian White decking Andrew Sheridan. One punch. Well, one retaliatory punch.

We were 17–10 ahead with twenty-one minutes gone and I was thinking: this captaincy lark is no bother. Then the grizzled English props locked horns. The Sharks shunted our scrum backwards before the ball was put in, so Wayne Barnes signalled for a free kick. As they broke apart, Sheridan leaned and Julian shoved him away aggressively. Sheridan used his superior reach to land a quick left jab. Julian's instinctive reaction was to counter with a perfect right cross that dropped Sheridan. In fairness to the big man, he got straight back up. It was about to blow up but the Sale forwards hesitated. None of them fancied going toe-to-toe with Julian, not even Scotland's hard-hitting flanker, Jason White, who was immediately on the scene but flinched away from Julian's re-cocked fist. The touch judge was inches away. The Sale captain, Juan Martín Fernández Lobbe, broke it up.

My first interaction with Wayne – or with any referee for that matter – as a captain went as follows:

'Clear punch, straight to the face . . .'

Be polite, a yellow card is coming. 'Yep,' I replied.

'No option.'

Out comes the red for Julian. Nothing for Sheridan. My jaw hit the floor. No idea what to do. There's Julian walking off the pitch, punished for landing a cleaner dig, basically. Lobbe called for another scrum.

So there I was on my first day leading the Tigers and we were reduced to fourteen men during a massive game at Welford Road. When I recovered from the initial shock, I realized this was a no-lose situation.

I looked around and everyone was switched on. With Julian gone, the other seven forwards built themselves into a bitter rage.

The Tigers' way of doing battle commenced. The seven-man pack was belligerent while Alex, Dan Hipkiss and myself made the necessary incisions out wide. Jesus, I ran hard that day. As captain of Leicester I was following some of the greatest men in English rugby history. I had to play well, talk later.

Not long after Julian walked, a high ball came dropping from the heavens just outside our 22. I knew my life depended on catching it. So I did, and then carried sixty metres upfield as well. The crowd went crazy on this, the last day before the old Cat stand was demolished. All 17,498 of them already believed they were attending a special occasion for that reason alone. And now it was being spoiled by this travesty! Julian White, who is practically a choir boy, sent off! They weren't having that. We are literally Tigers on days like this. Lads fire their bodies into everything, and it gets niggly – one thing about a red card is the referee tends to show only one per team per game.

Of course Julian deserved to be sent off, but when we're within the confines of that rectangular patch of grass for those eighty minutes we are detached from the reasoning of everyday life. It is warfare, focused violence. It is very hard to explain – the feeling of being out there – as everything is happening so fast. You are just in it.

In our eyes we have been wronged. How dare they do this to us in our house! The crowd react to our actions and the players are lifted by the reverberating sound in our ears. Kill or be killed. You can feel the hairs on the back of your neck stand up.

I remember the first time I experienced this sensation. At Gaelic football matches as a boy – the local club championship – when the early scalping dies down and scores start sailing over the bar, the crowd descends into an animalistic state of consciousness. It has to be intimidating to opponents. I remember the thrill as a boy watching my father, brothers and their friends work themselves into this rage. I realized: we are allowed to do this! Every so often I see a young boy, wide-eyed, watching the madness unfold at Welford Road. I know he will be a Tiger for life.

There is a belief that surges through the collective pysche in these moments. Manchester United and Munster have turned it into an art form: you just know when something goes wrong in a game that the performance levels of those clubs will improve, regardless of the personnel on the field. Some teams start arguing among themselves; Leicester players mould together into one being.

Thankfully, on my first day at the helm, the Leicester Way guided us home. We won 37–31, scoring five tries and thus gaining a bonus point that put us one point clear at the top of the Premiership.

It was a happy changing room afterwards. Lads were broken up, slumped against the dingy wall, legs sprawled, but everyone was smiling. Even Julian. No rush to the showers, just some old-fashioned banter among mates.

Someone was tugging at my arm, 'Interviews, Geordie.'

Of course. Being captain means occasionally missing those post-match moments with teammates.

It means a lot of things.

My relationship with Lucie had ended around the time I was made temporary captain, and I went through a tough period.

It was a perfect example of the old saying that when your career is going brilliantly your personal life must be in crisis. I couldn't mope around feeling sorry for myself. I had a new, all-consuming role at the club. I also had to give a lot more thought to what I would say to my teammates before games.

At the same time, I was waiting for everyone to see sense. Cozza or Aaron would return or the captaincy would be given to an English forward, which was the normal order of things.

I am the happy-go-lucky joker in the Leicester squad, always having a laugh, a laissez-faire attitude to everything away from rugby. It will be all right in the end, has always been my motto. Doesn't scream leader now, does it? Certainly not in the mould of the men I was following. I'm no Johnson or Corry.

Maybe it was because I'd played alongside these leaders that Cockers felt something must have rubbed off on me. Maybe he just wanted to go with someone he would be picking for most games.

Or maybe he just lost the plot. He was certainly taking a risk.

But, thinking about it now, I had become more vocal at team meetings since around 2006. When Johnno, Backy and several others departed I became a senior player. The captaincy was a natural progression.

Thankfully, the club hadn't heard about my involvement in a certain incident involving the Academy boys.

There is always a bit of fun to be had with young fellas at a club – harmless stuff where places get egged or somebody's car is filled with corn flakes or stealing car keys and moving the car so they think it is stolen.

A few of the Academy boys were getting out of hand, so the senior players intervened. We hired a big white van, got balaclavas, and tipped off one of the guys in the Academy house to leave the door unlocked.

We pulled up on this little street near the centre of Leicester, piled out of the van and into the house, where we terrified the three boys chilling on their couch. Andy Goode was in the kitchen smashing plates; others went upstairs, pretending to ransack the place (OK, they did ransack the place).

We tied the boys up and threw them into the van. A neighbour saw it. We were driving down Arbour Road when a police car cut us off.

'What's going on, gentlemen?'

'Nothing, officer.'

'Who's in the back?'

'Eh . . .'

'Open the doors, please.'

Balacavas were promptly removed and the Academy boys untied as several senior Leicester Tigers filed out of the van.

The police saw the funny side of it.

That 2008/9 campaign was probably the most hectic I ever experienced at the club. The Leicester board were determined to get the best possible coaching structures in place after the Loffreda season.

It was no great secret that, were it not for the politics of South African rugby, Heyneke Meyer would have been named Springbok coach ahead of Peter de Villiers in 2008. His record was impeccable, having guided the Blue Bulls to four Currie Cups and then, in 2007, become the first South African franchise to win the Super 14 title.

Yes, he had a ferociously talented pack at his disposal, including Victor Matfield, Bakkies Botha and Pierre Spies, along with one of the best scrumhalves of all time in Fourie du Preez, the kicking machine that is Morne Steyn and Bryan Habana on the wing. But Heyneke gelled it all together.

At Leicester he immediately gave off the air of a dictator. That is not meant as a slight; dictators have proven extremely successful throughout the history of team sports. It was a pity that Heyneke didn't get the opportunity to create a legacy of his own in English rugby, because he had the rugby brain coupled with the personal touch.

The man is extremely competitive. Unfortunately, that worked against him when we concocted a management race to break the monotony of a gruelling pre-season camp. Ireland have done this over the years as well and it's entertaining to watch the men wielding the whips (OK, whistles) slogging it out. Certain older coaches were given a ten- or fifteen-metre head start over a hundred-metre dash.

Heyneke was nervous about it as he was out of shape. After about twenty metres he went down, got up, battled on for about fifty

metres, down again, eventually hobbled over the line. He had ruptured his Achilles tendon.

We trudged off to the showers where the inevitable talk started.

'Jesus, we broke our latest coach in just three weeks!'

'That's a new club record.'

'What the hell is wrong with us?'

The injury made it very difficult for Heyneke to get a hold of
the group as he was largely confined to a golf buggy for the next
month or so.

Again, like Loffreda, the philosophy was perhaps a little too blunt
for our liking. The idea was to transfer the Bulls' direct approach to
the Tigers. Smash it up, smash it up and smash it up some more.
Replace Argentinian rugby with the South African model. It was
slightly more advanced, but still not transferable to a full Premier-
ship/European season.

Club rugby's main difference from international level is the
number of games. The direct approach simply cannot be adopted
week in, week out because most teams arrive at Welford Road thinking if they can front up, half the battle is won. We've been aware of
this for years, so we developed a versatile tactical approach. If we
don't have a range of different arrows in the quiver, then eventually
we are found out. An average rugby team can match their opponents
in a brawl, but come the definitive moments of any contest, the ability to pick off inferior opposition with skill and intelligence will
ultimately dictate the result.

Heyneke did introduce some really positive, lasting elements during his time at the club. We may not have agreed with all his tactical
ideas, but at least there was clarity to how he wanted us to play, and
I have no doubt he would have eventually mastered the northern
hemisphere club game.

Fitness standards were raised. We used to have these brutally tough
running sessions, and at the end Heyneke would ask for five players
to step forward. Each man had to kick a penalty from thirty metres
out or there would be extra circuits. It was about fostering a mentality of unity once the white heat of games descended. I'd know, just
by looking at a stockier teammate, that he didn't believe he could

make the kick, so I'd say something. He might need to relax or be given a routine, not having place-kicked for a while. Or ever.

(Later in the season, long after Heyneke had returned home, we would reap the benefits of this exercise.)

He also introduced an awards system that is still used at the club. The Buffalo award went to the forward who did the most work – tackles, carries, hitting rucks. The Ant award went to the hardest-working back. There'd be a mini-ceremony every Monday after a game. Really, it was a fresh, light-hearted way of analysing our stats. It worked. I always wanted to be the Ant. It got me into a few extra rucks and ensured some additional work was done on whatever part of my game dipped on the previous week's chart.

Heyneke was an old-fashioned Afrikaner with a deep attachment to rugby. He respected hard work above all else. It is not about the guy who scores three tries, it is about the unseen bruiser who smashes twenty-four rucks and makes twenty tackles. If he saw you clinging on in there, doing something worthwhile late in a game, he would seek you out for back slap.

We were playing Bath at The Rec in November. It was vicious stuff. The only way out was to grind it. With three minutes remaining I kicked a conversion after a try by Melfin Davies that put us ahead, having been 20–3 down at half-time.

We lost, due to a crazy bounce. Alex Crockett got there first and made an insane offload from the ground to put Butch James over for a try in injury time.

Bath's Aussie forwards coach Mark Bakewell came running into the in-goal area. 'HAVE SOME OF THAT!' he roared in my face. I don't know how I didn't smack him. I hesitated and he was gone. I'd have got a serious ban. Heyneke came up to me afterwards and thanked me for kicking the conversion. That impressed me.

I was back place-kicking owing to a number of unforeseen circumstances. Derick Hougaard, who had been capped eight times at outhalf by the Springboks, had joined us from the Bulls. Before arriving, Derick received a steroid injection in his ass to treat an injury, but it got infected. He turned up with a hole in his buttock a centimetre deep and the size of your palm, so he couldn't train. It was

horrendous. The club spent eight weeks trying to heal up his buttock, and then his appendix burst. He came back again, and something
else went. Derick ended up making just thirteen appearances for the
club.

Toby Flood was another new signing, leaving us well stocked at
ten, until he tore his Achilles. Sam Vesty took over at fly-half and our
new French scrumhalf, Julien Dupuy, became the primary place-
kicker that season. But he was off the field against Bath, so kicking
duties came back around to me.

Heyneke wisely brought in a new backroom team. Almost immediately Matty O'Connor won over the smaller, faster players since he
is another drenched in the ACT Brumbies' attacking philosophy.
However, John McFarland didn't work out as defensive coach. Again,
he came with a great reputation from the Bulls, but there were some
personality clashes with the players.

After Heyneke's departure, John phoned up Cockers, saying he
was having a tough time, and asked for a few days off. It was a Tuesday and we had a game Saturday so Cockers told him he could have
one day. He said he would return Monday. See you Thursday or don't
bother coming back at all, was the response. He never came back.

Cockers had slipped into the hot seat once again that December.
We all remember the iconic face-off with Norm Hewitt, the All Black
hooker, during the haka in his first Test match at Old Trafford in 1997.
No surprise that Darren Garforth was perched on his shoulder either.
A miracle that it didn't kick off before the kick-off. Cockers sidled up
to Johnno after the confrontation, expecting a nod of approval, but
Johnno was not happy: 'Cockers, what the fuck have you done?'

Richard's default mode is still anger – straight to red. But he is director of rugby now and has matured no end. Every step of the way,
he has learned and become a better coach and better manager. It
might not be evident on match days, but he is way more clinical in his
actions. He has to be.

Cockers has got in trouble for, eh, communicating with officials
and assessors during games. He was also caught on camera one time
wellying the wooden stand. A full-on freak-out. Better than kicking
a player, was the defence put forward. I suppose he's right.

There is a glass partition surrounding his area nowadays – Cockers' Cage we call it.

At the end of the season the board made Matt O'Connor head coach, with Richard promoted to Director of Rugby. Matt has a serious rugby brain, doing our attack and defensive tactics, while Cockers oversees everything. He still gets his hands dirty for breakdown work, scrums and lineouts, but Matt is the head coach. Ego doesn't get in the way of their working relationship. The partnership works, as results since January 2009 have proven.

In a repeat of 2006, we came up against Bath in the Heineken Cup quarter-finals at the Walkers Stadium. It was locked at 15-all entering the last ten minutes. My mind gets a little hazy when I try to recall anything from that match after my encounter with Matt Banahan. Sammy was right to fling out the skip pass, but I glanced up and knew the eighteen-stone winger was gambling all his chips on destroying me. This happens every now and again; you know the train is coming but you can't get off the tracks in time. I also knew Alex was on my inside shoulder, so I took the pass, offloaded and got obliterated.

We made maybe half a yard, but that's not the point. Alex did something similar to Nick Abendanon soon after, but he was slightly later and received a month's suspension for it.

The game ended in spectacular fashion. As we piled on the pressure, myself and Sammy slipped into drop-goal positions either side of an attacking ruck. Not only did it confuse the Bath blockers, but when Dupuy looked back he was unsure who to pass to, so he dummied and wheeled through the ruck, stepping the last man for a try under the posts.

Next stop: the Millennium Stadium against the Cardiff Blues. There was added motivation for me, with an Irish club waiting in the final: Leinster and Munster were scrapping it out in the other semi at Croke Park.

We were back in familiar territory: a season's run-in where each game could potentially define the campaign. Win, and move on. Lose, and it was over.

After Cardiff, Bath were again waiting in the Premiership

semi-final, followed by two finals on back-to-back weekends. If we made it that far. The double that we won in 2001 and 2002, and failed to complete in 2007, was back on the table.

We were coasting against Cardiff, up 26–12, thanks to my second-half try and the accuracy of Dupuy's boot, when everything fell apart.

First Toby Flood tore his Achilles; then I got sin-binned, for the second time in a competitive fixture, and again the referee was Alain Rolland.

It felt desperately harsh at the time, especially considering Craig Newby, our Kiwi flanker, was already cooling off for ten minutes. Cardiff had an overlap in our 22, so I went for the intercept, getting one hand to the ball before it went to ground. I couldn't believe he was calling me over.

I felt like saying, 'Rollers, I'm the captain!' But when the card comes out, all you can do is turn and jog off the field. Thirteen men against fifteen, Cardiff tore into us.

Newby returned just as Jamie Roberts powered over for a try. We were clinging on and the big Welsh centre was cutting us to ribbons. It was so hectic that Johne Murphy can be forgiven for not realizing I wasn't on the field. Roberts, again, made the initial break. Johne was covering their winger, Tom James, but not gunning for him. I could see from his body language that he thought I was covering in behind him. Now he was waiting for me to reappear in his peripheral vision. I could see it all happening in slow motion. James got over in the corner and even managed to knee Johne in the balls in the process (he couldn't walk properly for a week afterwards). Ben Blair kicked the conversion from the touchline. I returned to 26-all and extra time.

Our fitness seemed superior in those twenty additional minutes and we got into drop-goal range, but Johne's decent effort sailed wide.

We almost got in trouble over the Dan Hipkiss blood substitution. Dan had a cut on his head. They stitched him up, he had headgear on. He got another bang, took his headgear off, went over to the touch judge and showed him the opened stitches. It was only a trickle of blood, but the touch judge agreed. This meant we could bring Dupuy, a goal-kicker, back into the game only a couple of minutes before a likely place-kicking shoot-out.

This had the potential to become controversial. The 'bloodgate' affair during the Harlequins–Leinster quarter-final a few weeks earlier at The Stoop, when the officials were duped into thinking Tom Williams had a blood injury so Quins could get their kicker, Nick Evans, back on the field for a late penalty or drop goal, was a big talking-point.

But despite what Martin Offiah wrote in a newspaper column afterwards, the Dan Hipkiss decision was legitimate: he really was bleeding.

All we had to do was find Dupuy. Having been replaced, Julien had gone for a smoke, as French scrumhalves tend to do, with our director of operations, Simon Cohen.

Somebody found him, and he came trotting back on with his laces open.

A kick-off was uncharted territory for everyone. There was no planning. It was just a case of, 'Who wants to take one?'

Five guys raised their hands.

We led off with Dupuy, Sammy and then me, the solid, reliable kickers, although I thought for a split second I'd missed. Place-kick, dead centre on the 22, but it's desperately nerve-racking. As a thirteen-year-old I would've backed myself every time. In fact I have never missed anywhere near the posts, but I had a terrible mindset walking up. Was this to be the one time? What if the ground gives way like it did to David Beckham and John Terry? What if . . . Oh God. My strike was a bit of a wobbler but it got between the posts.

Johne had been working quite hard on his goal-kicking with Dusty Hare at the club, and had kicked for the seconds, but he pulled his shot left and wide. Four–three to Cardiff, with Tom James strolling up with a kick to make the final. He had been place-kicking in the Welsh camp with Neil Jenkins. This was over.

I called the lads into a huddle. Certain things needed saying. 'Be proud, none of us have let anyone down here today. We need to refocus immediately, we have a Premiership title to win . . .'

Really, I was thinking: fucking nightmare, we had this and we gave it away. Very un-Leicester-like of us, and it was on my watch. With Johnson or Corry as captain we would never have lost.

I glanced up to see James go through the usual kicker's routine, steps and everything, before shanking it well right.

Hello?

Scott Hamilton's kick sent it into sudden death. Tom Shanklin put his foot through their sixth penalty. Who is going to take our next one? Aaron Mauger walked up. You would bet the house on this world-class footballer delivering. Just like Italy wanted Roberto Baggio to be taking a penalty in the 1994 World Cup final . . . but that didn't go so well, now, did it? Again, the brain lets terrible thoughts creep in.

Despite his back injury, Aaron struck it perfectly.

Their scrumhalf, Richie Rees, approached the next penalty like a footballer and chipped it inches over the crossbar. He was smiling but I bet his insides had plummeted south.

Craig Newby stepped up next for us. Flanker or not, he's a Kiwi so most rugby skills are in the locker from childhood. The contact was mechanically sound, the ball flew high and true.

Six-all from seven shots.

Martyn Williams, a great player and the good guy of Welsh rugby, was up next. He missed.

Jordan Crane was next for us. He had been an underage goalkeeper with West Bromwich Albion, so we knew he could kick the ball. After that our cupboard was bare. We have a great pack of forwards, but they are absolute hackers. The ABC Club is legendary, but they will not win a penalty shoot-out.

I had no interest in celebrating after Jordan nailed his penalty – I just went and shook hands with the Cardiff players. It was no way to win a European semi-final. It is a soccer solution to a rugby problem and that didn't sit well with rugby people.

There was so much joking about it on the bus home that the following Tuesday at training those who didn't raise their hands were forced to kick for goal. Lewis Moody hit the corner flag while Julian White buried it in the bottom corner.

★

The same weekend that we beat Cardiff, in a dramatic power-shift in Irish rugby Leinster tanked Munster in the other semi-final at Croke Park.

Leinster, of course, it would have to be them. But that final was another twenty days away. We had to shelve Europe immediately as there was a six-day turnaround before facing Bath, again, at the Walkers Stadium in the Premiership semi-final. It was a comfortable victory this time, setting up a Twickenham meeting with London Irish and my old mate, Bob Casey.

The photo shoot for the programme cover was a good giggle. Kildare's finest leading out the two leading English clubs on the biggest day of the season. Although educated at Blackrock College, Bob hails from Maynooth. We played against each other during our schooldays, were teammates at Ireland under-21, and ever so briefly at senior level. He won his second cap against the USA in the summer of 2000 when I won my first.

I've catalogued my struggles under Eddie O'Sullivan's regime, but they pale in comparison to what Bob went through. While I have seventy-odd caps, Bob got seven – and none at all under Eddie, despite being considered one of the best locks in the Premiership during those years.

Bob's achievements at London Irish speak for themselves, but unfortunately there isn't a Premiership medal to go with them. We beat the Exiles 10–9 in a scrappy final. I ended up with the Man of the Match award. It rained, so plenty of ball was launched into the sky and I didn't drop any of it. It was a solid performance, but really the award was another case of the forwards being overlooked because my pretty touches were easier to see.

Martin Corry was still club captain so he lifted the trophy. I happily stepped aside. It was the end of his career as he was losing the race to make it back for one last game. Even to this day, you mention his name in my brother Ross's presence and he'll tell you the story, with deep affection, about how his good friend Martin Corry made Eric Miller slow down to ensure he found the way to Coventry in Jimmy Ferris's Datsun Cherry for my first big game, all those years ago. 'Honest, Coz, he even removed the bollards so I could park behind the team bus. Sound man. Sound man.'

★

In the space of twenty days we played the Millennium Stadium, the Walkers, Twickenham and finally Murrayfield. This is what Leicester Tigers are all about – moving from one great arena to the next.

There is a backstory to the Heineken Cup final I haven't spoken about before. I was half blind and badly struggling with a bilateral hernia.

Delon Armitage poked me in the eye during the first half of the Premiership final. He went to block down my kick near the corner flag and got his thumb stuck in my right eye, scratching my retina for a third time.

The pain of a scratched retina is incessant and untreatable. Pain-killers don't work – trust me, I've tried them. It is a paper cut on your eye. It started swelling on the Twickenham pitch after the game. I tried celebrating on the bus home but it wasn't happening. I immediately knew playing in Edinburgh was unlikely. Eye-drops help a little but it is a horrendous injury. I lay on my sofa, in complete darkness, for three full days, convinced I wasn't going to make it.

On Thursday I went training and tried to explain to the coaches that I couldn't see out of my right eye.

'Well, you can train, Geordie,' Matty and Cockers both agreed. They wanted me on the field. Cozza and Aaron were not being selected due to injury, and Lewis was only fit enough to make the bench. George Chuter and Ben Kay would be out there, but it was easily the most inexperienced Tigers side to contest a European final.

I went training on Tuesday in a pair of Adidas sunglasses. The boys were in hysterics even before I started dropping balls.

On the Wednesday we had another training session. The coaches asked to see me afterwards. Jogging over, I felt a darting pain in my stomach and was doubled up in agony.

I had thrown myself into the path of Delon's blockier little brother, Steffon Armitage, the previous Saturday. Steffon broke a tackle down the right touchline and picked up a head of steam. He's a cannonball, so I tried to get myself as low as possible, but he bowled me over on to my arse. I held on and got shredded. I felt a sharp pain in my pelvis but, Premiership final, you get up and play on.

I was more concerned about my lack of clear vision, until that sharp pain returned.

Cockers and Matty asked me straight out: 'Geordie, are you fit to play?'

They were more concerned about my eye than some abdominal complaint. It hadn't yet been established that my intestines were protruding through an ever-widening tear in the wall of my abdomen. It was my call.

'Hundred per cent. Ready to go.'

That's what they wanted to hear. That's what everyone wanted to hear. European final. Find me a player who would say otherwise and I'll show you a guy masquerading as a rugby player.

The team had lost its captain, two outhalves and an All Black playmaker. Half blind and flying on one wing will have to do. They gave me some anti-inflammatories before we travelled up to Scotland that afternoon.

Physically I may have been screwed, but mentally I was tuned in. I knew there might not be another day like this.

I looked like a plank at the pre-match interview, wearing the shades. Someone asked about the glasses. 'Just keeping the sponsors happy, looking for a new deal from Adidas.'

The *Irish Independent* put my mug on the front of their sports section: 'We'll put Leinster in the shade.' Most reports stated I had damaged my eye in the Premiership final, but the seriousness of it did not come out. Or so we thought.

The reporters were more interested in comments attributed to my parents that they would be cheering for Leinster. A reporter had called the house. George and Cecily were being polite. 'I think they were just put on the spot,' I explained, before joking, 'They'll be wearing Leicester colours or else they're not getting their tickets.'

Also, earlier in the week, I was adjudged to have made some mischievous comments about Leinster still being more of a Dublin club than representative of the entire province.

'A lot of my friends and people from my area have never really felt part of Leinster rugby, and it hardly helps when Naas have been given an allocation of just thirty tickets. Sure, I'll probably be sending home more than that many myself.

'A lot of people from places like Carlow, Kilkenny, Kildare and Wexford align themselves with Munster. That's because it's like the "country" team, whereas Leinster are the "city" boys.

'I know the lads will tell you Shane [Horgan] is from Meath and Rob [Kearney] is from Cooley. But they're Dublin boys. It will be strange playing a game of this magnitude against my native province. But I'm hoping Leicester will pick up a good bit of the Munster support.'

There was a bit of truth in this, and a bit of trouble-making. In the past few years, fuelled in part by their great success, Leinster's support base has widened across the province, but I knew what it was like to feel that if you were not in Dublin you were not on Leinster's radar.

On the way back to the hotel after the press conference, Cockers offered me the club captaincy on a permanent basis.

'If you have got no one better,' I said. 'I won't be offended if you find a forward to do the job.'

I still didn't know why he was asking me.

'Think about it, Geordie.'

I did think about it, and accepted a few days later. What I'd learned from captaining the side during that season was that the captaincy forces you into the firing line – as the guy who has to talk to the media, but also on the pitch. The really successful captains don't say a lot. They just do. Since becoming captain I had frequently launched myself into the sky for balls I would normally not be able to get. I caught a few and realized the lads expected me to do it all the time.

This was my role, but during the run-up to the Heineken Cup final my physical defects planted doubts in my mind. I hoped for an overcast day in Edinburgh so I could see the dropping ball.

Naturally, when I pulled the curtains back on the morning of the match I was greeted by heavenly rays and blue skies.

I went out for the coin toss. Bob Casey had been the opposing captain the week before; now it was Leo Cullen. Funny old world.

Leo called it in the air. We were on a ten-game winning streak and I'd lost the previous ten coin tosses, but this time Leo called it wrong.

'We'll receive the kick-off,' was all I said. It didn't matter. I had to win a toss eventually and a European final is different from anything else. The adrenalin had numbed the pain in my side. I didn't need to see clearly, just play from memory. I looked around the changing room and there was no Corry or Johnson, Back or Deano togging out, but I reminded each and every one of the men in that room what they were.

The Tigers went to work.

Saturday, 23 May 2009
Leinster v. Leicester Tigers, Murrayfield
Jonny Sexton drops the kick-off right down my throat.

'My ball!'

A blue jersey whizzes past. Isa Nacewa. I gather but Shaggy is there to wrap me up. The forwards pile in as I slip out the side of the maul. Leinster scrum, deep in our 22, dead in front of the posts. Worst start possible. Jenno trips someone so we get a relieving penalty.

I find a decent touch.

Ball comes back to me off next lineout and I belt it low towards Luke Fitzgerald in the Leinster 22. Jenno gives up another penalty. Dupuy misses.

Only five minutes gone in a hectic match, Sexton again comes looking to target me in the air out on Shaggy's wing, but he over-cooks the garryowen and I claim it over Scotty Hamilton's head.

'My ball . . . mark.'

They are definitely looking to put the ball in behind Alex and target me. Good. I am in pain, my vision is blurred, but my mind is in Cup final mode. I want the ball.

I catch the sweet spot, sending it over the Leinster 10-metre line and into touch. Darce takes it quickly and feeds it to Lukey, who goes up high again. Ben Woods spills it after Lukey's tackle and Jenno gallops into space. It gets to Rocky Elsom in a wide channel. He runs at Alex and bumps him off, but Ayoola Erinle is there to take him down.

The Leinster crowd let out a roar. Our defence realigns but it comes back to Drico, who sticks a drop goal, turning and heading back to halfway before it lands.

Six minutes, 0–3.

Everything is dimmer than it should be and my side is killing me. I already know there isn't eighty minutes in my tank.

Their main men – Drico and Rocky – have clearly settled. So have the entire Leinster team. Time to make my presence felt. Sexton sends another high ball. I take it, and hoist my own garryowen. Lukey fumbles and I pounce on it, twisting a yard or two along the ground. Quick ruck ball allows Dan Hipkiss to thunder into the 22. Jamie Heaslip doesn't roll away in the tackle.

Dupuy converts, 3–3, and our forwards seem nice and angry now.

Next I remember, we have a lineout inside our 22. Dupuy tries to clear but big Mal O'Kelly blocks down. Myself and Mal are in a sprint as the ball trickles over the try-line. He has a few yards' head start, but I get there ahead of him and walk up to take the drop out, which I send long. It goes straight to Shaggy, who launches it straight back up to me. Even Shaggy is sending it up! No question, they are targeting me.

I gather but get smashed by Jamie. My offload bounces off Jamie's head and into Rocky's hands on our 22. We eventually force a turnover and Dupuy gives it to Sam Vesty, whose punt doesn't find touch, but it's in their half again so we should be OK.

Sexton gets it and fires a massive drop goal from the halfway line, about fifteen metres in from touch.

Ah Jesus, 3–6.

It gets worse. George Chuter doesn't find Ben Kay at the back of a lineout in our 22, Sexton half breaks and offloads to Darce, who is flying. This is a try. No. Woods and Newby hold him up, but we are in all sorts of trouble. Every Leinster player has shown up.

Rocky batters off three attempted tackles. Drico draws a penalty from Nigel Owens. Sexton steps up to make it 3–9. Amazing to think the twenty-three-year-old couldn't get on the Leinster bench a few months ago. Only injury to Felipe Contepomi saw him come into the semi-final against Munster.

We are trying everything to get into this game. We kick the restart to the blindside wing, away from the forwards, where Scotty gets above Nacewa but knocks on. Jordan Crane is not right, so Lewis Deacon comes on and Crofty moves to the backrow.

Leinster put it into our 22 again. Danny Hipkiss has clearly had enough, setting off on a forty-metre dash before grubbering towards the Leinster line. Crofty is haring after it but he is blocked by Lukey as Jonny fly hacks into touch.

Finally, after thirty minutes we have an attacking lineout five metres out. You must score in finals when these opportunities arise. Crofty takes Chuter's throw off the top and Alex is launched towards Jonny. Jenno gets across and hits him low.

We work the phases, like we always do. I slip in to first receiver, show to pass wide, step Jackman but get tackled by Leo. Dupuy goes back the short side and offloads to Sammy, but Stan Wright takes a gamble and nails him before the ball arrives. Flag is out. Wright is off to the bin with a little pat from his opposite number, Castro.

Dupuy makes it 6–9. Not bad for what we have had to weather. A try would have been nice, though.

The momentum swings our way. Danny is playing sensational rugby with the ball tucked under his arm. Crofty is carrying well too. Dupuy is directing operations from the base. We keep breaking the gainline. Leinster sprinted out of the blocks, but they might be blowing. That happens in finals.

Sammy gets the ball out of contact to Ben Woods, who bounces Nacewa and carries Darce over the line.

Dupuy's conversion makes it 13–9.

I'm a passenger now. The adrenalin has worn off and I am in agony – playing a European final with a double hernia. The medics missed it because I was at home all week, lying in a dark room.

I can feel one of my organs bulging into a sac just above my groin. I'm in tatters. The ball is ping-ponging around and I'm not even looking for it. I need the changing room. Eventually it ends up in Ben Kay's mitts. He fires it back to me.

The pain is forgotten. I could kick it dead but Leinster are behind, let's send it back to them and see if they make a mistake – that's what finals are about: you pressurize your opponents into error – but Nacewa kicks it dead.

The coaches are keen for me to head back out, and because it's a European final I agree, but I know I'm a liability to the team now. I may have fooled the Leinster players up to now, but they are about to notice a glaring weak link in their opponents' backfield.

Five minutes into the second half, Rocky makes another rampaging run down our right wing, going through three men. Crofty gets back to collar him and the next ball is for Jackman on the charge. I am at the edge of the ruck, so Cian Healy cleans me out.

From the impact, I lose the will to live. I go down on one knee in agony. Drico sees as much and puts a dink in behind. It is a Leinster lineout in our 22. I can't go on. Nigel Owens asks if I'm all right. I walk off as Matt Smith comes on and Scotty switches to fullback.

Murrayfield – the place will never give me peace.

From the lineout Jenno drives Jamie over our line. Jonny's conversion makes it 16-all. The final goes on without me.

The match descends into brutal hand-to-hand combat. Jonny's penalty on seventy minutes decides it.

The lads did brilliantly, performing like Tigers, to be in with a chance at the death, but I still feel we should've done better. It still hurts. We had been the best team in England that year by some distance. We had coped excellently with everything thrown at us.

Experience won it for Leinster. Brian O'Driscoll, Leo Cullen, Shane Jennings, Shane Horgan – men who can find their way home on a pitch-black night from memory alone.

It was their time, but I can't help thinking about what Martin Corry would have done. I have no doubt he would have made it his dying act as a rugby player to smash Elsom, halt him in his tracks.

16. Twenty-five Slam Minutes

During an interview a few years ago Declan Kidney was asked his biggest regret in rugby. He said it was cutting young fellas from the cup team in Pres Cork. When he became Ireland head coach in 2008 I suppose I felt like one of the schoolboys he had to leave out when he was a teacher. More often than not, he couldn't find room for me in his starting XV.

I don't know if Deccie knows the game as well as Eddie, but he is approachable. He's a decent man and a clever motivator, and I enjoyed working with him throughout my career, from Ireland under-19s, to 'A' level and up to his time as assistant coach.

In October 2008, in the run-up to his first set of autumn internationals as head coach, Deccie and the new team manager, Paul McNaughton, travelled to England to meet Irish players there. This gave all of us hope. False hope, as it turned out. The problem wasn't the new Irish coaching ticket; it was Premier League Rugby (PLR), the umbrella group for top-tier English clubs which decreed that no player could be released for national squad sessions outside the IRB Test window. By contrast, players with the Irish provinces are centrally contracted with the IRFU, so Deccie can take them whenever he likes. Leicester always understood my desire to represent my country, but if they released me the PLR could hit them with a fine or even dock them points.

This was a real disadvantage for Irish guys playing in England. Mike Ross, for example, didn't get his opportunity until he moved from Harlequins to Leinster. The PLR rule also dented Bob Casey's chances of ending his eight-year exile. For my own part, I saw the departure of Eddie and the arrival of Deccie as my chance to nail down the number fifteen jersey which had proved so elusive since I was dropped in 2006.

★

I was named in the squad for the November matches against Canada, New Zealand and Argentina, but because I had been released by Leicester just two days before the team was selected, I missed a week of Ireland camp. It was not a surprise when Keith Earls was picked at fullback to play Canada in Thomond Park, but I was disappointed when Girvan was named at fullback for the All Blacks match, with Rob and Tommy on the wings and Earlsey on the bench.

Ireland were convincingly beaten by New Zealand – in what proved Girv's last international – and I was recalled at fullback to face Argentina. Six of our starting fifteen – Rob and Tommy on the wings, Luke Fitzgerald at inside centre, Tomás O'Leary at scrumhalf, and Stephen Ferris and Jamie Heaslip in the backrow – were young players who had not even been in the squad that had faced the Pumas at the World Cup just over a year earlier.

There would be serious repercussions if Ireland lost. The new coaching team, comprising Declan, Alan Gaffney, Gert Smal and Les Kiss, with Mark Tainton and Mervyn Murphy kept on, were only too aware that defeat against the Pumas at Croke Park would see us ranked ninth in the world and therefore third seeds for the 2011 World Cup draw that followed a week later. That would probably mean an even tougher pool than the one we encountered as second seeds in 2007.

The whole Argentinian-Irish rivalry had become extremely bitter, as a result of some messy incidents over the years. As Rog had put it, they don't like us and we don't like them. Rog (for Munster or Ireland) and Felipe Contepomi (for Leinster or Argentina) had been at each other for years. The Pumas had also handed us a couple of painful World Cup defeats, and so it became a grudge match every time we stepped on the field. It felt awfully like hatred.

We won handily enough, 17–3, helped enormously by Felipe being injured and Juan Martín Hernández pulling up in the warm-up. Rog delivered an enormous performance that included a massive drop goal, despite a constant hail of abuse from his Latin friends – especially Rodrigo Roncero. He put the icing on the cake late on with a fine cross-field kick for Tommy's try. We didn't play well, we hardly attacked through the hands, but we won and secured a second seeding for the World Cup.

I had missed two crucial weeks in Deccie's new dawn as coach and was due to miss another gathering at the Johnstown House Hotel in Enfield, Co. Meath, over Christmas because it wasn't a sanctioned international window. I would have disobeyed the ruling, if only to sneak over for a day trip, but if the PLR found out Leicester would have been severely punished.

The Enfield gathering proved to be a watershed.

The boys told me what happened. Marcus Horan flared up on Rob Kearney for saying the Munster boys seemed prouder to play in red than green. The exchange had pointed out the elephant in the room.

In Ireland there will always be a little bit of segregation when we come together. It is natural, if you play for Munster or Leinster or Ulster, to be a bit closer to your provincial teammates. You socialize together at home and travel down to Ireland camp together. You are not going to just ignore each other when you get out of the car. There are exceptions, like Best and Leams, who have been thick as thieves for years, but with two or three provinces supplying most of the squad it is no surprise that there are cliques.

I never had that problem in Ireland camp. Living in England and being from Naas meant I was an outsider from the very start. I ended up gravitating towards guys I respected or got on well with regardless of their address: Bestie, Shaggy, Drico, Rog, Leams, Tommy and Donners (or, to stereotype them: Protestant Armagh farmer, half-Kiwi Meath man, Clontarf-Blackrock boy, Cork legend, Cashel lunatic, Monaghan GAA-head and resident of planet Zog). All over the place, basically. That's the way it has always been for me.

And, of course, The Bull. Everyone liked John Hayes, because he's such a decent man. He used to giggle when telling me, 'Go on back to England with you.' Lads would, with mock surprise, say I was from Naas. 'Nah, he's from England, go on back there, Geordie.'

I always got a laugh out of that.

Rob, still only twenty-two years old, had taken a brave stance. Munster players love playing for Ireland. It's just that they had unearthed something special down in Thomond Park. I related to that from my own experiences with Leicester. Leinster were not long finding it themselves, and I know Ulster will remember where they left it soon enough.

The Maori call it manna.

The theory that Munster players perform better in red than green was familiar – a similar charge had been levelled at me over the years. For my own part, I knew I never made any less effort for Ireland than for Leicester; it was just that there was a dynamic at the club that we weren't often able to replicate in the national team. I was sure the same was true for the Munster lads, but Rob's comments had a useful effect. They proved the catalyst to everyone doubling their efforts to play for each other, come the Six Nations.

In Leicester's final Heineken Cup pool game before the Six Nations, we played the Ospreys away, losing 12–9 but knowing the bonus point was enough to get us through. I got Man of the Match in a high-intensity game. It was a nuts-and-bolts fullback display. Kearns had done something similar for Leinster against Edinburgh.

Now that Girv was gone, I went into camp thinking I would be retained as the Irish fullback. As well as Rob was performing, he had yet to establish himself at Test level.

But a few days before France came to Dublin, Deccie sat me down and told me he was going with Rob. I was number twenty-two. I sucked it up, knowing it was important to Kearns that I was supportive. I am a good-natured person and I couldn't let my disappointment change that. I pulled down a mask. I got three minutes in what is now seen as a watershed 30–21 victory in which Jamie and Brian scored cracking tries, while Darce came back from a long-term arm injury to twist over for a third.

Then we went to Rome and won 38–9. I replaced Rob with two minutes to go – another irrelevant cap. One fleeting touch of the ball and I was back in the changing room without a bead of sweat on my forehead.

My form was strong, every facet of my game at a peak, but I wasn't used at all in the 14–13 defeat of England at Croke Park as the campaign started to gain serious momentum. Again, the lads were brilliant, Drico in particular. He won the game for us with his try, despite being clearly targeted by some high and late hits from Riki Flutey and Delon Armitage.

We were on a roll. Then, without any warning, Deccie surprised everyone by changing a winning team for the trip to Murrayfield.

Every player who was on the cusp of inclusion got his opportunity: Darce was back at twelve for Paddy Wallace, Leams came in for Jamie, Strings replaced Tomás and Bestie got the nod over Fla.

Deccie stopped me in the corridor of the hotel: 'I just want to stick with Rob. Let him find his form. I don't know what else to say to you.'

I respected the honesty of the man, but my levels of frustration were unreal. The only try came from a Strings break, finished off by an ultra-pumped-up Jamie. The boys got their chances and took them.

I got on for the end of a messy encounter to bring my total up to eleven minutes in three games.

The Lions squad for the tour of South Africa that summer was being picked on Six Nations form – Ian McGeechan, returning as head coach for the first time since 1997, had made that very clear – and I had no form to speak of. Lee Byrne of Wales looked a certainty, and now Rob had found the form Deccie hoped to see.

The pair of them would be squaring off in the last game at the Millennium Stadium, where we would be playing for the Grand Slam. Wales still had a shot at the championship, if they could beat us by 13 or more.

Rob went down early in the first half. It looked serious. Merv said, 'Rob's done. Warm up, Geordie.'

I got myself ready. The first quarter is the perfect time to come off the bench. You don't have time to mentally switch off, sitting in the stand, and you can feel your way into the game's rhythm because it hasn't settled.

'You are going on in five, Geordie.'

Finally, I'm going to have a say in this championship, I'm going to . . .

'Hang on, Geordie. We're giving Rob time to recover.'

I sat down and pulled my tracksuit top back over my head. Rob made it to half-time, when he could get treatment. I was bursting to get on. I remember saying, to nobody in particular, 'Give me a run! Give me a run!'

When Tommy went over for his try early in the second half, to give us a 14–6 lead, I looked at Rob and he seemed to be struggling. But, as with all of them, a limb would have to be hanging off for him to leave that field voluntarily.

Wales kicked two penalties shortly after Tommy's try and at 14–12, as the minutes ticked on, the match became the ultimate arm-wrestle. No back wants to arrive into that type of contest.

'Warm-up, Geordie.'

By the time I ran on, with sixty-six minutes on the clock, my adrenalin levels had dipped. Yes, I was focused, but now I just didn't want to be the guy who messed up. I know Strings and Paddy Wallace were thinking the same thing. Lewis Moody said something similar about arriving into extra-time of a World Cup final. Jesus, I don't want to go on now!

It's a terrible frame of mind for a fullback in a cup-final situation, with both teams kicking long and waiting for the other to make a mistake.

Sure enough, a ball came down from the sky. Strings called it, but I remember thinking I should have. He caught it and I thought he shuffled as though to launch it back down the field, so I went focused on the chase – but he flung it to me. Nobody's fault, wires crossed by two subs who were not in the flow of the game.

The ball went to ground; I thought it went backwards, but Barnes awarded a scrum to Wales. It was the platform that led to Stephen Jones's drop goal that put them 15–14 ahead.

We went straight downfield and Rog dropped a goal with three minutes remaining, to put us ahead 17–15. All I remember is being off to the left of Rog before he dropped into the slot. I could have positioned myself to attempt a drop goal, but Rog is the man for that job. Every time.

Rog turned and did a little jig before switching back on. Three minutes is a very long time in a two-point game.

Now all we had to do was cling on. I leaped up for the restart with plenty of Welsh and Irish forwards joining me in the air. It ended up in Paulie's hands.

With fifty seconds remaining, Alun Wyn Jones carried over half-way. Paddy Wallace came through the gate and turned his body, getting hands on the ball and then promptly releasing. Barnes had been shouting about 'hands' for several rucks now, without blowing his whistle. He started to say it again, but then put his arm out to give Jones a forty-eight-metre penalty to win it. And crush us.

Paddy came walking back, apologizing to everyone, 'Sorry, lads.'

'Don't worry about it, next job, next job.'

It was then that I looked up at the clock and realized that at best there would be only one more job.

The lads who had played eighty minutes looked shattered, hands on knees, all believing the dream was about to become a horrible nightmare. Not me. I was fresh as a daisy and thinking about 'what if' scenarios.

There were forty seconds on the clock when the penalty was awarded. If Stephen missed, I was going to be the man who caught it: any dropping ball belongs to the fullback. There might still be ten seconds remaining, so if he missed I planned to run into the corner. If no one chased me I would run to the other corner and waste another four or five seconds. I was going to kill that clock.

As soon as the kick reached the apex of its flight I knew it wouldn't carry the crossbar. I was right underneath it.

'My ball.'

Rog appeared beside me: 'My ball.'

'No, mine!'

Rog: 'No, mine!'

'MY FUCKING BALL.'

Rog moved a split second before I caught it. I had to be sure my foot was in the in-goal area, because if I was in the field of play I would have had to kick to touch. When I caught it I ran behind the posts. I shook my leg at Barnes: I was inside; yeah, he nodded as if to agree, so I knew it was going to be a 22. I thought there might be a few seconds left – I was too focused on catching the ball to see the clock tick into red – so I ran for the corner. When I saw Paulie take off on an obscene, arm-twirling gallop up the pitch, I knew we were Grand Slam champions. I touched it down and boom – into the River Taff with ya! I didn't succeed, but probably got row Z of the third tier.

Back in the changing room, one of the lads was getting his shirt signed when it dawned on me. Ah, fuck. What is it like to have the Grand Slam-winning ball in your hands? Amazing. What did I do? Lost the head and booted away an incomparable piece of memorabilia.

A Welsh man called the IRFU a few days later, saying he had the ball and asking if he could get it signed. They asked him to drop it in – or we could give you a pre-signed one and some other bits and pieces in exchange? He hung up. So somebody still has it. Feel free to drop it into Oval Park in Leicester. Maybe we can come to an accommodation. Then again, he probably realizes it's hardly devaluing as the years pass and we don't win another Slam.

A great session followed.

Donncha O'Callaghan is the chief messer in camp. He baked a cake once up in our old Killiney base, Fitzpatrick's Castle, and came into a room in front of all of us, only to trip over and splat it in his own face.

You tell non-rugby friends what we get up to and they say, 'Are you not grown men, what are you at?' But we are not in a normal adult environment. So many aspects of camp remind us of our childhood.

Even the word 'camp'. It is big boys playing sport. We are given everything, told what to eat, and we must work off a rigid timetable. There are different uniforms for whatever we are doing, and that includes our travel gear – tracksuit, white polo shirt and matching tops so we look the part. Just like school. So it is no wonder that the boy in us all tends to resurface.

Throw boredom into the mix and anything can happen. The week of that Welsh game was worse than usual because of all the Slam talk floating about the place, so Donners played his part in diluting stress levels.

Wednesday before travelling to Cardiff was our down day. This can be dangerous if lads don't have some place to go. All the clean laundry is left outside Rala's room (Patrick 'Rala' O'Reilly being the Ireland baggage master for as long as I can remember – there is a great book in that strange yet wonderful human being). Anyway, Donners got into the bag and cut shapes out of the back of the polo shirts.

My T-shirt was one of the innocent victims in this child's play. One option was to wear my tracksuit zipped up on travel day, but it gets stifling hot in the airport so I headed up to Rala's for a spare. There was already a queue halfway down the corridor. Only XL shirts were left over.

Knowing it had to be Donners, I plotted a revenge assault. I sneaked into his room and cut the legs of his tux trousers to three-quarter length. See how Huckleberry Finn looks, come Saturday night.

Of course, Donners had the last laugh simply because he didn't care. He strolled down for the post-match function wearing his vandalized formals, looking brilliant, with black socks pulled up to his knees.

He said I was a nemesis he could respect. The management sent him back upstairs to change.

After the post-match reception some boys ventured out into Cardiff, but I was content to sit in the team room that night. Most of the lads had partners with them and eventually headed up to bed, but myself, Tommy and Merv stayed put. At dawn we popped open a bottle of champagne each. Someone came in to us at 8 a.m. and said the bus was leaving in an hour. We were in great shape. On the ride to the airport we started singing 'The Black Velvet Band' without noticing we barely knew the lyrics for the chorus, never mind a verse or two. A long old day followed, but a merry one.

By the time we got to the Mansion House in Dublin for the public reception, we hadn't had a beer for a few hours and were flagging.

Can we have another beer? No. I'd love another beer? No. We were dying. No sleep. Not Tommy, though. Somebody suggested he should sing his song.

What about her eyes, Tommy!

'Ah yeah, the lads will join in.'

I tried to save him, 'Tommy, you are mental if you think they'll join in.'

'Nah, they will, won't you, lads?'

Aw yeah, Tommy, we'll all join in.

'Tommy . . .'

He grabbed the mic and took centre stage.

'Her eyes they shine like diamonds . . .'

On realizing that he had no verses and that no help was forthcoming, he just belted out the chorus again before the MC, Des Cahill, let him off. It was a disaster but everyone loved it.

I couldn't save Tommy because I didn't know where I was. Deccie asked me to thank the crowd. I had a mic in my hand. I have no idea what I said, but I spoke. I think the TV cameras were gone.

For me, winning the Slam was all that mattered. The Triple Crowns were great but, after the third one, in 2007, they lost their value. We needed the Grand Slam. So we went and got one. Finally.

Early in the 2009/10 season I wrecked my shoulder, requiring total reconstructive surgery that meant five months of rehabilitation. I was given the green light to return for Leicester in February 2010. The Six Nations was already underway, but I was hoping to squeeze back into the reckoning just like in 2004. I came off the bench against Northampton on 6 February and against Leeds a week later, before getting eighty minutes against Gloucester, when I scored a try. I was so excited that I swan-dived over the line, winding myself even before Lote Tuqiri bear-hugged me.

You overdo it sometimes after being out for a while, and the jolt of the physicality makes you want to curl up and die. But, like anything, you go again and it comes back to you.

I wasn't considered for Italy but Rob got injured in the defeat to France in Paris so I was parachuted straight back in against England and Lewis.

I remember Twickenham in 2010 because we beat them 20–16 and I had one of my better days in a green jersey. I also remember it because of Moody. I could tell before the kick-off that my best mate wanted to melt me into the dirt. You could see from the way he was standing, nostrils flaring and hoof stamping, that he had been told where the ball was going. Yeah, even Jonny Wilkinson's stance was confirmation. Good thing I had the Gloucester match banked because this was going to get bloody very quickly.

Lewis told me afterwards that he planned to massacre me. He requested the ball be dropped down my throat so he could shred my bad shoulder, like all good friends should, and maybe orchestrate an English score in the first minute. But Jonny topped it, one-in-a-hundred kick-offs for him, so he didn't get near me. No English player did. For me it was one of those rare days when you feel like you are floating.

Rob was fit for Wales, but Deccie stuck with his veteran fullback. 'Geordan was playing well all last season and he answered the call last week. I thought he played well enough against England to warrant a second run out.

'Rob has been working really hard to get back in, it's not like he's done anything wrong, I just went with Geordan on this one.'

We won again, so I was retained for the last rugby international at Croke Park, against Scotland, before the return to Lansdowne Road. Another Triple Crown was on offer.

I can't explain how we lost. It's one of those inexplicable Irish performances of the sort that rears its head once a season. I lasted twenty minutes. We were leading, thanks to a try from Brian, created by Jonny Sexton, but the game opened up thereafter and we allowed Scotland to play their loose, wide, attacking game. Their number eight, Johnnie Beattie, broke down the left wing and I came across to tackle him as Paulie was thinking the same, from behind. The pair of them steamrolled over me as Beattie got over for a try. I piled into a ruck soon after and got kneed in the back. My right butt cheek went completely numb. I tried to run it off, but my arse, hamstring and back all seized up.

The renting of Croke Park ended in the same way as it began, with our opponents snatching victory at the death. Same old story: play my way into the team, do enough to hold my place, only for injury to intervene.

New Zealand hammered us 66–28 that summer after Jamie was sent off for kneeing Richie McCaw in the head. Fifteen minutes gone, and we were already 10–0 down when Darce was tackled, inches shy of the line. McCaw did his usual, coming in from the side of the ruck, body spread across the ball, making it impossible to get quick ball. Barnes – him again, but he's actually a good referee! – shouted, 'Hands away, black,' but nothing happened so Jamie took matters into his own hands. The All Black forwards went to town on him as the whistle went.

'A deliberate knee to the head,' said Barnes as he pulled out the red. Game over. Keven Mealamu got nothing for unloading on Jamie. When Rog got sin-binned as well, they ran riot, but with fourteen men we scored four tries in the second half to take something out of the game.

I'll always remember that tour, because Deccie asked me to captain Ireland against New Zealand Maori in Rotorua the following week-end. My old pal Daryl Gibson was their coach and had explained how important the fixture was, as it was the team's centenary season. That haka, led by Hosea Gear, was particularly chilling.

It was the first time Irish teammates got to see me in a role I had been carrying out at the biggest club in England for two years. Donners and Rog said they were impressed. I knew what I was doing and transferred my weekly behaviour at Leicester to the national set-up. The team leaders must take control at some point in the lead-up to a game, as the coaches are little help come kick-off, so I spoke more than usual.

It was a ferocious contest. Myself and Paddy combined for a try that saw us 25–21 in front around the hour mark. The response was epic. I sent a really good kick deep into their 22 that slid out for a lineout. Typical Maoris – they saw this as an attacking opportunity, taking a quick throw and immediately spreading it wide right. Sean Maitland carried over halfway in an instant before they switched it wide left, through six pairs of hands, to cross for a sensational try thirty seconds after my long punt. You can coach that, but it must be done when players are knee height. They won 31–28.

★

In November 2010 the IRFU scheduled a Test match against the Springboks outside the IRB window to ensure rugby was the first international sport played at the shiny new Aviva Stadium. They got in just ahead of the soccer match against Argentina a few days later. It meant I had the same problem as in November 2008, and couldn't be considered for this historic game.

Leicester had Australia at Welford Road the following Tuesday night and Cockers wanted to pick me, so he contacted Deccie on the Sunday night, after the South Africa match, to see if I was needed for Samoa the following Saturday. Deccie couldn't say for certain. Matty O'Connor was so frustrated he got on to him as well; Deccie said it would be unfair on the other guys if he made a decision on me before announcing the rest of the squad.

I called him and asked him straight: should I play for Leicester against the Wallabies or show up in Dublin, or do both? Go play for Leicester was the answer. There was no problem, I could always talk straight with Deccie, ever since I was a teenager. He may be hard to read, but you can speak your mind without any repercussions. The only problem, for me, was that the issue of club versus country kept arising in a way it never did for the guys with the Irish provinces.

Luke was picked for Samoa. Rob returned for the All Blacks, and I was again left out of the twenty-two.

Rob badly damaged knee ligaments in the 38–18 defeat to an awesome New Zealand (during which Brian scored a magical try, scooping the ball off the floor at full pace and riding two tacklers before twisting over the line – genius!). So I came in for the Argentina match.

Again, for what seemed my thousandth comeback, I was patrolling the Irish backfield. I had it all planned. The 2011 Six Nations would be my swansong. I would play my heart out and finish up in New Zealand as the resident Irish fullback. Then I would be done with the jersey. Rob or whoever else could scrap over it.

Of course, in January I mangled my foot against Northampton, so Lukey got his opportunity while I started out on another long and lonely road back.

17. End of the Line

Wednesday, 12 October 2011, Leicester
Arrived home yesterday from New Zealand. It's odd being here in the house by myself after so many weeks away. On tour the abnormal becomes the norm. You don't speak in the language of everyday life. I am constantly expecting Tommy or Besty or Jenno to come walking through the door and slip into our secret dialect. It's rugby-speak, male-speak, thirty-men-cooped-up-in-a-hotel-speak.

Being on the road with Ireland was like being in a bubble, but it has burst. I am no longer a part of that.

The World Cup is not over but it is for us, and for England too, so the boys will trickle back into Oval Park this week. I'll go down tomorrow. Just need some time to myself after the anticlimax I just experienced.

In the run-up to the quarter-final against Wales, the mood in camp was as good as it had ever been, with the bus journeys getting ever more vicious. Ferg McFadden was up for joke of the day on the way from Wellington airport. It wasn't accepted as funny enough, so he was told to make his own way to the hotel. He had to knock on some random punter's front door and ask for a lift. Sean Cronin was in charge of informing the group about Wellington as a city. His presentation wasn't accepted as interesting enough, so he was thrown off the bus as well. It was lashing down, so we gave him a rain jacket. Twenty-minute drive to our hotel. Pretty cruel, but it was worth it just to see Sean standing there in the pouring rain as we drove away. It was a city he was supposed to know so much about anyway.

Mob rule had taken over.

I introduced a dice game to the group. You have to roll if the ethics committee deems you are misbehaving. If you roll a one it is a reroll, if you roll a six you have to take a card. There are several punishments written on the cards – get a spray tan, dye your hair, shave your eyebrows. Lads are obviously terrified of the cards. It made the internal discipline a hugely powerful tool, but really it was just fun. If you were late, you wore a clock.

We had grown into a tight bunch.

It was a very light week, only two sessions. The lads were battle-hardened by now, so contact wasn't needed in training, and anyway the majority of them were carrying injuries. At the indoor session on Tuesday one new move was introduced – a short side sweep to Tommy. We repped it a few times, but the game plan was rigidly in place.

On the Wednesday we had a rugby session. The Assassins became Wales. We were trying to impersonate Shane Williams and Lee Byrne, who we expected to be at fifteen.

Everyone assumed Rory Best had broken his collarbone against Italy, but it turned out to be an A/C shoulder-joint problem. The Assassins had planned a night out on Wednesday, but when Deccie asked for volunteers to do a fitness test with Rory on Thursday morning, myself, Jenno and Ferg raised our hands. He had been icing the joint all week so I didn't think he had any shot of playing. Sean Cronin was in line to start, with Damien Varley on the bench and Mike Sherry flown out as cover. By Wednesday Rory was still nervous but felt a little better.

The night out was supposed to be fairly tame – that is, until we ran into our Welsh counterparts. It was like one of those Westerns when your sworn enemies come through the swinging saloon doors.

The piano man stopped playing (there was no piano man), the can-can girls stopped dancing (no girls either) and the place went deathly silent (it didn't). Stephen Jones, Andy Powell and the others staring us down. After the sambuca experience with Lewis and myself in Leicester a few years earlier, Stephen was ready this time. A round of shots was ordered and away we went. All good-natured, half-slagging stuff, but it went on a little late, making it a struggle to rise for Rory's fitness session at 10.30 a.m.

We started off with pads, pushing and twisting him. Then he tackled us. Then we landed on him with pads. He never even winced.

I already knew he was a tough bastard, just like his brother, Simon. Rory doesn't lift anything that impressive in the gym, nor is he a freakish athlete, but he has that farmer's strength. He is an Ulster-born forward. That means he's hard.

Game Day

Tommy was my room-mate and he wanted to get some sleep so I turned off the TV and kept myself occupied on the iPhone. It was about four hours before the 6.30 p.m. kick-off, but a massive crowd had gathered outside the hotel. They were already singing their favourite song, 'We all dream of a team of Tommy Bowes', to the tune of 'Yellow Submarine'.

I'm giggling away so he wakes up.

'What are they singing?'

Just listen.

'Number one, there's Tommy Bowe . . .' We opened the window and it was like nothing we'd ever heard, or seen, before. Pandemonium.

That's the only decent memory I have from the day.

I thought the game would be close, but it just didn't pan out for us. They thundered into us. Jamie Roberts nearly destroyed Donners in the first collision. Shane Williams switched to the right wing, to avoid marking his much taller Ospreys teammate Tommy, and was over for a try before we had settled into our seats.

Our game plan was so simplistic that when we had to chase scores we struggled badly to surprise the Welsh. The systems simply weren't in place to punch holes after three or four phases.

Wales had done their homework. They chopped down our primary ball-carriers, dropping the hips and hitting at ankle level. They got one or two players, usually Warburton, over the tackled man. That meant three or four green jerseys were needed to clean them out, so that our ball was slowed, meaning they could reorganize themselves and do it all over again. We lacked the structures to go at them in a different manner. The effectiveness of Seanie, Jamie and Stevie in possession was quickly neutralized. It didn't matter how good our finishers were outside because they weren't going to get any space. We hadn't prepared to break down the Welsh by any means other than a battering ram.

Rog had won back the number ten jersey for the Italy match and held it against Wales. The wind was swirling at pitch level, as it tends to do in Wellington. We passed up a few seemingly kickable penalties early on – but if Rog felt they were kickable he would have taken them. We went to the touchline instead, but just couldn't score a try. Nobody made any bad decisions. God knows, Rog can play the percentages better than anybody else. The Welsh broke us by denying a pathway to the try-line from our attacking lineouts. Their defence silenced the Irish crowd.

We kept pounding away. Keith Earls got over for a try early in the second half and Rog's touchline conversion made it 10-all. I thought we had them. But Wales had another gear and we didn't. Maybe we put so much effort into our attack that our defence suffered. In any case, their two tries were terribly soft. Mike Phillips got over at the corner flag when Darce and Tommy, in a microsecond of confusion, both vacated the same position. Philips saw his opportunity and exposed us.

The real killer came two minutes after Keith's try. I remember Phil Larder drilled it into us over ten years ago at Leicester when we were winning everything: if a team lands a heavy blow and you can counter, they will falter. When you're the team that had landed the heavy blow, it is all about consolidating. Do your next task correctly. That didn't happen.

We know what it sounded like to make a World Cup semi-final, because the changing rooms were right beside each other. Their music went on and the sounds were excruciating. Some of our guys were in shock, some distraught. Nobody moved for a while. There was a sick feeling hanging over the whole room like a dense fog. I went into the smaller room down the back to check my messages.

Aaron Mauger texted, 'Everyone is going to be down. Don't let them hang their heads too much. Be a positive influence around the team.' Aaron, of course, had been in my exact situation four years ago: in a distraught changing room, having not been part of the twenty-two after the All Blacks lost that quarter-final to France in Cardiff.

I made Tommy a cup of tea. Tried chatting to a few lads. That was pretty much it, really. There was nothing else to say. You get up and leave.

I don't think Auckland would have been able to cope with an Irish invasion for the semi-final.

So many people were poised to book their flight as soon as the full-time whistle sounded. But we were beaten by a better team on the day.

Deccie had the bus driver pull over five minutes out from the hotel. He spoke about disappointments in life. He didn't see it as total failure. He commended us. But there wasn't much he could say.

There was a big crowd in the lobby. The saddest sight at all was seeing a grown man standing there in floods of tears, his face paint being washed away. Everyone was decked out for a party, but it had been cancelled.

We had a team room on the first floor. Most guys sat in to watch France beat England and had a few drinks. Some went out. I stayed in the team room, just like I did after the 2009 Grand Slam match in Cardiff when the mood was so different. Damien Varley's guitar helped. He played for ages and we had a real Irish sing-song. It felt like a wake, the passing of someone great, someone that will never come into our lives again.

We were not flying home until Monday afternoon, so Sunday was always going to become a massive session. I went for a walk, had some lunch and then into an Irish bar around 2 p.m. Mayhem was waiting for us. Camera phones were out again. We escaped to a coffee shop down the road, where the owner kindly let us turn it into a private function after closing time. We had a good crew – Jenno, Leo, Paddy Wallace, Leamy, Ferris, Tommy, Rog, Paulie and a few others. Partners and girlfriends too. Earlsey, Varls and Mike Sherry also came in.

I ended up with Tommy and Rog. Despite Australia and South Africa having played that day, there were Irish people everywhere. The next morning we woke up to pictures of Tommy and Rog doing the rounds on emails back home. Rog's shirt was ripped. I felt really sorry for him – he can't go for a few pints to drown his sorrows without that shite. I was right beside them but didn't get into the photos.

I didn't make the cut! Not that it would bother me. Rog just gets too much attention. I told him to ban cameras from his life. Never pose for one again unless it's at home with the family.

Deccie spoke to me at the airport about my thoughts on the future. I had said to Kissy and Merv that I was probably done, and they'd relayed it to Deccie. He asked me to wait a month before deciding anything and then call.

'You are still in my plans,' was how he left it.

I appreciated it, but it felt like the end. I'd say he felt the same, but it was decent of him to leave the door open, and smart too, in case he did need me again.

I spoke to Rog about it. He would go on. After the Italy match he had given a very emotional interview in which he said it would all be over with Ireland after the World Cup, but he backtracked a few days later. (Now it seems like he is looking to emulate Brett Favre, the great NFL quarterback, who played until he was forty-one! Rog never misses a trick. I remember years back he allowed the rumour he was off to the Miami Dolphins as a kicker to grow wings. No coincidence that he was negotiating a new contract at the time.)

Paulie asked me if this was it.

I said, 'Yeah, probably.'

He said, 'Thanks for everything, Geordie.'

I would love to play another game for Ireland. Finishing off on the bench against Russia is a downer. But I have to walk away some time. Leicester are down the bottom of the league. I need to play my part. That's what matters now.

The English boys will all return after a shocking tournament. Their 2011 was like our 2007. The media got stuck into them, a siege mentality descended, and they didn't perform on the pitch.

New Zealand's obsession with winning the tournament has become unhealthy. I was talking to Drico about the Dan Carter injury – he tore his groin during place-kicking practice. That muscle must be so strong from the thousands of kicks he has done. It would be like me tearing a hamstring walking to the training pitch. We surmised that it must have had something to do with the pressure and stress on his body. Otherwise, why now?

If they don't win the tournament, well, Jesus, the country may never recover. They take their rugby way too seriously. The levels of hatred – and that is the right word – directed towards opponents was getting pretty nasty when we left. The poison directed at the Lions in 2005 had been transferred on to Quade Cooper and Australia.

Nevertheless I think they will still win the whole thing. They are just so strong. Not that I care any more. Can't wait for it to end properly.

Deccie said to wait a month. So I will. Felix might not be back playing in time for the Six Nations. That leaves only one established fullback in Ireland. If Rob got injured I might still be needed. Maybe. Even now, after everything, I find it impossible to turn my back on my country. I'd rather my country discards me when I am no longer needed. I would happily take that as my international epitaph.

He came, he served, he was discarded. But he came again whenever he was called.

18. The Derby

Friday, 2 December 2011
Leicester

The neighbours are popping over tomorrow for afternoon tea.

Last time the Northampton Saints visited, in May for the Premiership semi-final, Manu Tuilagi took his sledgehammer fists to Chris Ashton's face in the middle of the pitch. The officials deemed it a sin-binning offence, but the slow-motion replays were fairly damning and Manu served a five-week suspension.

'I know I did wrong, Geordie, but that was the biggest game of my career. In the changing room beforehand I was told they were coming to our house to beat us up! Kick in the front door and rob your stuff. I felt like crying.'

What can you say to that? He is a Tiger to his fingertips and has a potentially great career ahead of him for us and for England.

'Hopefully I will learn from it, but if I feel like that again I don't know what I'll do, Geordie.'

Manu knows he 'did wrong', but he was driven to it by the sound of those creaking wooden rafters. I know the feeling well. To reach the grass we must come from underneath the wooden stand. The natives are stamping their feet and roaring, 'Tigers, Tigers.'

It sounds a little like the old Lansdowne Road west stand when the train used to rattle past. There is thunder in your ears when the changing-room door opens. Your eyes are rolling in the back of your head as you jog through the crowd.

As captain, at the front of the line, I make the boys walk, force them to soak up every last drop of the raw emotion.

Nah, I couldn't blame Manu for losing it when Ashton pushed him. It was a miracle he was only sin-binned, yet we felt wronged. Our blood still boiled. We love to have a cause. If we don't have one, we'll create one.

Who wouldn't want to be involved in such beautiful madness?

I was stranded on the sideline that day, decked out in my suit. Crocked. But I am leading them out tomorrow.

This must be the performance to ignite our campaign.

The problem with being the Leicester Tigers is that the 'crumbling of an empire' talk always starts as soon as we lose a few games. Especially at home. We shipped two heavy defeats against Saracens and Harlequins at Welford Road during the World Cup. Regardless of missing internationals and injury lists and other excuses, we are Leicester; we set such high standards that the expectation to deliver will always be enormous. Now we are tenth in the league. Time to move on up.

But enough of rugby for tonight. Family is a welcome distraction; George and Cecily are over for the weekend. I won't be home for Christmas: we're training on the 24th and 26th, and we visit Worcester on the 27th, so I can't even squeeze in a day trip this year.

It's nice having them visit every couple of months. I think they get a kick out of the whole Welford Road experience too. They'll be at the match with Aneka and her parents.

OK, it's not Christmas but the festive lights are already up around Market Harborough. That's where we are tonight – dinner at Timo, the restaurant I own with Marco Castrogiovanni, but only after Aneka takes them to evening mass in the idyllic church down the road.

I'm not much of a mass-goer myself, but I will join Mum for the 8.30 a.m. service Sunday morning. Body permitting, that is, as I'm already booked in for a physio session with Bobby Sourbutts at ten. No harm saying a few prayers every now and then. Ah, I am a Catholic boy at heart, I suppose.

George is in good spirits tonight. He gets talking about old times – UN patrols of the Lebanon–Israel border, where one side was a barren wasteland, the other populated by vast rows of citrus trees; the Cyprus/Turkish donkey incident (don't ask); our brief El Salvadorian adventure – Mum, Dad and me – until peace broke out and we were sent home, but not before my trip to the Guatemalan border with Sammy, the Indian UN officer.

'We probably shouldn't have let you go,' said Mum.

'Ah, I wanted to go with Sammy.'

'And when he wanted to go somewhere, who could stop him?'

True.

We eat and head home early, but not before saluting Castro and the Argentinians, Marcos Ayzera and Horacio 'Ringo' Agulla, who are down below, sipping water with friends and family. Everyone is on duty tomorrow.

Ireland is still on my mind. I haven't officially retired from international rugby yet. Still holding out for another run at Lansdowne Road – sorry, the Aviva – as a way to close that book for good.

I'm not keen on being a thirty-three-year-old tackle bag in Carton House, and Deccie made it clear with his initial World Cup squad that he wants to move on. But Felix Jones isn't back yet from injury and Keith Earls will be filling in for Brian at centre, so there's no obvious cover for Rob, who is the undisputed fullback now. Even Leinster shifted Isa Nacewa (arguably the best number fifteen in Europe these past two years) to wing to accommodate Kearns.

After all these years, it looks like I'm still one injury away from another cap. Just saying. Can't help thinking that way. It's hard to let go. My body is fine: foot, shoulder, everything well oiled and operating. I'm back playing well, and more physical than ever before. Or so Jimmy Ferris told me the other day.

If Deccie wants to move on and try someone else, fine. I could take a week off in February and another in March. Get away, finally, on a little holiday. Brace the body for the months ahead.

But I would love one more crack at the Six Nations.

I called Drico the other day to catch up and feel him out. He has his own problems, rehabbing after surgery, a cervical fusion to ease a constant nagging pain from shoulder to neck that he carried for over a year. For a while he thought he might miss the World Cup. But he made it and performed. He always has.

Deccie and I agreed to talk before he selects the next squad. But it is the end. I know this. Ideally, I will agree to hold off my retirement until after the Six Nations so I can be called up as a replacement should Rob get injured.

A retired pro said it recently: you can control many things in your career, or at least influence them, but not the end. That comes without your consent. It comes and that's it.

Maybe I'll coach. If I'm let. Les Kiss has taken over as Ireland attack coach for the Six Nations. He touched base with Matt O'Connor, as they know each other from Australia. I think he will do a decent job. Mervyn Murphy is another with plenty to offer in this regard, and his responsibilities have been expanded. But the evolution of Irish back play is coming too late for me, I'm afraid.

Anyway, that's enough fretting over something that is out of my control. Ah yes, a rugby cliché – control the controllables. Chris Ashton and Ben Foden will come steaming down the tracks tomorrow. Saints have picked Tom May at inside centre over Jimmy Downey, so that indicates they are going to kick a lot. To me.

I hope they kick to me. I can't wait.

Saturday, 3 December 2011
Up for breakfast at 9 a.m. I'll be eating again at 11 as it is a 2.15 p.m. kick-off. Fuelling the body for war.

Head down to the shop to get the old man his newspapers. Watch some American college football on ESPN. Set the box to record our match so I can hear Austin Healey's take on everything later. Austin has no concerns about sticking the boot into his old club or anyone else for that matter. He's made for punditry, I guess.

It may be Leicester against Northampton, but it is also Cockers against Dorian West – two men who scrapped over the Leicester B/two jersey for several years. Westy is Saints' forwards coach nowadays.

Or is it the Tuilagis against Chris Ashton?

This game is bound to boil over. I might speak to Wayne Barnes beforehand about how we can keep the lid on it.

Crofty is my neighbour and usual match-day chauffeur but he's injured, so Matt Smith picks me up at 12.15 and we head to the ground. Matt's a decent bloke, big centre who starts today as Manu and Anthony Allen are injured.

Matty is one of the few uncapped players in our place. He is

Leicester by birth and hugely underrated. Ian Smith, his father, captained and coached the club before becoming director of rugby over at Oakham School.

Smithy earns small money by professional standards, but I'd like to be his agent: he is worth much more and could start regularly for most Premiership sides. Thing is, he just loves playing for Leicester. I've never heard him moan. If Manu and Ant come back next week and he is benched it would be, 'Yep, no worries.' That kind of guy. He is twenty-six and just needs a break.

He seems nice and relaxed on the drive in.

We have a quick meeting, where we run over the game plan. We want to put them under pressure at set-piece. Keep them from offloading so rapid ball can't make it to their main strike runners, Foden and Ashton. It has to be a physical affair against Northampton.

I see Wayne heading out to the pitch and we have a brief chat. I ask him to be vigilant about their second-man assists at the breakdown because Northampton are always at this. It's illegal and I want him to call it consistently as a penalty for us.

I know the stakes are high because of the recent history so I say, 'You can help me out there by being pretty tight on things in the first twenty minutes because it is going to be ready to go.'

'No worries. Make sure your guys are whiter than white.'

'Yeah, we'll be fine.'

We've a decent side out today. Ben Youngs and Toby Flood are back at halfback. Marcos Ayerza, George Chuter and Dan Cole are the ABC club, with Castro waiting to be sprung off the bench. Coley just signed a new contract – look around the best club teams anywhere in the world and they have two top-notch tighthead props on their roster. Louis Deacon and George Skivington are in the second row, with Steve Mafi, Julian Salvi and Thomas Waldrom making up a powerful, athletic backrow.

Alex has a sore knee so he might not make it, but Ringo is on the other wing, with Scotty Hamilton to step up and Manu doing the warm-up in case his brother doesn't make it. Manu is edging back from injury since the World Cup and has been dying to feature today after last May's madness.

The big brother makes it through the warm-up without any problem, so Manu must calm down and head up to the stand.

As the Tigers jog back up through the crowd, I remain on the pitch
for my pre-game routine with Paul Burke. I like to catch three garryowens, throw a long pass off my right and another off my left, then
boot the third into touch.

It's probably going to be the first thing I have to do in the game.
Keep it implicit. I'm going into my game trance.

There are about four or five minutes to go when I get into the
dressing room. Deacs, my lieutenant, is talking to the pack. All the
boys are putting on their final trappings.

Cockers goes all profound on us: 'In 1880 both these clubs were
formed. A hundred and thirty years of this . . . playing big derby
matches against Northampton. It means a lot to the community . . .'

Two-minute warning, I bring the lads in. I know they're listening
now. You've got to make it sharp. I repeat Cockers' words: 'It means
a lot to the community but it must mean a lot to us as well.'

The crowd are in good spirits today, 24,000 in the full house. They
love this fixture and everyone is expecting something to happen. The
big brother is marking Ashton this time.

I lead the boys on to the field, followed by Deacs and Coley, nice
and slow until we hit the grass.

Ryan Lamb kicks off. The Saints' pack thunders into us with Barnes
getting accidentally bowled over by Dylan Hartley. They get a penalty. Lamb kicks it, 0–3.

Tom May sends a grubber my way, I boot it away but Ashton hits
me with a late shoulder. I barely notice, but the crowd are simmer-
ing, the fuse lit.

Typical Ashton, getting his dig in first, he's always like that. That's
his character. Others would keep the head down and let the rugby do
their talking, but he's an extrovert, shoving and poking, running
across lines, dropping the shoulder when he doesn't need to.

This game's gonna blow.

★

Nine minutes: Foden comes across a ruck and head-butts me in the eye. Accidental, but it's my bad eye. I think it could be scratched again. Bobby comes on to examine me. The vision returns, but it is blurry. I can play, and even if I couldn't nobody is leaving the field after nine minutes unless they are carried off.

May sends another low bobbling ball my way. This is a tactic all right. I deal with it and we shuffle downfield, getting a penalty. Toby opens his account, 3–3.

Sixteen minutes: The bomb goes off. We attack left at pace, shipping the ball to Alex, who bumps Ashton, but Ashton recovers to grab him, dragging him into touch. By his hair. Ringo and Alex pile into him at the advertising hoardings, and when Courtney Lawes arrives throwing haymakers it descends into complete chaos. I arrive as a peacemaker, but Tom Wood cracks Ringo with an uppercut and elbows me too, so he can wind up another big punch; I lose it, flinging a few over-arm digs until Wood shoves me away. I dive straight back into the middle of it.

Manu is tearing down the touchline but, thankfully, never makes it to the brawl. He's not even a sub! He would have got a massive ban. Richard Blaze, our lineout coach, takes him into the changing room.

Barnes: 'Leicester winger [Alex] punched the white fourteen [Ashton] numerous times.'

Touch judge: 'White seven [Wood] comes in clearly with a retaliatory action. Punches.'

'Captain and eleven.'

Barnes shows Alex the red. I go to remonstrate (with jaw firmly in place, three years on from my first ever chat with the same referee in the Sale game when Julian was sent off) but Wayne knows my question, 'Yes, I am dealing with them too.'

Wood also walks.

Alex's sending off is blatantly about what his brother did the last time we played Saints. The officials have got this completely wrong: what man wouldn't retaliate on a rugby field after having his hair pulled?

Still, it's fourteen versus fourteen and they just lost an international flanker while we lost a winger. I know which I would choose. It makes life more difficult for me, but they have to put Tom May into their scrums. And there is one coming up right now.

We mince them. Penalty. The Saints have a big, powerful front-row – Soane Tonga'uiha, Hartley and Brian Mujati – but I think we have the better scrum. Ayerza is a massively underrated operator.

Our guys are playing with rage in their hearts.

Twenty-eight minutes: Matty Smith powers over for a brilliant try. Taking it off Billy Twelvetrees on their 22, he runs straight between the English internationals, Ashton and Foden. Ashton gets a good grip on him but he carries him over at the corner flag, freeing his hands, despite the attention, to touch down. Alex would have been proud of that strength and finish. Toby misses the touchline conversion but 8–3 signifies first blood.

Thirty-two minutes: Clean up another May grubber – the tactic is clearly to launch Ashton into my face, and here he is. I'm forced to snap it into touch in our 22, but Hartley's throw is crooked.

I rarely thrive in these claustrophobic games, but I enjoy them. The shitty stuff has to be done against Northampton. There is a lot of running and covering and directing, now we're down a winger. The Saints are desperately trying to expose our weakness before we punish their seven forwards.

Thirty-three minutes: We are rampant up front. Steve Mafi sees a row of skittles in front of him, bowling through four tackles for our second try. Toby converts for 15–3. The crowd are delirious.

Thirty-six minutes: Lamb sticks a penalty for 15–6. They will keep coming at us. They have too much quality to lie down. We get a penalty but Toby is wide.

Half-time: As we head off, I have a brief chat with Wayne about the second man, again, but we are in complete control – two scores clear with a strong second-half gale behind us.

Behind the changing-room door Mafi, our six, is told to cover the blindside wing at all times. He's athletic enough to do the job. Ben Youngs is to assist.

Forty-two minutes: Toby's penalty makes it 18–6. The Saints must score next or it is curtains.

Forty-six minutes: They finally exploit our vacant wing. Quick hands get the ball to Foden in my alley. I hit him, but he puts Ashton away. Ryan misses the conversion but 18–11 changes everything.

I begin slipping in to first or second receiver. I've always done that at Leicester, especially in recent seasons. In the past I would see a try coming and know Paddy Howard or Rod or Daryl or Aaron would get it wide, so I'd time my run in the wider channels. If it gets through three pairs of hands I'm home free, whereas now I get the ball into those spaces for others. Leicester let me use my passing game, they encourage it. Go get the ball, Geordie.

Fifty-eight minutes: Get smashed late by Lawes. More smelling salts from Bobby or Dave Orton – no idea which one, I'm out of it.

My groin was tight at half-time so Bobby/Dave ask if that's why I'm down.

'Huh, my groin?'

'Yes, Geordie, your groin.'

'No, my groin is fine.'

Dave/Bobby get me on my feet, 'Get back in the play . . .'

I don't know where I am. Ah, yes, Welford Road. I know this place.

One moment we are on the attack – and then a turnover, and they look certain to score, until their giant second-row replacement, Samu Manoa, fumbles. It's that sort of game. Hectic.

I come back to my senses.

Fifty-nine minutes: After a brilliant turnover by Salvi, Benny Youngs appears to wrap up the victory, sneaking over for a try near the ruck. Toby misses the conversion and another penalty, but at 23–11 we are coasting. The season has, finally, kicked off.

Sixty minutes: In a ruck Ryan Lamb sticks his face up over the para-
pet just as I go to clean him out. I break his nose. An accident.

Sixty-three to sixty-six minutes: Three disastrous minutes change
everything. Tom May crosses for an avoidable try. We are trying to
play inventive rugby when we should be shoving the ball down the
tramline. We give them quick ball; they break a few tackles, very
sloppy. I'm outside Mafi, our six playing wing, but, when we drift,
Mafi is not accustomed to this and makes the tackle in front of him
like any good flanker. This proves costly and May gets over. Stephen
Myler, on for Lamb, nails the touchline conversion.

They catch the restart, we miss a few more tackles and they strike
again. Ashton is haring after a kick through. Ringo and Benny both
ease off, thinking it will roll into touch, but it bounces into Ashton's
hands and he puts Phil Dowson over for a try under the posts. Myler's
conversion makes it 23–25.

How the fuck did that just happen?

Cockers and Matty are going to go bananas at Monday's review
session. We've been guilty of going flat at times this season, but
against Northampton? This is terrible.

Under the posts, I'm relaxed. I still think at two points down with
fourteen minutes to go, if we can get our hands on the ball, play
patiently until we get into penalty range, this one is still ours for the
taking. Take the three points and walk away.

But some really frustrating decisions go against us. Flood gets
done for not releasing, even though Dowson wasn't the tackler, second man in – exactly what I had talked about beforehand.

'That's our penalty, Wayne!'

Then Castro tackles their nine, Lee Dickson. He and Marcos burst
straight through the middle of the ruck. He can't touch the ball – the
laws are a bit shady here – but the two boys have counter-rucked and
the rule is you can't tackle the nine either. So what are they supposed
to do when Dickson grabs the ball? This is when you want a rugby
player refereeing the game.

★

Seventy-three minutes: I carry from outhalf but get absolutely creamed by Samu Manoa, their replacement lock. More treatment from Bobby. I've damaged my ribs. We'll deal with it tomorrow, but I'm flying on one wing now.

There are no gaps, no offloads coming off, and we are going backwards. It needs something.

Floody hits me with a flat pass, Chutes tells me to carry. Their second man, replacement backrower Ben Nutley, pulls it off me on the ground.

'Ref!?'

'Nah, he's done it in the tackle.'

'Has he fucking really . . .'

Me and Wayne are no longer friends.

Seventy-five minutes: Then it comes. The Welford effect. If we are to score, it must be on autopilot. I am desperate to contribute in some way, but again I get smashed by Manoa. It's a bit late, but no penalty. I'm rattled. Wheezing. Zinged. Bobby is checking my neck.

Ashton offloads to a backtracking Chutes; turnover ball! Chutes pops it off to Benny. The space is wide left. I see Foden tracking across to snuff out the danger. There are bodies strewn everywhere. I might just get away with this.

'I gotta go . . .'

'Where are you going?' asks Bobby Sourbutts, now acting as more a medic in a war zone than a physio.

'Back in the line.'

'The line is that way, Geordie.'

I'm running like a newborn foal, but I'm completely focused on my next task. Foden is homing in on the match-saving tackle on Ringo, unless . . .

Benny feeds Toby, who can create a two-on-two situation if he forces Myler to commit. Two strides and a pass, before Myler nails him. Ed Slater gathers just over our 22 with Ringo outside.

Suddenly it is a two-on-one as I come from Foden's blind spot and give him a little bump. He makes a massive deal of it, which I would do too. Did I do that? Oops, awfully sorry. I get into the slipstream of Ringo as Ed puts him streaking clear. Fodes appeals, arms outstretched, but he catches Ashton, one of the few men with the pace to catch Ringo.

Double whammy.

Ringo knows from the halfway line that he is going to score. The crowd love his Chris Ashton-style celebration, swan-diving over the line, to secure the victory and a bonus point.

Game over, surely? No, it's not. Barnes isn't finished.

He penalizes us at the next scrum for an early engagement and walks us ten metres when someone chirps up. That's terrible indiscipline. The review on Monday will be hard all right. Scotty Harrison puts in a big hit. Then Barnes penalizes us in another scrum. We somehow get it back and Sammy Harrison boots it into touch.

The whistle goes. I try to catch my breath.

Ben Foden comes over to me, he's smiling, 'Can't believe you got away with that.'

'Yeah, sorry, mate. I know it's not ideal.'

He gets it. He wants to win as much as I do. Ashton had done the same to us. I just did it at the most important moment to create a try, not to make a cynical statement in the opening minutes.

Interview on the pitch with ESPN, then into the changing room for a long-overdue shave of the ginger beard. A minute with the boys, a drink and down to the media room.

I meet Wayne again in the corridor. He's actually a really good referee. He gives me some constructive criticism, saying, what with the game that was in it, I spoke too much.

'Shut your mouth a little bit.'

I appreciate him saying it. Maybe I whinged when I shouldn't have. Something I can work on. The English referees will have dialogue with captains. That's so important. Others seem arrogant, as if the game is about them, and they won't talk to you.

Into the media scrum I go.

'Howya, lads.'

Straight away they want my view on the fracas.

'I didn't really see it because I was stuck in the middle of it! It probably looked worse on TV. Nothing really connected, really just the referee putting his stamp on the game.

'Load of handbags. I've spoken to all the Northampton boys. They are all decent blokes. That's the way rugby should be. We'll all go over and have a beer.'

The Foden incident?

'I was a little dazed as I was hit late by big Samu. I was lying in the backfield, a little bit pinged, a little bit dizzy. The physio was beside me. I don't know. It happened to me a few times today, trying to get support lines, and people will niggle or get in your way. Just one of those things.'

It always takes a while to get across the pitch to the members' bar. Plenty of kids have been waiting for a very long time to get an autograph. It costs nothing to sign away and pose for photos with people who have supported me for years.

Upstairs, our boys are convinced I caught Ringo with one of my digs. I'll never be seen as a hard man at this club. I let them have their laugh.

I'm shattered and a little broken up. Don't even have a beer. We head home for a family dinner, me, Aneka and our folks.

Afterwards we go to Timo for the party but don't stay long. I've had enough wild nights recently – Bestie and Stevie Ferris stuck around after the Heineken Cup match against Ulster a few weeks ago.

Anyway, I've got mass in the morning.

Sunday, 4 December 2011

Up early with Mum. Say my prayers. Watch the game again and then head for my MOT with Bobby Sourbutts in Oval Park. My shoulder is a bit sore from the second hit by Samu Manoa. He popped some rib cartilage with the first hit. Bobby pokes around, loosens it up. A few bumps and bruises, dead legs. The usual after a game like that.

Home for lunch, then off to Leicester General Hospital. The Tigers visit the children's ward twice a year.

I am wrecked, emotionally and physically drained, but something magical happens.

We go into intensive care, where a premature baby boy has lung and heart problems. There are tubes everywhere. A chilling sight.

He would fit comfortably into Castro's massive hand. The big, grizzled Italian prop – with wild hair down to his shoulders and a scraggly beard – kneels down beside the baby and looks at him through the incubator.

The heart monitor starts beeping faster, so Castro starts making faces. The baby can see us! The heart rate keeps increasing. I get nervous.

'No, no, it's all right. He is just getting excited,' says a nurse.

We lean in and the little guy is smiling out at us. An unbelievable sight.

I drive home with a glowing feeling. Can't wait to tell Aneka and my parents.

The season doesn't stop now – we've got back-to-back matches in the Heineken Cup against Clermont coming up – but for tonight I relax. I am the Leicester Tigers' captain, and twenty-four hours ago we stuck it to Northampton, by hook or by crook. I know Deano would've liked my late contribution. Probably made Johnno and Backy smile too.

Tuesday, 6 December 2011

I got a level-one citing – equivalent to a yellow card – for my part in the brawl against Northampton. Ashton got four weeks for the hair-pulling. Alesana Tuilagi got no suspension.

Cockers seemed happy Wednesday morning. Well, he didn't actually look 'happy', he wasn't smiling or anything; but he didn't look like he was going to murder someone, so that's progress.

We move on, we move up. The Leicester Way. The only way I know.

Epilogue

Tuesday, 29 May 2012
Bangkok Airport, Thailand
Myself and Aneka are waiting for our connecting flight to Koh Samui. This is the last holiday before my final season contracted to Leicester.

With that in mind, I'm only taking two weeks of the four-week break on offer. I'll go straight back to Oval Park on our return home. Need to get an edge on the rest of them, what with now being an old man in rugby years. Thirty-four is ancient to the guys breaking into the game. I remember thinking that, back when I was breaking in, and it's still true.

Anyway, it's getting close to the end, but I'm not done yet. The club and I have agreed to see how my body is around Christmas time before deciding whether to extend my contract for another year. Clubs have to be smart about this nowadays – there have been too many unfit players signing contracts.

I've nothing concrete in place for when I retire. I do have Timo, the restaurant I own with Castro in Market Harborough, but the next year or two will have to be my springboard into something else. I will do my level-three coaching certificate, and that means I'll need to get hands-on coaching a team.

The club have been very good, even knowing that the end is in sight. They completely supported me last year, even after the surgeon believed I was finished. I'd like to stay involved in some shape or form, and they seem amenable to the idea as well. We'll wait and see what happens.

But I want to keep playing. Good luck finding a professional athlete who doesn't want to fight on for a few more rounds when they know they aren't spent. Having been crocked for most of 2011

I really enjoyed this campaign. I appreciated every moment in the changing room before games and leading the boys out.

I know these unique feelings will soon be gone for ever. My priority is to hold on to the number 15 jersey, and being the last man to wear the letter O on my back I've a responsibility to make the likes of Niall Morris or Matt Tait tear it off my back. Or maybe our Fijian signing, Vereniki Goneva, will want to play fullback. Wingers Miles Benjamin and Adam Thompstone are coming in as well, and there are others coming through the Academy, so I'll need to stay sharp.

At pre-season, everyone will see a thirty-four-year-old. I'll need to show them something else. Hence the early return from sitting by a pool in Southeast Asia. I'll be fighting for my existence as a rugby player. Wouldn't have it any other way.

Yeah, I've really enjoyed these past few months, being back on the pitch, winning in Tiger stripes.

With one fairly significant exception – last Saturday's defeat at Twickenham.

I'd better tell you how I almost won my eighth Premiership medal.

The Saracens drop goal – 19 February 2012

We were still suffering from the World Cup hangover. The team wasn't settled. Then we lost down at Exeter. The coaches were livid, but the senior players intervened. No point getting spoon-fed all the time – let's sort this out among ourselves. So we got Simon Barber, our video analyst, to turn the Monday-morning video session into a players' meeting. We critiqued ourselves, called our own individual mistakes.

It worked.

The worst thing we had to watch on the screen was the Exeter players celebrating afterwards. You could see what it meant for them to beat us. We needed to see that.

The run-in thereafter was fairly tough – including Saracens at Vicarage Road a week later. They were defending champions, on the top of the Premiership table, and hadn't lost at home in the league in over a year. We had fallen out of the top four.

It came down to our pack rumbling phase after phase, inch after inch, until they laid siege to the Sarries' try-line. The clock was past eighty minutes and we trailed 19–17. It was going to be them or us, and there was no way through. From the bottom of a ruck I could see Ringo was in position to strike a drop goal – but I knew he was not exactly a drop-goal specialist. I was shattered, but as captain it was a moment when I needed to put it all on the line. I pulled myself up off the turf and we went through a couple more phases.

Toby moved off to the right, so I called it on myself while wishing I could transform into Rog for those ten seconds. James Grindal whipped it back cleanly but I dropped it horrendously. For a drop at goal, the ball should land on the point, but it was on its side. Normally you just strike it, like a golf swing, but because of the way it dropped I drove my foot against it.

Somehow it squeezed between two attempted blockers' heads. I was the last to know it had skimmed over the crossbar because a Sarries forward splatted me. Then I got mugged by the Tigers pack. I think that's when my nose got split open.

The win ignited our campaign. Finally.

300

The following Saturday I made my 300th appearance for the club, against Newcastle Falcons. The club made a presentation afterwards. I didn't want any of this attention. Especially not mid-season.

People had made me aware I was closing in on the milestone. Aneka wanted me to admit that it was a big deal; my own attitude was that next week it would be 301, the week after that 302. It was just another game.

Cockers used it in the team talk. That was awfully flattering. He spoke about the effort of people who had served this club over the years.

We ran out 42–15 winners. It was the middle of a Six Nations weekend and I was conscious that the 19,000 crowd wanted to catch the second half of England v. Wales at Twickenham. Many of them remained in their seats when Peter Wheeler came on to the pitch to give a speech. About me.

He went way back in time: 'A young Irishman joined us in 1997 . . .' I was standing there by myself initially, but I drifted back to the guys to grab a drink before finally coming to the conclusion that this was going on far too long. I interrupted him, 'Look, Peter, I think they know who you are going on about.'

I was given a lovely decanter and some engraved, silver glasses. Later that night, having a few beers, Matt Smith said something that hit home. 'Not many professionals will reach 300 games for their club and seventy-odd for their country again.'

They are decent numbers, I suppose.

Saints again, and again

A month later we made the LV Cup final. So did Northampton. George Ford won Man of the Match for his performance in the semi-final victory over Bath – the same kid I remember playing around at Irish training sessions when his dad, Mike, was our defence coach. George is nineteen now and he did a fine job covering when Toby went down injured.

I'd been given that week off, so I joined Aneka, skiing at a chalet in France. Obviously, I didn't ski. I watched the Bath game down there and immediately wanted to play in the final.

The coaches knew the Saints were going to pick a side close to full strength, so we did likewise. Same old drill, yet another war with our neighbours. This time there was silverware for the taking.

I was chatting to Dorian West, the Saints forwards coach and my old teammate, before the game and I think I managed to piss him off. The topic was not a clever one – the Stephen Ferris/Dylan Hartley incident at Twickenham only twenty-four hours earlier. Hartley subsequently got an eight-week ban for biting Stevie's finger.

I was sin-binned, my fifth yellow card ever, but we were two scores up with about ten minutes to go in the game, so thankfully it didn't hurt us. Matt had made a tackle on their centre under the posts and hurt his knee. Smithy is a hard boy, he doesn't go down, but I could see by the noises coming from him that he was in trouble. I wanted the referee to stop the play – it was a penalty against me anyway for being offside – so I just put my hands on the ball as well. Out came the card.

There was an ugly incident earlier in that game when Calum Clark broke our hooker Rob Hawkins's elbow in a ruck. Everything got a little heated. I didn't see it but I heard the crack and Rob's scream. Our boys were saying the man bent the arm back, and it left a bad feeling afterwards.

When Julian White's last act as a rugby player was to pick up the trophy, I went down the tunnel and crossed paths with Dorian outside the Northampton changing room.

'Fucking hell, Nobby, that's bad.'

Again, we should have left it for another time. He squared up to me, saying what a prick I was, and how much I had changed. I used to be a good lad but now I'm a prick.

We were having a bit of a set-to when Cockers came steamrollering down the corridor, having just had a word with Clark out on the pitch. Nobby and Cockers are old sparring partners, having overlapped as Tigers hookers.

All I could think was: If this kicks off – and it was about to – we were right outside the Northampton changing room. A massive fight with just me and Cockers against the entire Saints squad. I pulled my coach back to our changing room and sorted it out with Nobby later on in the week. I haven't changed after all, thankfully. It was heat-of-the-moment stuff.

Clark was banned until November, so he'll return around the same time as Rob. I feel bad for him as, at just twenty-two and a really good player, from now on every game he plays he'll have to be whiter than white.

I scratched my flippin' eye, for the fourth time, the week of the next Saints game in April. We were doing some three-on-two drills and I was defending. I went to tag Toby, who threw out a gentle handoff, but his finger went straight into my eye. The boys were taking the piss out of me for going down like a sack of spuds, until I didn't get up. You can't do anything but lie in bed for two or three days, in agony, with both eyes remaining closed, because you can't open either without feeling an even worse stinging sensation.

Harlequins were next, and we needed the win to secure a home semi-final. Crofty broke his neck tackling Nick Easter. He is in a cast, having had everything put back together in surgery, and is expected to return within six months. We played some impressive rugby, winning 43–33 at The Stoop, to make sure that Saracens came to Welford Road. I managed to put Chief over for a try in the corner to bring us back into it before Thomas Waldrom's try and Toby's boot dragged us clear; but it was ultimately our pack that ground Quins down. In the last twenty minutes we had more in the tank.

To beat any South African-style side – like Sarries – all the rugby must be played in their half. That means a kicking game must be employed to combat theirs. Alex made a crucial tackle on their winger David Strettle, who seemed certain to score a try. He tap-tackled him with his inside hand, and the TMO said no try. We won 24–15, thanks in part to some assured kicking by George Ford after he replaced an injured Toby. Next up, a final against Quins at Twickenham. Alesana got another try on his last ever game at Welford Road, before heading to Japan, while myself and Craig Newby contributed with quick offloads to put Steve Mafi over for our crucial second try.

Having sat out these massive occasions last season, it was great knowing I would be leading the team out at Twickenham. I didn't even think about the old hoodoo of beating Wasps in regular season games but losing to them in the final.

International retirement

It was a question asked in the lead-up to the final. I was doing my captain duties, chatting away to the media, when someone asked if I was disappointed to be missing out on the tour to New Zealand. I had already moved on, having booked flights to Thailand with Aneka a few months beforehand.

I just assumed Deccie saw it the same as me. The reporter came at me as if I should be disappointed. I just said there comes a time when a player has to hang up his boots. It had been almost a year since I had been involved.

Next morning I woke up to 'GEORDAN MURPHY RETIRES FROM INTERNATIONAL RUGBY' moving across the Sky Sports News ticker-tape.

I felt bad about not speaking to Deccie. I rang him straight away. He called me back that evening and was typically sound about it.

'It doesn't matter if you have retired or not, Geordan ... If I needed a fullback I'd ring you.'

But that is it. Finally official.

It felt strange running out at Twickenham without Crofty or Lewis Deacon, who was also injured, but it felt far worse watching Harlequins explode out of the blocks. It was brave of them to throw the ball around in a final. Their offloading game ensured we didn't see much possession in those opening fifteen minutes.

The sun was splitting the stones. I was confident we were the better side and that they would eventually fade. They never did. Scrum penalties hurt us, and so did Thomas Waldrom's sin-binning in the first half. I had tackled Danny Care and could see Nick Easter's hands on the ball. It seemed fine, but the Quins boys were smart to make a big deal about it and Wayne Barnes produced his yellow card. Moments of inspiration from Ben Youngs and Anthony Allen ensured we were in touching distance of extra time. But Quins were excellent in the last twenty, finding new levels of energy to repel us time and again. When we were camped on their line at the end I thought we'd get the try and convert it to force extra time – you always feel like that in a Tigers jersey. But it didn't happen, and we lost 30–23.

We gathered in a huddle afterwards. I knew I had to say something, but what can you say? That rugby hurts you more than it rewards you? That you lose more big games than you win? Even at Leicester. They are listening, but really most of the boys are numb, lost in their own anguish.

That pain lingers. But that's a good thing. It will make most of them Tigers for life. I've said it before, this club seeps into your very being if you hang around long enough. There will be more opportunities like this because you crave them like any addiction.

I mentioned guys who were leaving by name. George Skivington, Horacio, Billy Twelvetrees. And Alex, of course. Guys who had put the work in to get us to Twickenham yet again when the rest of the country had written us off a few months ago.

'Finals are won and lost on very fine margins. We didn't play a lot of rugby in the game but at the end we were still there, battering away. Just like the previous two years.

'Sometimes you win, sometimes you lose, but at Leicester we will always be battering away at the gates at the end. Not a lot we can do now but concentrate on next year.'

I'll get one more go at it, maybe two. Depends on the body. But eventually I'll slow down and have to be content wearing my green tie on match days and having a drink with David Matthews and the other former Tigers.

At least I know Leicester will always keep going. That's enough for me.

Acknowledgements

Being the baby in a big family, I have to start by thanking them for everything they have done for me. As far back as I can remember, someone in my clan has been looking out for 'Geordie' – even before Ross became my personal on-field bodyguard in that one season playing for Naas RFC.

Mam and Dad have been constant supporters, year upon year. It has always been one of the toughest things to see the sadness in their faces after defeats or poor performances, but the awareness of how proud they are of me always makes the disappointment fade quickly. The same goes for my big brothers and sister (nieces and nephews, too). We have an expression in my family, 'If you are wrong you are still right,' and I'm acutely aware that it always applies when I'm around you all.

Special thanks to Gavin Cummiskey for all his efforts in deciphering my ramblings. It has been a real pleasure working with Gav, ever since our first meeting in Naas, followed by those long sessions in Carton House, random chats from the World Cup in New Zealand, and Leicester weekends (when, coincidentally or not, Northampton were always our opponents – which has certainly ensured good copy!).

To everyone at Penguin, particularly Michael McLoughlin and Brendan Barrington, thanks for making this possible. Thanks also to Ray McManus at Sportsfile.

I consider myself very lucky to have played with some great players (and even more brave ones) and been coached by some fantastic rugby men. I mention them in these pages but I'd like to thank them here for imparting their wisdom and, more importantly, becoming good friends along the way.

This rugby journey started in Newbridge College and, via Naas, will probably end in Leicester, with some unforgettable memories in the Ireland camp thrown in for good measure. They say you can choose your friends but I seem to get stuck with them! Maybe it's because I have spent my entire adult life living in the East Midlands that many of my English-based mates have become like extended family anyway. I won't name names as I'm bound to forget someone, so this is for you (don't say I didn't mention you). Seriously though, from the moment myself and Jimmy arrived at Oval Park in that black cab you have all made it one hell of a ride.

Also, I want to acknowledge the people who have supported me for both Leicester and Ireland over the years. It has been a privilege to play in front of such passionate crowds.

Last but not least, I'd like to give a special mention to my girlfriend Aneka. I always say you have to have bad times to appreciate the good, but you always make the dark moments seem a lot brighter. I know I can be difficult, especially when I'm on crutches or – even worse – when the Tigers lose, so thanks for putting up with me. Hopefully there will be a lot more good times in the future.

Geordan Murphy

July 2012

Index